MEMORY IN THE REAL WORLD

MEMORY IN THE REAL WORLD

Gillian Cohen

The Open University, Milton Keynes, U.K.

LEA LAWRENCE ERLBAUM ASSOCIATES, PUBLISHERS LEA
Hove and London (UK)   Hillsdale (USA)

Lawrence Erlbaum Associates Ltd., Publishers
27 Palmeira Mansions
Church Road
Hove
East Sussex, BN3 2FA
U.K.

British Library Cataloguing in Publication Data

Cohen, Gillian
  Memory in the real world.
  1. Man. Memory.
  I. Title
  153.1'2

  ISBN 0-86377-101-7
  ISBN 0-86377-102-5 Pbk

Typeset by Ponting–Green Ltd., London
Printed and bound by A. Wheaton & Co. Ltd., Exeter

Contents

1 The Study of Everyday Memory

HISTORICAL BACKGROUND

A Hundred Years in the Laboratory

Psychologists have been studying memory for about one hundred years but, with some exceptions, most of this time has been spent in the laboratory using formal experimental techniques to answer theoretical questions about the general principles that govern the mechanisms of memory. In its relatively short history psychology has often seemed to proceed by a series of reactions, discarding one approach in favour of a new one, and then swinging back again to revive and reinstate the original ideas. This kind of oscillation is especially evident in the study of memory.

Around the turn of the century, psychologists began to react against the philosophical, introspective approach exemplified in William James's (1890) reflections on memory. In an attempt to give psychology a status of genuine scientific respectability the objective experimental methods employed by Ebbinghaus (1885) were enthusiastically adopted and developed. The majority of these experiments were concerned with verbal learning. A typical experiment of this kind tests memory performance in situations where a few of the relevant factors are isolated, and rigorously controlled and manipulated. All the myriads of other factors that may normally influence memory in everyday life are deliberately excluded. Using stimuli such as nonsense syllables which are almost entirely devoid of meaning and of previously acquired associations, the experimenter controls the number, duration, and timing of the presentation of these stimuli. The subjects are carefully selected and instructed; the environment is standardised; the delay before recall is fixed and the mental events that occur during this retention interval are controlled as far as possible. Finally, the instructions for recall are presented and the experimenter can record the number and type of items that are recalled, and the order and timing of the responses.

Experiments like these reveal the limits of memory capacity and define the constraints that govern the system. Some general principles have emerged which have proved robust and reliable, and which generalise across a range of experimental situations. For example, the division of memory into a short-term store and a long-term store is widely accepted, and phenomena such as the bow-shaped curve of serial learning; the rate of decay; the role of rehearsal; and the effects of interference are well established. And, on the basis of these findings, theoretical models of memory have been constructed and tested such as, for example, HAM, the human associative memory model (Anderson & Bower, 1973); or ACT, the adaptive control of thought model (Anderson, 1983). Research of this kind has accumulated over many years and still continues. However, over the last decade there has been a marked change of direction in the study of memory.

The Winds of Change

In 1976, at a conference on Practical Aspects of Memory, Ulric Neisser gave a talk (later published in 1978) entitled "Memory: What are the important questions?" in which he dismissed the work of the past 100 years as largely worthless. This talk was undoubtedly a milestone in the psychology of memory. Neisser believes that the important questions about memory are those that arise out of everyday experience. We ought, he claimed, to be finding out how memory works in the natural context of daily life at school, in the home, or at work. We ought to be finding out what people remember from their formal education; why some people have "better" memories than others; why we remember some things and not others; and how we remember such diverse things as poems and town layouts, people's names, and events from our childhood. The traditional laboratory experiments, according to Neisser, have failed to study all the most interesting and significant problems and have shed no light on them. He claimed that the experimental findings are trivial, pointless, or obvious, and fail to generalise outside the laboratory. He advocated a new approach, concentrating on the detailed examination of naturally occurring memory phenomena in the real world, and paying special attention to individual differences. According to this approach, psychologists should adopt an ethological approach, studying human memory in the same way that ethologists study animal behaviour. In Neisser's own phrase, memory research should have *ecological validity*. By this he means that it should apply to naturally occurring behaviour in the natural context of the real world.

Neisser's ideas had an enthusiastic reception and the wind of change has blown strongly since 1978, bringing with it a rapidly accumulating, richly varied, and extremely interesting body of research into everyday memory. Indeed, this new wave of interest in the more practical aspects of cognition is not confined to the study of memory alone. Ecological validity has become something of a catchword and vigorous efforts are under way to relate many areas of cognitive psychology to the mental activities of ordinary people going about their daily lives. Problems such as how doctors decide on a medical diagnosis; how gamblers decide how to place their stakes; how juries assess the credibility of a witness; the skills involved in holding conversations, planning routes, and recognising disguised faces are all being studied. In 1987, when the second conference on Practical Aspects of Memory was held, it was apparent that, since Neisser's original talk, a very wide variety of naturally occurring memory phenomena ranging from memory for the names of birds and flowers to memory for the faces of war criminals have attracted the attention of psychologists.

Precursors of the Change

So how did this change come about? It would be quite wrong to suppose that research into everyday memory only began abruptly as a result of Neisser's talk. Both Galton (1883), and later, Bartlett (1932) had long ago addressed themselves to important questions about the rich and complex functioning of memory in natural contexts. Although their ideas were allowed to lapse for many years, ecologically valid research began again both in Britain and in the United States during the Second World War. There was a new growth of applied psychology, when answers were urgently sought to practical questions about human performance in tasks like air traffic control (Broadbent, 1958), work on production lines (Welford, 1958) or Morse code operation (Keller, 1953).

More recently, the new school of cognitive psychology which evolved in the late 1960s adopted a much broader and more speculative approach to memory research than that of the traditional verbal learning experiments. Researchers confronted problems about memory strategies, and these led them to investigate many of the phenomena that characterise the use of memory in everyday life, such as the use of imagery and mnemonics (Paivio, 1969), the tip-of-the-tongue phenomenon (Brown & McNeill, 1966), and the advantages of categorical organisation (Mandler, 1967).

Research into topics like these broadened the scope of memory research and awakened interest in how memory functions in natural contexts outside the laboratory. Developmental studies of children's memory and neuropsychological studies of memory impairment have, in any case, always tended to be hybrid in character, with one foot in the laboratory and one foot in the real world. The winds of change were already beginning to blow, and Neisser voiced ideas that were already beginning to take shape. Nevertheless, the rapid growth of everyday memory research since 1978 is proof that his forceful expression of these ideas has undoubtedly had great influence.

IN THE LABORATORY OR OUT IN THE REAL WORLD?

It is important, now that the study of everyday memory is well launched, to try to assess it critically, to identify its strengths and weaknesses and, in particular, to determine what precisely is the relationship between the two approaches, the traditional laboratory experimental method and the everyday, ecologically valid approach. Are they antagonistic or should they be viewed as complementary? What follows is an attempt to compare the two methodologies in terms of aims, methods, scope, advantages, and limitations.

Two arguments are advanced here. First, the distinction between the two approaches is by no means clear cut. Rather, there is a continuum from studying performance in a memory task that is as natural as possible, like observing a shopper in a supermarket and noting how many items he or she forgets to purchase (Anschutz, Camp, Markley, & Kramer, 1985), to studying performance in a task that is entirely artificial, like having subjects try to memorise a string of unrelated letters while simultaneously repeating "the-the-the" (Wilding & Mohindra, 1980). In between these extremes are laboratory experiments that mimic everyday situations, and studies of everyday behaviour that incorporate some constraints and controls. Second, in so far as they are distinct, the two methodologies should not be viewed as competing alternatives. They are not two different ways of doing the same thing, one of which is better than the other. They are two equally valid ways of doing two different, but equally important, jobs.

Aims and Scope

Studies of everyday memory and traditional laboratory experiments have fundamentally different aims. Research into everyday memory is concerned with how memory normally operates in ordinary circumstances. It is essentially about *norms and habits*. The typical laboratory experiment, on the other hand, is concerned with *capacities*; with pushing the system to its limits and observing the effects on performance. The primary aim of this type of research is to infer the nature of the mechanism, to deduce general principles, to construct and test theoretical models. It is probably true to say that, in everyday life, naturally occurring memory tasks rarely tax capacity to its limits. People tend to use written reminders or memory aids when the memory load is high. Normal function does not reflect the limits of capacity very closely. In the laboratory, on the other hand, everyday norms and habits are often irrelevant, either because of the unfamiliarity of the task, or because the subjects are constrained to perform according to the instructions and not according to their usual habits. Because of this difference in aim the two methods are not very closely related and are unlikely to yield parallel findings.

The two approaches also differ in the *level of explanation* they are aiming to supply. The traditional experimental approach seeks a high-level explanation, aiming to construct an abstract model of behaviour; to expose the basic underlying operating principles of memory mechanisms stripped of all extraneous factors and particular variations. High-level models of this kind are intended to apply across a wide range of different types of memory. By contrast, everyday memory research provides low-level explanations which are much more concrete and apply only to specific tasks and situations.

Everyday memory research has a more functional approach with practical aims and useful implications. It is not just an exercise in natural history of a purely descriptive kind, but can also be predictive. If we know how memory normally functions in everyday life, we can sometimes predict performance in natural contexts; we can give practical advice about how to achieve the best results. The findings should help us to structure a lecture or to frame instructions for using a gadget, to shape the advice a doctor gives to a patient, to assess whether someone's memory is impaired, and to devise memory therapy and memory aids. Of course, there are many real-world situations in which no accurate predictions can be made because the causal factors are so numerous, so complex, or so little understood. It is much easier to make predictions about the restricted repertoire of responses in the limited setting of a typical laboratory experiment. It is easier to predict the shape of a learning curve for a list of nonsense syllables in an experiment than it is to predict the grade an adolescent will achieve in an examination.

If everyday memory research is to have maximum ecological validity, this entails that the behaviour and the context of its occurrence should not be tampered with or distorted in any way. Researchers should observe and record, but not intervene. To achieve real ecological validity, the study of everyday memory should aim to include all the relevant factors, not just those that the researcher decides are of most theoretical interest. But is this approach feasible?

The kind of things people remember in everyday life include a great variety of different items such as remembering a shopping list or a recipe, remembering to telephone a relative or to fill up the car with petrol, recounting the arguments put forward at a meeting or the plot of a play seen on television, or the amount of a bill that has to be paid. These experiences are embedded in a rich context of ongoing events and scenes; they are influenced by a lifetime of past experiences, by history and culture, by current motives and emotions, by intelligence and personality traits, by future goals and plans. Because all these factors are involved, a given act of memory is different for each individual performing it, and it is difficult or impossible to generalise about it.

The Unitary Approach

Some psychologists (e.g. Norman, 1980; Zimbardo, 1984;) have explicitly advocated a *unitary psychology* adopting an all-inclusive *integrated approach* that tries to take account of all these factors. They have reacted against the way psychology has become fragmented into splinter groups, each concerned with a highly specific area. Until recently, for example, the study of memory was divorced from the study of emotion and of personality. They argue that these demarcations are artificial and claim that human behaviour can only be understood as an integrated unitary system. Their views are in opposition to those who argue that the mind is organised as a set of modular sub-systems which can be understood as separate and independent entities (see Fodor, 1983, for a discussion of these views).

The unitary approach has considerable appeal, but, even if the human brain is a unitary system, it may not be possible to study it in a unitary way. The researcher is liable to be so overwhelmed by the richness and complexity of the data that no conclusions can be drawn from it. Integrative studies with no restrictions of scope and complexity are liable to be purely descriptive, and to lack any explanatory and predictive power. Bruce (1985) argues that ecological memory research must be concerned with both how and why. It must ask how memory operates in everyday life, identifying causes and processes; what functions it serves, and why it has evolved both ontogenetically and evolutionarily in this way. But if everyday memory research is ever to answer Bruce's questions a certain amount of ecological validity must be sacrificed to ensure that manageable and informative results are produced. The researcher must classify and compare; must exclude or ignore some variables and focus on others; must impose some form of measurement or testing; must interpret the findings and extract generalisations from them. In doing so, it is inevitable that the natural context of the memory act is changed to some extent. Everyday memory research is usually a form of compromise between complete non-intervention with unsullied ecological validity, and the need to impose some structure on the data that are collected. If the researcher cannot examine everyday life in the raw, he or she must try to ascertain that memory in the more structured research context preserves the essential aspects of memory in the natural context.

METHODS OF EVERYDAY MEMORY RESEARCH

Everyday memory research has mainly employed two different methods. The first relies on self-reports; the second method involves the use of naturalistic experiments.

Self-reports

Self-reports seem to provide a simple way of finding out how people's memories work in everyday life by asking them. The researcher can record people's own observations about the way their memories function, collecting reports from individuals about the things they remember and the things they forget; the tricks and devices they use to prop up memory; the particular circumstances that are associated with success or failure. The use of self-reports may involve collecting oral histories and reminiscences or it may involve the administration of formal questionnaires about memory. Subjects may be asked to supply self-ratings of their own memory ability, or to think aloud while they solve problems and produce a verbal protocol, or to keep a diary recording the occurrence of memory phenomena such as absent-minded lapses. All these procedures rely on introspection.

The Validity of Introspective Evidence

The recent use of introspective evidence by psychologists is another example of the way the history of psychology exemplifies a kind of swings-and-roundabouts progression, with ideas being enthusiastically adopted, then discredited, and then reinstated. Early psychologists like Wundt and Freud based their theories on the introspections of their subjects or patients, but, during the behaviourist period (roughly from the 1920s to the 1950s), only overt measurable behavioural responses were considered admissible as evidence. The importance, and even the existence, of mental events were discounted. However, the advent of cognitive psychology in the 1960s brought renewed interest in covert, unobservable mental processes such as imaging, reasoning, deciding, and planning. Although it is to some extent possible, with carefully designed experiments, to infer the nature of covert thought processes from the nature of the overt responses that are made, the subject's own introspections can provide valuable corroboration or can suggest alternative hypotheses. Introspective methods have been brought back into use and are now employed extensively in studying aspects of cognition like problem solving and decision making as well as everyday memory.

This resurrection of introspective methods has not been without its critics (Nisbett & Wilson,1977). It is recognised that many of the very rapid mental processes that underlie activities like perceiving a complex scene, recognising a word, or speaking a grammatical sentence are simply not accessible to conscious awareness. Another mental process which takes place without conscious awareness is the so-called *pop-up* phenomenon described in Chapter 4, p.103. You may have the experience of finding that you cannot recall something, such as a person's name, although this may be a name that you know quite well. Such a retrieval block may persist, despite your best efforts, for hours or even days. Then, when you have given up and are thinking about something quite different, the forgotten name suddenly pops up into consciousness. In this situation, people are usually unable to report anything about the mental processes that produced the pop-up. Introspection fails to yield any information. In such cases, people are conscious of the end product of the mental operations, but not of the processes themselves. Nobody can introspect and make verbal reports about what is going on below the level of consciousness, and much of mental activity is unconscious.

Nevertheless, there are some thought processes that do take place consciously, and with some effort and practice, people can become quite good at describing them. This is particularly true of the so-called slow processes—long drawn-out mental processes like figuring out solutions to tricky problems or attempting to reconstruct a personal memory from childhood. Self-reports are more accurate if they are concurrent with the mental events being described since delay tends to introduce distortion. Reports that are produced afterwards are less likely to be accurate. The researcher must also avoid giving any hints that might bias the report by indicating what is expected of the subject (Ericsson & Simon, 1980). Even so, some mental events may be difficult or impossible to express in words, or, in some cases, the act of trying to verbalise what is going on in the head may interfere with or change the nature of the mental activity under scrutiny. Trying to introspect about how you read silently, for example, will almost certainly change the way you read, causing you to read more slowly and in a more word-by-word manner than you usually do when you are not thinking about it.

Verbal Protocols

Verbal protocols are a record of what people say when they are asked to think aloud as they perform a task. For example, when people are asked to try to recall some event from their past lives, they can be asked to verbalise the processes of search. Their speech is recorded and later transcribed so that the mental processes that are reported can be analysed. The use of verbal protocols is a form of concurrent introspection. Concurrent introspection has certain advantages over retrospective introspection in that there is less opportunity for editing and rationalising the report, and less chance of forgetting some of the mental processes. The protocol reveals the temporal sequence of mental operations, and the location and duration of the pauses in verbalisation convey information about the choice points. It is especially useful as a research tool for studying complex tasks of fairly long duration which involve operations that are easy to verbalise. So, for example, a practised subject can report the reasoning processes underlying the selection of a chess move. One disadvantage of using verbal protocols is that they are necessarily incomplete and they give no indication of what has been omitted. As already noted, some mental processes are not accessible to conscious introspection. Unconscious processes cannot be reported and unspoken thoughts remain mysterious. Another disadvantage is that individual subjects may differ in the ease and spontaneity with which they can produce a running commentary on their thinking, and in the level of detail they report, so individual differences in the underlying thought processes may be obscured by individual differences in the spoken commentary. Verbal protocols may also be inaccurate if subjects are trying to please the experimenter or to present themselves in a good light. They may not like to reveal the confused and muddled state of their mental processes and may tidy up the reported version so as to seem more impressive. Nisbett and Wilson (1977) have emphasised the shortcomings of verbal protocols, but Ericsson and Simon (1980) have defended the use of concurrent introspections and they have proved to be an informative way to study problem solving and planning (see Chapter 2, pp.39–47).

Questionnaires and Self-ratings

It is worth discussing the use of questionnaires at some length since many examples will be found in later chapters. Several different kinds of questionnaire can be distinguished. One type of memory questionnaire is a straightforward test of factual knowledge and asks questions like "What is the date of the battle of Waterloo?" or "Who was the composer of Rigoletto?". Another type has been called a *metamemory questionnaire* because it queries beliefs about memory. Metamemory questionnaires are not tests. They are more like opinion surveys. Questions in metamemory questionnaires take a variety of different forms. Some are self-assessment questions which ask people to assess their own memory abilities by choosing the appropriate rating (e.g. Very Good; Good; Fair; Poor; or Very Poor) in response to questions like "How good is your memory for the words of songs or poems?" or "How good is your memory for routes to places?". Alternatively, subjects may be asked to assess the frequency of certain specified lapses of memory, as in "How often do you forget appointments?" or "How often do you want to tell a joke, but find you cannot remember it?" by rating the frequency of occurrence as Very Often, Often, Occasionally, Rarely, or Never.

As well as asking for ratings of memory ability, metamemory questionnaires may ask subjects what memory strategies, mnemonics, or reminders they employ; or whether they have detected any changes over time in their memory ability; or what beliefs and expectations they have about the way that memory works in general.

Self-assessments of memory ability are based on direct first-hand experience of success and failure in a wide range of everyday tasks over a long period. It seems reasonable, therefore, to assume that people should know about their own memory performance and be able to assess it accurately, but many researchers (e.g. Morris, 1984) have expressed serious doubts about the validity of self-ratings. These ratings have proved to have high reliability (that is, if subjects are asked to work through a questionnaire, and then it is administered again at a later date, there is a strong correlation between the original and the repeat ratings). However, validity appears to be low, since when the ratings are correlated with scores on formal tests of memory ability, such as digit span (the number of digits which can be repeated back in the correct order) or free recall of word lists, the correlations are low or nonexistent. For example, self-rated ability to remember telephone numbers correlates with digit span at only 0.4, and self-rated ability to remember faces correlates with tests of ability to recognise photographs of faces at 0.3 (Herrman, 1984). Several reasons for this low validity have been identified:

1. Self-assessments may reflect a person's self image rather than his or her performance, and be distorted by modesty or pride.
2. The *metamemory paradox* may operate, so that people who make most errors are least likely to report them because they forget they have occurred.
3. Individual variation in the opportunity for error may also distort results. For example, some individuals may assess their memory for faces as excellent, but have few demands made on it because they seldom meet many new people.
4. Using memory aids like diaries, address books, shopping lists or knotted handkerchiefs may protect an individual from memory failures, so that few actually occur, even though memory is poor.
5. Questions that ask "how often" or "how good" are ambiguous unless they specify a reference point. Providing an objective scale (e.g.

instructing the subjects that "Often" should be taken to mean about once a week) or specifying comparisons (e.g. how good are you as compared with an average person of your own age) helps to lessen this ambiguity.

6. Response biases may operate that inflate or reduce estimates of frequency. For example, the elderly may be anxious about the possibility of cognitive deterioration and be sensitised to errors. Zelinski, Gilewski, and Thompson (1980) found that whereas young people's self-assessments were quite unrelated to their test scores, elderly people's ratings had greater validity.

7. Low correlations between laboratory tests and self-assessments may be due simply to the fact that they are measuring different things.

The factors that govern the everyday performance on which self-assessments are based are different in so many ways from the factors that operate in formal laboratory tests that the lack of agreement is not surprising. The subjective memory beliefs expressed in self-assessment questionnaires should be validated against objective observations of everyday performance, rather than against laboratory tests. Some researchers (e.g. Broadbent, Cooper, Fitzgerald, & Parkes, 1982; Sunderland, Harris, & Baddeley, 1983) have tried to check the validity of self-assessments by having a spouse or close relative provide a parallel set of ratings. If I rate my tendency to lose objects as very rare, this can then be checked against my spouse's observations. These third-party ratings do correlate reasonably well with self-ratings. What is wanted, though, are more studies correlating self-assessments with ecologically valid tests that are close analogues of everyday situations, such as some of the tests in the Rivermead Behavioural Memory test battery (Wilson, Baddeley, & Hutchins, 1984) or Martin's (1986) study in which she validated subjects' ratings of their own ability to keep appointments with objective records of how often they had missed appointments while serving on the subject panel.

In spite of some doubts about their validity, self-assessment questionnaires have proved valuable in a number of ways. They have clearly indicated that people view their own memories as a set of specific abilities with specific strengths and weaknesses. Memory is not seen as being "good" or "bad" overall. Instead, people recognise that they may be good at remembering some things and poor at others. Self-assessment questionnaires provide a "profile" of memory ability that is considered more revealing than overall scores (Chaffin & Herrman, 1983).

These profiles have produced evidence for individual differences in memory style. Sehulster (Note 9) claims to have identified three factors in memory ability. A verbal factor includes memory for words, stories, facts, and jokes; an autobiographical factor includes memory for personal experiences, emotions, dreams, scenes, smells, and music; the third factor is prospective memory, which is essentially memory for things that have to be done, and includes memory for actions, plans, anniversaries, paying bills, appointments, etc. Sehulster has developed a typology of memory which characterises individuals according to their pattern of scores on these three factors.

As well as being used to differentiate individuals, questionnaires provide an instrument for examining differences between groups like the young and the old (Cohen & Faulkner, 1984; Perlmutter, 1978) or studying changes over time following head injuries (Sunderland et al., 1983). In general, it is useful to know what people think about their memories because beliefs and expectations about memory performance affect many aspects of everyday behaviour, including people's preferences, the kind of tasks they are willing to tackle, and the way they respond to information dissemination.

In spite of some reservations and difficulties, if self-report data derived from protocols and questionnaires are used and interpreted with care and caution, they can be a valid and valuable source of information about memory in everyday life.

Naturalistic Experiments

The other main approach to the study of everyday memory retains the experimental method, but attempts to devise experiments that are more naturalistic, more ecologically valid or representative of real life than the traditional laboratory experiment. Typically, such experiments involve testing people's memory for more natural material such as stories, films, or maps instead of the traditional lists of nonsense syllables, letters, or digits. In some cases, they may test memory for events that occurred naturally in the subject's daily life rather than for material selected and constructed by the experimenter. So, for example, researchers have studied college teachers' ability to remember the names or faces of their former students (Bahrick, 1984) or John Dean's ability to remember conversations with President Nixon (Neisser, 1982a). In other examples, naturalistic experiments may involve testing memory for specially constructed materials, but are carried out in natural environments outside the laboratory, such as Baddeley's (1982) study, which tested deep-sea divers' ability to remember information while they were on the sea-bed.

The naturalistic experiment is essentially a compromise in which the researcher tries to make the task and conditions as close to those that obtain in real life as possible, while at the same time imposing enough control and standardisation of the procedure so that definite conclusions can be drawn from the findings. Of course, an experimental procedure can never be exactly the same as a real-life situation. In an experiment, subjects know they are being tested. They may be anxious, bored or eager to impress, and the material, or task, is liable to be more simplified and more orderly than real events.

Another approach to the study of everyday memory relies on neuropsychological evidence. The relationship between types of memory impairment and their effects on memory function in everyday life can throw light on the mechanisms involved (Parkin, 1987). However, the focus of this book is on normal memory function and neuropsychological research lies outside its scope.

LIMITATIONS AND ADVANTAGES OF EVERYDAY MEMORY RESEARCH

The limitations and problems inherent in everyday memory research stem from weaknesses in the methodology that have already been noted. How can we draw conclusions about what causes people to forget something in everyday life when we have no control over potentially relevant factors? Consider, for example, memory for faces. In the real-world situation, the researcher has no control over the initial learning phase; the degree of attention paid to the face when it was encountered; the number and duration of encounters; the importance and affective quality of the encounters; and the number and similarity of the faces encountered during the intervening period. How, then, can we conclude what causes X to forget Y's face? The combination of lack of control, and, in some cases, the absence of a strong theoretical framework, means that everyday memory research is in danger of producing only a mass of interesting, but uninterpreted, observations and untested speculations. Because of these problems some researchers are inclined to dismiss everyday memory research as "soft" psychology, in contrast to the rigour and precision of the traditional experimental methods.

However, the great advantages of everyday memory research are relevance and interest. It generates practical predictions. It poses a host of new, important, and challenging questions. Another advantage of studying memory in the real world is that it takes more account of individual differences. Differences of age, culture, sex, personality, socio-economic and educational background are important factors in everyday memory performance. Laboratory studies have often seemed to operate on the assumption that all human beings behave in the same way, basing generalisations on tests carried out on a fairly homogeneous sample of young college students. Once the researcher emerges into the real world, the great range and variety of human responses to the same situation has to be confronted. Moreover, the rigorous methodology of the laboratory is no guarantee that the results will be of interest. It is possible to design experiments which conform to the highest standards of control and produce elegant quantitative data, but which only show how subjects respond in that particular experimental paradigm and shed no light on how memory functions in any other situations.

The Relationship Between the Two Approaches

As Baddeley and Wilkins (1984) have pointed out, everyday memory research provides a testing ground for the theories and findings that have resulted from 100 years of laboratory experiments. Studies of everyday memory test the range of situations to which the laboratory-based findings apply. Do they generalise to the real world? Can they be applied to naturally occurring phenomena? This relationship between the two approaches works to ensure that the laboratory experiments are not sterile. Laboratory research has a tendency, left to itself, to become incestuous, endlessly exploring its own paradigms. Everyday research acts as a corrective to this tendency by opening up new lines of inquiry. The functional questions about what memory is for, which arise in the everyday context, provide a better basis for laboratory research than theory building for its own sake.

The benefits do not flow in one direction only. Everyday research also draws heavily on what has been learned in the laboratory. Although the results obtained in the laboratory are unlikely to be replicated precisely in the real world, some of the general principles, the organising concepts, and the distinctions and classifications derived from traditional studies can be carried over and used to give shape and structure to research on everyday memory. Throughout the chapters that follow, the studies of everyday memory that are described illustrate the debt which everyday memory research owes to the traditional approach. The findings are commonly interpreted in terms of these general principles even if the fit is, at times, rather loose. Distinctions like those between episodic and semantic memory or attentional and automatic processes or constructive and copy theories are frequently employed. Models such as schema theory and production systems are applied and concepts such as levels of processing, metamemory, and scripts are used to make sense of the data and supply a guiding framework for further research. It would be unrealistic to suppose, though, that the data from everyday memory research are going to fit very neatly and precisely into the theoretical models it borrows. Because of the complex and wide-ranging nature of the topics studied it is not to be expected that any one model should be able to account for all of the findings. A decade after his talk, it begins to seem as if Neisser was reacting too strongly in writing off the last 100 years of laboratory research as misguided. At the second conference on Practical Aspects of Memory, in 1987, it was apparent that the two kinds of memory research continue to co-exist, and it becomes increasingly clear that the relationship between memory in the laboratory and memory out in the real world is one of cross-fertilisation. The two approaches are not antagonistic because of the differences in aims and scope. Instead, their relationship is a complementary one: They exert a useful and mutually beneficial influence on each other. Laboratory research is enriched and extended; everyday research is disciplined and guided.

In the chapters that follow different aspects of everyday memory are loosely grouped together according to the type of memory function. These groupings are often rather arbitrary because, in practice, different types of memory function overlap and interact in most everyday activities. Chapter 2 examines memory for actions and includes monitoring ongoing sequences of actions, remembering what to do and when to do it, and planning how to carry out complex actions. Chapter 3 concentrates on the use of visual memory and includes remembering maps and routes, remembering the location and appearance of objects, and remembering events that have been witnessed. Chapter 4 is concerned with memory for people. This chapter includes a section on memory for faces and a section on memory for proper names, both of which turn out to be distinct and peculiar types of memory. Chapter 5 focuses on memory for personal experiences. Of course, memory for personal experiences includes remembering places and faces, objects, and events. Chapter 6 discusses both general knowledge and specialist knowledge. These kinds of knowledge, though not so obviously "everyday", are nevertheless used in many daily activities. Chapter 7 is concerned with verbal memory, with remembering spoken information and written information.

In each of these chapters, the findings, observations, and phenomena are described, and cognitive models and theories are introduced where relevant to show how these can help to explain and illuminate the workings of memory in the real world. More comprehensive accounts of these theories can be found elsewhere. Here they are presented only in enough detail to show how they apply to real-world memory. In the explanation and inter-pretation of memory function, common sense intuitions are frequently invoked. Everyday memory research is an area where common-sense has a good deal to contribute. In particular, where theory or data offend against common sense it is a powerful indication that they should be carefully re-examined.

2 Memory for Plans and Actions

Everyday memory does not only consist of a record of past events. As well as remembering what has happened in the past, we also use memory in everyday life to remember plans, to keep track of ongoing actions and of the actions we intend to carry out in the future. This function of memory has been greatly neglected, but in recent years its practical and theoretical importance has been recognised.

Studies of memory for plans and actions fall into two major categories, although these are not very sharply distinguished. One is concerned with absent-mindedness and slips of action. As defined by Norman (1981, p.1), "a slip is an error that occurs when a person does an action that is not intended." Errors of this kind arise during the performance of an action sequence. The other group of studies is concerned with what is called prospective memory, defined as "remembering to do things". Errors of prospective memory involve failing to carry out a plan or comply with an instruction to do something. So, whereas the absent-minded slips of action usually take the form of doing the wrong thing, errors of prospective memory take the form of forgetting to do it at all. However, before they can be carried out, plans have to be formulated in the first place. Before embarking on an action sequence which is novel or complex, we usually spend some time thinking what we are going to do, how best to achieve the goal, in what order to perform the individual actions, and how much time and effort will need to be allocated to the task. Memory is involved in formulating such plans, holding the elements and sequence in mind while the plan is being assembled, evaluated, revised, and implemented. For large-scale plans like how to start a business or write a book we would not rely on internal memory alone, but would employ external aids in the form of written schedules and memos. Less ambitious plans like packing for a holiday or organising a party may be formulated in memory. When it comes to implementation of the plan, the component actions are assembled in some form of output buffer and the memory system monitors the output of actions from the buffer to ensure that the plan is implemented correctly

ABSENT-MINDEDNESS AND SLIPS OF ACTION

Slips of action are a common experience in daily life and occur both in speech and in nonverbal behaviour. In this chapter we will be concerned with errors in nonverbal actions. We all find ourselves, from time to time, doing things like pouring coffee into the sugar bowl, throwing cheques into the waste-basket, or driving towards one destination when we actually intended to go to quite a different one. By analysing the nature and incidence of these kinds of slips, researchers have been able to infer some of the characteristics of the mechanisms that control the performance of action sequences.

Classifying Slips of Action

Reason (1979) asked 35 volunteers to keep a diary record of their slips of action. In 2 weeks the diaries yielded 400 of these slips, and Reason was able to identify several different categories of error:

1. *Repetition errors:* forgetting that an action has already been performed and repeating it, e.g. "I started to pour a second kettle of boiling water into the teapot, forgetting I had just filled it." Reason called these storage failures and 40% of his corpus consisted of repetition errors of this kind.
2. *Goal switches:* forgetting the goal of a sequence of actions and switching to a different goal, e.g. "I intended to drive to a friend's house but found myself driving to work instead" or "I went upstairs to fetch the dirty washing and came down without the washing, having tidied the bathroom instead." These slips (which Reason called test failures) formed 20% of his corpus.
3. *Omissions and reversals:* omitting or wrongly ordering the component actions of a sequence, e.g. filling the kettle but failing to switch it on, or putting the lid on a container before putting something in it. In Reason's study 18% of the errors were of this kind.

4. *Confusions/blends:* confusing objects involved in one action sequence with those involved in another sequence, e.g. taking a tin opener instead of scissors into the garden to cut flowers. Or confusing the actions from one sequence with actions from another sequence, as in the case of a woman who reported throwing her earrings to the dog and trying to clip dog biscuits onto her ears. In these cases, there has been crosstalk between two programs and different action sequences have been confused with each other. About 16% of Reason's errors were confusions.

Although the diary records produced good descriptive evidence for the occurrence of these different types of error, the reported incidence of each kind may not be a very accurate record of actual incidence. A particular kind of slip may be reported as more frequent because it is more disruptive and therefore more noticeable. Slips that involve confusions are likely to be particularly memorable because they tend to produce rather ludicrous results, but other slips of action may go unnoticed.

Automatic and Attentional Processes

From the classification of slips, some characteristic features have been identified. The most important finding is that slips of action occur predominantly with highly practised, overlearned, routine activities. Making cups of tea and coffee, for example, are activities that give rise to many of the reported slips of action. This is partly because actions that occur very frequently provide more opportunities for slips to occur. However, the predominance of tea and coffee errors is not just evidence of a national obsession, but also arises because these are routine, repeated actions. To understand the underlying mechanism, researchers have applied the distinction between *automatic* and *attentional processes* formulated by Shiffrin and Schneider (1977). Highly practised actions become automatic and can then be carried out according to pre-set instructions, with little or no conscious monitoring. Reason and Mycielska (1982) called this mode of action control an "open-loop" system.

Automatic, or open-loop, processes differ from attentional, or "closed-loop" processes. Attentional processes are under moment-to-moment control by a central processor, which monitors and guides the action sequence, modifying performance according to feedback about changes in external circumstances and internal needs and intentions. A good example of this distinction between automatic and attentional processes is provided by driving a car. Emerging from a road junction is (or ought to be) an attentional process. The traffic must be scanned, distances and speeds assessed, and the driver is consciously thinking about the actions that need to be implemented. In contrast, for the practised driver, changing gears is an automatic process. The actions involved do not need to be consciously monitored, and can usually be carried out successfully while the driver is attending to something quite different, like chatting to a passenger or calculating petrol consumption. Automatic action sequences have the advantage that they can be carried out while the conscious mind is freed to engage in other parallel activities. However, automatisation can lead to slips of action. Even automatic actions may need intermittent attention to keep them on the right track, and slips of action occur if attention is not shifted to the ongoing action at a critical point in the sequence.

Strong Habit Intrusions

An action sequence (or program) that is in frequent use is "stronger" than one that is used less often. There is a tendency for a stronger program to take over from a weaker program, particularly if some component stages are common to both. Slips of action often occur at junctions where two programs share a particular component and there is an involuntary switch-over to the stronger program. William James (1890) describes these switch-overs as "strong habit intrusions". In his example, a person went into the bedroom to change his clothes, took off his jacket and then got undressed completely and went to bed. The stronger "going to bed" program took over from the "changing clothes" program because both shared the common components of entering the bedroom and removing the jacket. The types of slip classed as goal switches and confusions may both occur because of strong habit intrusions.

Predisposing Conditions

Another predisposing condition, besides automaticity and competition from stronger habits, has been identified by Reason (1984). Any form of change in a well-established routine is liable to produce errors. In one of his examples, someone who had decided to give up sugar on cornflakes sprinkled it on as before. In the same way, the ex-smoker's hand goes to his pocket. Changing the locations of familiar objects can also disrupt routine actions. Eighteen months after my kitchen was re-designed I continue to throw the table-cloth into the rubbish bin from time to time.

In addition to these predisposing circumstances, there are predisposing internal states. Some individuals are much more prone to make these kinds of errors than other people, but many people find that slips of action increase with tiredness, illness, or stress.

Broadbent et al. (1982) developed the Cognitive Failures Questionnaire (CFQ) to serve as an index of an individual's susceptibility to slips of action, as well as other failures of memory and perception. Respondents were asked to assess the frequency with which they experienced specific examples of cognitive failure, e.g. "Do you forget whether you've turned off the light or fire, or locked the door?", on a five-point scale ranging from Never to Very Often. Broadbent et al. established that CFQ scores were not related to performance on tests of immediate and delayed memory, or to perception as measured by performance on a word-identification task. Martin and Jones (1984) later attempted to establish whether CFQ scores were related to any other aspects of cognitive ability, or to personality traits and internal states. They found that CFQ scores correlated significantly with ability to perform two tasks at the same time, indicating that poor ability to deploy attention and allocate processing resources effectively, is associated with frequent slips of actions as well as other forms of cognitive failure. CFQ scores were also related to forward digit span (the ability to repeat back a sequence of digits in the correct order). This ability to remember serial order is also involved in carrying out action sequences and the kind of slips classified as omissions and reversals arise as a result of breakdown in the maintenance of the correct serial order for components in an action sequence. Besides these measures of cognitive ability, Martin and Jones also reported an association between frequent cognitive failures and high anxiety, and cited studies by Parkes (1980) comparing nurses working on high-stress wards and low-stress wards, which suggested that cognitive failures are related to vulnerability to the effects of stress.

Models of Slips of Action

Both Reason (1984) and Norman (1981) have developed explanatory models of action control to account for absent-minded slips of action. Common to both models is the concept of an *action schema*. An action schema is a knowledge structure representing the sensorimotor knowledge that constitutes an action sequence. Schemas are linked together in related sets, and several action schemas may be operative simultaneously. Schema theory is described in more detail in Chapter 3, p.71.

Reason's Model

In Reason's model there are three levels of control. At the schema level, control is by automatic pre-programmed instructions built into the schemas; the activation of a particular schema initiates the action sequence. Schemas can be activated by sensory information or by another, already active schema. At this level, activation is influenced by recency and frequency of use. Schemas that have been implemented more recently or more frequently (the "strong habit" schemas) have lower thresholds and are more easily activated. The second level of control in Reason's model is the intention system, which generates goals, and can also activate the schemas that are appropriate for achieving these goals. The intention system assembles plans, monitors ongoing activity, and corrects errors. It has a limited capacity, so that only one plan is maximally active at any one time. At the third level, the attentional control system acts to energize or suppress the activation of particular schemas, deploying attentional resources in accordance with the goals of the intention system. Reason conceptualises the complete set of schemas as a "cognitive board" on which attentional resources in the form of an "attentional blob" are moved around and may be concentrated on one particular schema or diffused over several (see Fig. 2.1).

In this model, some action sequences require little or no attentional resources. These are the automatic, open-loop, schema-driven ones. Other, higher-level, closed-loop action sequences involving complex decision making require much more attention. Slips of action result from the faulty deployment of attention.

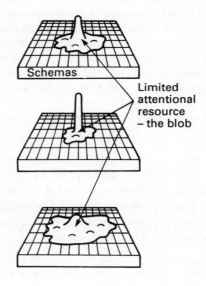

FIG. 2.1   The cognitive board with attentional resources more or less concentrated (from Reason, 1984).

Norman's Model

Norman's model emphasises the hierarchical organisation of schemas, which work together in organised groups as in Fig. 2.2. He calls the highest level "parent schemas". These correspond to global intentions or goals (like "having a cup of tea"). Subordinate level "child schemas" or

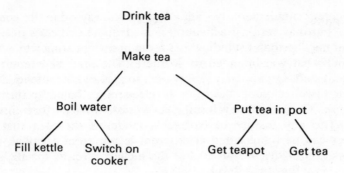

FIG. 2.2   A hierarchy of action schemas for making tea.

subschemas correspond to component actions necessary to achieve the overall goal (like "getting out the teapot" or "boiling water"). The activation level of each schema is determined by internal events (plans, needs, intentions) and by external events (the current situation). Each schema also has a set of triggering conditions that must be fulfilled for it to be implemented. These consist of external events and circumstances. A given schema operates when the activation level is above threshold, and the current situation matches the triggering conditions. So, in the tea-drinking example, the intention to have a cup of tea activates the whole set of schemas related to this goal, and the state of the boiling water might constitute the triggering condition for initiating the teapot-filling subschema.

According to Norman's model, slips of action result from faulty specification of the overall intention, faulty activation of the schemas, or faulty triggering. Particular examples of slips can be classified in terms of these causes. The specification of the intention to go to work may be inadequate if it fails to specify the intended form of transport, and could result in getting in the car when you meant to take the bus. Strong habit intrusions or goal switches, like driving to the wrong destination, can be explained as faulty activation. So, for example, the frequently used "going to work" schemas are more highly activated and may take over from the less frequent, less activated "visiting a friend" schemas. In Norman's terminology, this is a *capture error*. Tidying up the bathroom instead of fetching the washing is also a case of faulty activation. The mess in the bathroom matches the triggering conditions for the bathroom-tidying schema and causes it to be activated. Norman calls this kind of slip a *data-driven error* because the switch originates from externally cued activation. Reversals and repetitions occur when the triggering of an action sequence is faulty, and blends or confusions result if two different schemas are triggered simultaneously. Slips are not always due to competing schemas, but may result if activation is inadequate or fizzles out. In this case, you may be found standing in a room and wondering why you went there, and what you intended to do there. The original intention is no longer activated. Or, you may simply omit to perform the intended action, forgetting to collect your coat from the cleaners, or failing to turn off the electric fire. The activation is insufficient to sustain the performance of the actions. The key feature of Norman's model is the idea that action sequences can be represented at different levels, from a global, general representation of the overall goal at the highest level to specific subordinate actions at the lowest level.

The two models obviously have a good deal in common. In Norman's model, the postulated mechanism for action control is able to account for the different types of error that are observed. Reason's model does not offer such a fine-grained explanation. However, his claim that slips of action can be ascribed to faulty deployment of attention is supported by Martin and Jones's finding that ability to divide attention efficiently is related to the incidence of slips.

PROSPECTIVE MEMORY

What is Prospective Memory?

Retrospective memory involves remembering events experienced in the past, but prospective memory is memory for a future act. Prospective memory includes remembering a plan of action (i.e. what to do) and also remembering to do it. In most cases, the planned action has to be performed at a specified time, or within some time limits, so prospective memory also involves remembering when to perform the act. In everyday life, prospective memory is almost continuously active. We go through the day employing prospective memory to remember to pay the gas bill; to phone a relative; to buy some more cat food; to raise a point at a meeting; to look up a reference in the library; and so on. In spite of its undoubted importance, prospective memory had, until very recently, hardly been studied at all.

Baddeley and Wilkins (1984) have pointed out that the distinction betwen prospective and retrospective memory is not absolutely clear cut since prospective memory necessarily includes some elements of retrospective memory. In remembering my plan to phone my mother, I also remember, retrospectively, her number and how to use the phone, and not to call while she is watching "Dallas". However, in spite of this overlap between the two kinds of memory, there are numerous distinguishing features (West, Note 12). Prospective memory differs from retrospective memory at the encoding stage, since prospective plans are usually self-generated and do not involve initial learning, but the difference between the two is perhaps more marked at the retrieval stage. With retrospective memory the test of success is the accuracy and completeness of recall; with prospective memory the test of success is the execution of a plan that is appropriate and timely. It is no good implementing the plan too early or too late, and there is no particular value in sticking accurately to the original plan if circumstances have changed. Prospective plans have to be modified continually to meet changing conditions. It is no good raising a point at a meeting, as you intended, if someone else has made it first; it is pointless to phone a relative who has just phoned you.

Types of Prospective Memory

Prospective memory is probably much too broad a category to be useful. As research in this area progresses, distinctions between different types of prospective memory will need to be made. One obvious distinction is between self-imposed prospective tasks, and prospective tasks imposed by someone else. Another distinction is between prospective plans that are *routine plans* and involve remembering to perform familiar, often-performed, routine actions; and prospective plans that are *novel plans* and involve novel actions or modifications of familiar actions, such as performing familiar actions at different times or in novel contexts. A prospective plan may be for a single isolated action, or it may be part of a whole network of related plans. Some prospective plans are highly specific and detailed (e.g. going to a particular shop and buying a particular brand of cat food), and others are vaguer and more general (e.g. doing the shopping). This distinction is one of *level of formulation* and relates to Norman's ideas about a hierarchy of schemas. The prospective plan may involve only a high-level "parent" schema, or it may be formulated at a lower level and include specific subschemas. This point about specificity also applies to the *timing*, as well as the content, of the plan. Prospective memory involves time monitoring as well as remembering. A prospective plan may specify an exact time at which it must be implemented (e.g. 3.15 on Tuesday afternoon) or a much more indefinite one (e.g. before the library closes; next time I see him; after I've finished everything else I have to do today). Consideration of variations in the specificity of timing leads to a further distinction which rests on *priority*. Some plans are of vital importance and have high priority; others are much less important and have low priority. It is not necessarily the case that a prospective plan is implemented if it is remembered. Different plans may compete with each other for implementation time. Busy people have whole sets of prospective plans that are stacked up like planes over an airport, waiting to be implemented. Some will be postponed; some will be truncated; and some will be discarded altogether. These differences between various types of prospective memory are significant because they are likely to influence its efficiency. Both theoretical and common-sense considerations suggest that novel, high-priority plans that are part of a network of related plans are more likely to be remembered.

Methods of Studying Prospective Memory

Methods for studying prospective memory are still in early stages of development. So far, the methods adopted take the form of either questionnaires or naturalistic experiments. Questions about prospective memory have been incorporated in a number of questionnaires, e.g. "How often do you forget to keep appointments?", or "How often do you forget to take things with you when you go out?", or "How often do you forget to say something you intended to say?". Problems about the validity of self-assessments of this kind were discussed at greater length in Chapter 1, pp.9–11. One difficulty is that subjects may not always be aware of failures of prospective memory. Of course, failure to implement some plans is noticed because it brings serious consequences or earns bitter reproaches, but other failures may well pass unnoticed. In an experimental prospective memory task, Wilkins and Baddeley (1978) noted that although subjects remembered when they had performed planned actions, they tended to be unaware of omissions. This finding suggests that self-assessment of prospective memory is likely to be inaccurate. Several studies have reported that elderly people assess their prospective memory as better than young people assess theirs (Harris & Sunderland, Note 2). Logically this could arise if they more often fail to notice their errors, or, having noticed them at the time, they forget about them later, but Martin (1986) found that elderly people were essentially accurate in their self-assessment. However, the apparent superiority of elderly people could arise if their lifestyle is more relaxed so that the demands on prospective memory are less severe for them than for the young.

Naturalistic experiments provide more objective evidence of success or failure. Researchers on prospective memory set subjects a specific task, such as remembering to post a postcard or make a phone call to the experimenter at a designated time. This method allows the experimenter to vary factors such as the retention interval; the number and spacing of the to-be-remembered actions, and the incentives that are offered for successful performance.

Sometimes prospective memory tasks are incorporated in an interview (West, Note 11). In her study, remembering to keep the interview appointment was one test of prospective memory. Subjects were also told at the beginning of the interview that they should remember to locate a folder and hand it to the interviewer at the end of the session. Sinnott (Note 10) used a combination of questionnaire and experimental methods. Subjects at a research centre for a 2–3 day stay were quizzed on their memory for actions, objects, and persons experienced during the visit. Some of the items queried were classed as incidental (e.g. irrelevant objects in rooms), and other items were classed as prospective/intentional. These were defined as information useful for future actions, such as routes to the cafeteria, procedures for paying for meals, and arrangements for the next visit. Memory for the prospective information was more durable than memory for the incidental information.

A number of problems arise with naturalistic experiments like these. Although the experimenter can manipulate some of the relevant variables, there is no way of controlling other, potentially relevant, variables operating during the retention interval, such as the amount of rehearsal and the number of competing tasks. These experiments are examples of ones that have high ecological validity, retaining a close resemblance to the naturally occurring tasks of everyday life, but in so doing they sacrifice the element of control and are therefore difficult to interpret.

Issues in Prospective Memory

Research on prospective memory has reached a stage at which some of the interesting and important issues have been identified, although few questions have yet been resolved.

The Use of Reminders

The strategies that are used in prospective memory consist in setting up cues to remind the actor of the prospective task. Meacham and Leiman (Note 6) gave people postcards to post back at varying intervals up to 32 days later. Half the subjects were given coloured tags to hang on their key chains as a reminder, and there was some evidence that this improved performance. Levy and Loftus (1984) reviewed the effects of sending written reminders on whether patients remembered to attend for medical appointments. Without reminders only 40–50% kept their appointments, but both telephone and postal reminders produced a 10–20% increase in the number of people keeping their appointments.

However, many subjects spontaneously devise their own reminders, such as leaving the postcards in a prominent place. Moscovitch (1982) suggested that the superior performance of the elderly in some prospective memory tasks is due to increasing reliance on external reminders. Elderly people are known to make more use of written reminders in diaries and notes, and Harris (1980) also reported that middle-aged women made extensive use of reminders such as calendars and wall charts to remember family birthdays and social commitments. Other people make knots in handkerchiefs, leave objects where the eye will fall on them, or write in biro on their hands. Other strategies include mentally linking the prospective task to another routine event or activity, like scheduling prospective phone calls for coffee-break time, or linking picking up the dry-cleaning with going to work, so that one action cues another.

Differences in the extent to which people devise internal and external reminders, and use them efficiently, may underlie observed differences in prospective task performance between individuals, age groups, or sexe.

Motivation

Another important factor in prospective memory is motivation. This operates in two ways, affecting both compliance and memory. For a prospective act to be performed, the actor must not only remember to perform it, but also be willing to perform it. A patient may remember a hospital appointment, but not feel like going; or may remember to take prescribed medication, but decide not to take it. These are examples where poor motivation has caused a failure of compliance, rather than a failure of prospective memory. But the level of motivation may also affect whether the prospective act is remembered. It is a truism that very important appointments are rarely missed. When a job interview is make-or-break, you get there on time. A high level of motivation may ensure that an elaborate reminder system is set up and the sequence of events is carefully planned and frequently rehearsed.

These common-sense observations have been confirmed experimentally. Meacham and Singer (1977) gave subjects eight postcards to post back one a week for eight weeks. One group was offered a cash incentive for posting on time, which produced a small improvement in performance. The effects of experimental manipulation of motivation by incentives are not very striking, but there is reason to believe that self-generated motivation in naturally occurring prospective memory tasks is a more powerful factor.

Time Factors

Another factor that has been studied experimentally is timing. Time factors such as the length of the retention interval, the time of day, and the regularity of target times have been manipulated. Wilkins and Baddeley (1978) designed a study to simulate remembering to take pills at specified times. Subjects had to press a button on a small box at 8.30 a.m., 1.00 p.m., 5.30 p.m. and 10 p.m. each day for 7 days. The apparatus in the box recorded the time of each button press. Lateness of response increased across the 7 days and across each day, with 8.30 a.m. responses being more accurate than later ones. This time-of-day effect might be due to the distracting effect of competing activities later in the day.

By analogy with retrospective memory, it would be expected that prospective memory would decline as the retention interval increased. However, Wilkins (1976) varied the retention interval in a postcard task from 2 to 36 days, but found no effect of increasing delay. The fact that prospective memory does not operate like retrospective memory was underlined by Wilkins and Baddeley's finding that subjects with low scores on a free recall task did better on a prospective memory task. In this case, people who have poor retrospective memory, as measured by a conventional laboratory task, perform well on a more naturalistic prospective memory task.

Harris and Wilkins (1982) studied the effect of response spacing. Subjects were asked to hold up a card at 3-minute or 9-minute intervals while watching a film. They found no effect of response spacing and no effect of the stage of the film. The interesting finding in this study was that subjects sometimes forgot to make the response even though they had checked the time within the previous 10 seconds. In this situation, with the competing activity of watching the film, it was difficult to hold prospective intentions in mind even for a very short time. Everyday life often involves concurrent tasks, and we are often distracted from our prospective intentions as, absorbed in one activity, we forget to interrupt it and do something else. The amount and type of concurrent activity are likely to be important factors in naturally occurring prospective memory, but have yet to be investigated systematically. Common sense suggests that busy people with a lot on their minds might perform differently from those with a more relaxed schedule.

Plan Schemas

Studies that are indirectly relevant to prospective memory were carried out by Lichtenstein and Brewer (1980) and Brewer and Dupree (1983). They were investigating memory for actions that had already been performed, rather than memory for future actions. They adopted a theoretical framework similar to Norman's (1981) hierarchy of schemas, and proposed that goal-directed sequences of actions are organised within an overall plan schema. Within the plan schema, the actions are linked by the *in-order-to* relationship to an overall goal. In their example, the actor takes keys from pocket in-order-to unlock the door in-order-to open the door in-order-to go into the house, etc. The overall goal is getting into the house. Lichtenstein and Brewer found that subjects who viewed videotapes of action sequences showed good agreement in segmenting the sequences and identifying subgoals. In a recall test, actions higher up in the goal hierarchy were remembered better than those lower down, and actions that did not relate directly to the main goal (e.g. putting keys back in pocket) were also less well remembered. They concluded that plan schemas have a strong influence on recall of actions. Brewer and Dupree, in a further series of experiments, were able to clarify the role of plan schemas. Their results indicated that, over time, information about actions was progressively lost from the hierarchy in a bottom-up direction, but the plan schema was used to reconstruct the whole action sequence at the retrieval stage. In everyday life, prospective plans are commonly embedded within each other. For example, my plan to remember to buy some eggs is embedded in a higher-order plan to make a birthday cake. If prospective plans are like retrospective actions in being better remembered when they are embedded in a plan schema, then experiments on prospective memory may be under-estimating everyday ability by using isolated tasks that do not form part of a plan schema.

Other factors that are potentially relevant to prospective memory have so far received little attention. These include emotions and personality traits and states such as levels of anxiety and stress, and the effects of fatigue and illness.

Modelling Prospective Memory

Levy and Loftus (1984) attempted to construct a theoretical model to predict performance in prospective memory tasks. In this model, the probability of remembering to perform an act is given by the joint probability of G (the probability of generating a cue to carry out the action at the proper time); R (given the cue, the probability of remembering what the action is); and A (given that the cue is generated and the action remembered, the probability of actually carrying it out). They suggested that research should aim to discover which of these probabilities is influenced by factors that are known to affect prospective memory, such as incentives and timing. This more analytic, theoretical approach to the study of prospective memory is, in principle, the best way to integrate the findings but, in practice, prospective memory takes so many different forms and is influenced by so many different factors, that it is doubtful how successful a predictive model of this kind could hope to be.

REALITY MONITORING

What is Reality Monitoring?

One aspect of prospective memory that has not been discussed so far is remembering whether an act has been performed. It is no good remembering to do something if you do not know whether you have already done it. You need to be able to distinguish between the memory of an action and the memory of an intention or plan to perform that action. Sometimes it may be difficult to distinguish these two kinds of memory, as for example, when you are uncertain whether you actually locked the door, or turned off the lights, or whether you intended to do so but have not in fact performed the actions. The ability to make such distinctions is part of a more general ability that has been called reality monitoring.

Reality monitoring is the ability to discriminate between externally derived memories that originate from perceptions, and internally derived memories that originate from imagination. External memories represent events that really occurred, objects that were perceived, actions that were performed, words that were spoken or written. Internal memories are of events that have only been imagined, actions that were planned, considered or intended, words that were thought but never uttered. The ability to distinguish between what goes on in the head and what goes on in the real world, between fact and fantasy, is a crucial aspect of competence in everyday life.

The distinction between internal and external memories may seem like a trivially easy one. You may think that nobody in their right minds can fail to make it. But second thoughts bring to mind many examples of confusions and uncertainty. Many memories are in fact a mixture of perceived and self-generated material. When you remember events from your early childhood, for example, what you remember of the original experience is typically overlaid and interwoven with what you have heard other people tell you about it, and with your own imaginative reconstructions, which have filled in gaps, and may have transformed the original event. Similarly, we often hear someone telling an anecdote that improves with each re-telling, being imaginatively embellished by the narrator until he himself can no longer distinguish truth from fiction.

Cognitive psychologists are in agreement with these common-sense observations. From Bartlett (1932) to Bransford and Franks (1972), the constructivist view of memory has emphasised the role of elaboration, interpretation, and reconstruction based on prior experience and stored knowledge. On this view, memory is not a direct copy of the physical information received through the senses. Remembering is not just a process of passively receiving impressions, but of creatively constructing a representation. Of course, some memories are much closer to an exact copy and some rely to a greater extent on construction, but most externally derived memories contain some elements that are internally generated.

Failures of Reality Monitoring

In spite of the fact that many memories are a joint product of external and internal elements, people are usually fairly competent at distinguishing fact from fantasy. Failures of reality monitoring are characteristic of schizophrenia, dementia, delirium, intoxication, and other states of mental abnormality which involve hallucinations or obsessions. In these disorders there is usually inability to distinguish between the real and the imaginary in current experience as well as in past experience. Developmental psychologists have also suggested that in early childhood the borderline between what is real and what is imaginary is not a clear one (Flavell, Flavell, & Green, 1983). However, failures of reality monitoring are not confined to abnormal or immature individuals. In everyday life imperfect reality monitoring is quite common in normal intelligent adults, and is an important source of errors in judgements, in action, and in belief.

Some types of slips of action and failures of prospective memory originate because the memory of an action planned is confused with the memory of an action performed. For example, you may be uncertain whether you have added salt to the soup or only thought of doing so. Sometimes you may find yourself thinking "I know I thought I must remember to lock the back door but did I actually do it?" Or you may be confused about whether you said something or only intended to say it. Misplacing objects can result from a similar kind of confusion. You thought you put the missing keys, diary, or whatever in the usual place, but in fact you only planned the action and never carried it out. Occasionally you may be uncertain whether an event really happened or whether it occurred in a particularly vivid dream. We all have these experiences.

It is important to note that the direction of confusion affects the type of error that is made. When a plan or imagined act is mistaken for the memory of a real act, the consequence is an omission error. If you mistakenly think that you have already put salt in the soup or locked the door, the result is that the soup is left unsalted or the door unlocked. If, on the other hand, the memory of a performed action is mistaken for the memory of a plan, the result is a repetition error. The soup gets salted twice over, or a second dose of medicine is taken, or you go to lock the door only to find it already done. Everyday experience and questionnaire data such as Reason's 1979 study suggest that these errors are more commonly associated with routine, frequently performed actions. With these actions the difficulty lies in deciding whether a memory of performing the action is today's memory or yesterday's. (A colleague told me she often had to check whether her toothbrush was wet in order to decide whether she had brushed her teeth.) Strictly speaking, these are not errors of reality monitoring but problems of temporal dating. It is not so much a question of distinguishing between plan and action but between a recently performed action and a less recent performance of the same action.

Repetition Errors

Koriat and Ben-Zur (Note 3) attributed repetition errors, when people repeat an action because they are unaware that they have already performed it, to defective output monitoring. They distinguished between two modes of output monitoring: on-line cancellation and retrospective judgements. On-line cancellation processes may operate to erase or tag a plan once it has been executed, just as I might strike out or tick the items on a shopping list when I have bought them, or executed plans may simply lose activation so that they are unlikely to be re-activated. In the absence of cancellation processes, retrospective checks may establish whether an act has been performed. These checks may be external or internal. We can check the external consequences, by tasting the soup, or by trying the door handle. Alternatively, we can carry out an internal check, examining the memory trace of the act and making a reality monitoring judgement about it.

Another type of reality monitoring error affects judgements of frequency. The judged frequency of occurrence of a particular event may be inflated if that event is frequently imagined. The internally generated memories are added to the externally derived ones. Johnson (1985) suggests that people's subjective estimates of how often they have been ill or unhappy could be influenced by the frequency with which episodes of illness or unhappiness have been thought about.

Models of Reality Monitoring

Johnson and Raye (1981) have put forward a model to explain how reality monitoring decisions are made, and they and their colleagues have tested the predictions of the model in a series of experiments. According to this model, there are two ways in which external memories can be distinguished from internally generated ones.

Evaluation of Qualitative Attributes

The first method depends on the evaluation of qualitative features of the memory trace. The differences between the two kinds of memory trace are listed in Table 2.1.

External memories are characterised by being relatively richer in sensory attributes such as sound, colour, and texture. They are set in a context of time and place of occurrence and other ongoing events, and are more detailed. Internal memories are more schematic and lacking in sensory and contextual details. They are also more likely to contain traces of the cognitive operations (such as reasoning, inferring, imaging) that generated

TABLE 2.1
Qualitative Differences Between External and Internal Memories

Attributes	External Memories	Internal Memories
Contextual attributes – space and time	+	–
Sensory attributes – visual, auditory, haptic	+	–
Detail and complexity	+	–
Coherence	+	–
Schematic quality	–	+
Cognitive operations – imaging, reasoning, decision processes	–	+

them. According to the model, the origin of a memory can generally be determined by the extent to which it possesses these characteristics. Figure 2.3 shows how memories are evaluated according to the amount of contextual information they incorporate.

However, qualitative differences would not invariably provide a clear indication of origin. Some internal memories can be unusually vivid and detailed. Shepard (1984) has pointed out that the memory representations generated for prospective planning must be accurate and detailed if they are to be any use. If you are mentally planning how to change the furniture around, or deciding whether you can get into a parking space, or whether a particular wallpaper would look well in your living room, you need to be

Probable internal   Uncertain origin   Probable external

Strength or amount of contextual information

FIG. 2.3   Representation of a set of decision rules for judging the origin of a memory on the basis of the amount of contextual information it includes (triangles = externally derived memories; circles = internally derived memories) (from Johnson & Raye, 1981). Copyright (1981) by the American Psychological Association. Reprinted by permission of the author.

able to generate internal representations that are a good match with external reality. And, of course, failures of reality monitoring confirm that internal and external representations can sometimes be confused with each other.

Coherence and Plausibility. For memories that fall in the region of uncertainty in Fig. 2.3, different methods of evaluation could be employed. One method is to invoke criteria of coherence and plausibility. External memories ought to make sense in terms of our knowledge of the world. Internal memories, like fantasies and dreams, can sometimes be recognised because they violate natural laws or conflict with other knowledge. A dream in which you can fly or are invisible is unlikely to be true, and if the fantasy in which you tell your boss exactly what you think of him were a real event you would be out of a job. People can sometimes check on the reality of a memory by trying to recall supporting context. If you can remember that when you locked the back door the key was stiff, and the cat was on the wrong side, the memory is probably of a performed action and not an imagined one.

Another criterion is based on confidence. People appear to operate a strategy that has been called the "It had to be you" effect (Johnson & Raye, 1981). This strategy is used to determine whether a memory is of an action performed by oneself or by someone else. People assume that if the memory was something they had done or said themselves, they would be quite confident about its origin ("I'd know it if I'd done it"). If they are not confident they attribute the action to another person ("It had to be you").

Experimental Evidence

Johnson and her colleagues have tested this model of reality monitoring processes in a series of experiments, manipulating the attributes of internal and external memories and observing the effects on reality-monitoring judgements.

The Effect of Qualitative Similarity

Johnson, Raye, Wang, and Taylor (1979) tested the prediction that people who are unusually good at forming vivid and detailed visual images should be poor at making reality monitoring judgements because the vividness of their self-generated images would make them qualitatively similar to externally derived memories. Conversely, people who are poor at imaging should be better able to distinguish their vaguer images from real memories. Prior to the experiment, subjects were divided into good and poor imagers on the basis of scores in a test requiring them to recall visual details of a picture they had seen. (In fact this was a test of visual memory rather than of visual imagery and was not altogether appropriate for the rationale of this experiment.) In the experimental session, subjects were shown pictures of common objects, but interspersed with the pictures were trials in which they were given the name of an object and told to imagine it. The number of times a particular object was displayed as a picture, and the number of times it was imagined, were varied. Later, subjects were unexpectedly asked to judge the number of times each picture had been actually seen, ignoring the times it had been imagined. As predicted, for good imagers, the judged frequency was inflated by the number of times they had imagined the item. Poor imagers were less affected. Apparently, rich imagery makes reality monitoring harder.

The Role of Cognitive Operations

The cognitive content of memories has also been manipulated in several experiments. The experimenters worked on two assumptions: (1) that the more difficult an item is to generate in thought, the greater the amount of cognitive operations that will be present in the memory trace; and (2) that the greater the amount of cognitive operations in the trace, the more easily it will be recognised as self-generated.

In one experiment Johnson, Raye, Foley, and Foley (1981) compared subjects' ability to identify which words they had generated and spoken themselves and which words had been generated and spoken by the experimenter. The words were instances (e.g."dog") generated in response to category cues (e.g."animal"). When a first-letter cue was added to the category cue (e.g."animal, d—"), the identification of origin was less accurate. Johnson et al. argued that the added cue elicited the response automatically and so reduced the need for cognitive operations in generating the response, and the reduced cognitive component made the memory harder to identify as self-generated. This interpretation rests on the distinction between automatic and attentional processes described on pp.19–20, and the idea that automatic processes occur without involving cognitive operations such as search and selection. In a further experiment, they found that it was also harder to identify the origin of highly typical (and hence more easily elicited) instances of a category than to identify the origin of more unusual instances. So, for example, a subject who generated the typical instance "apple" to the category cue "fruit" would be more likely to mistake its origin than one who generated "pomegranate".

Johnson (1985) pointed out that the recall of memories under hypnosis can be explained in terms of the reality monitoring model. It has been shown (Dywan & Bowers, 1983) that attempts to enhance recall by hypnosis yield more false memories. Johnson suggested that memories generated under hypnosis may be like dreams. They have great vividness, but because they are produced without the exercise of cognitive control, they would lack any trace of cognitive operations. Internally generated false memories might then be indistinguishable from genuine, externally derived memories.

Further evidence in support of the general principles of Johnson and Raye's model comes from Anderson's study (1984). She compared Johnson's claim that errors in reality monitoring are caused by confusability of the memory traces, and an alternative explanation whereby origin information is coded directly on the memory trace in the form of a tag and errors occur when the tag is lost. According to the confusability explanation, different kinds of self-generated memories, such as memories of performed actions and memories of imagined actions, are more similar to each other, and less similar to the other-generated memory traces derived from other people's actions. The confusability explanation predicts that errors should reflect a gradient of similarity; that is, the greater the similarity between origins, the greater the probability of confusing them. The origin-tag explanation, on the other hand, predicts that all types of confusion would be equally likely since, once a tag is lost, origin identification must be pure guesswork. Her experiments used simple line drawings as stimuli. Subjects had to trace the drawings (the Perform condition); imagine tracing them (Imagine); or watch someone else trace them (Look). She found that subjects were most likely to confuse the more similar self-generated memories (Perform and Imagine) than to confuse the self-generated memories with other-generated (Look) memories. She concluded that these results were consistent with Johnson and Raye's model. Subjects judged the origin of memories by evaluating qualities of the trace rather than by inspecting origin tags.

Some of Johnson's assumptions are simplistic, the observed effects are not very large, and in some cases, there is no independent evidence that the attempt to manipulate the nature of the mental representation and covert processes was successful. Nevertheless, a substantial body of confirmation for her model has accumulated.

Developmental Studies of Reality Monitoring

Some developmental studies have explored age differences in reality monitoring ability. Foley, Johnson, and Raye (1983) tested 6-, 9- and 17-year-olds in a task that required them to discriminate between words that had been said and those that had been heard (Say vs. Listen); or between those that had been said and those that had been thought (Say vs. Think). The young children had no difficulty in the say–listen condition in discriminating between what they had said themselves and what someone else had said. They were also able to discriminate between words spoken by two different speakers (i.e. two external sources), but 6-year-olds were more likely to confuse the two self-generated sources, saying and thinking. Foley and Johnson (1985) also noted a similar developmental pattern in memory for the origin of actions. The younger children distinguished doing and watching, but not doing and imagining. At the other end of the developmental spectrum, Cohen and Faulkner (1988b) found that elderly people made more false positive errors in a reality-monitoring task. They were more likely to misidentify actions they had only imagined, or actions that had not occurred at all, as ones they had performed themselves. There was evidence that elderly people have a lower criterion for deciding that a memory is a "real" externally derived one, but age-related deficits in the very young and very old may also partly be due to failure to encode distinctive features on the memory trace.

None of these experiments are very closely analogous to reality monitoring in everyday life, and Cohen and Faulkner noted that the self-rated incidence of reality-monitoring errors in daily life correlated only weakly with errors in their experimental task. In the laboratory tasks, when words are used as stimuli, they are isolated words occurring without context and do not form part of a meaningful message. When actions are the stimuli, they are not goal directed and do not form part of an overall plan schema. The experimental tasks are not sufficiently like naturally occurring instances of reality monitoring for us to be able to draw conclusions about how people normally distinguish internal and external memories in everyday life.

PLANNING

What is Planning?

Prospective memory involves remembering what to do and when to do it. Planning and mental rehearsal are concerned with *how* to do it. As defined by Hayes-Roth and Hayes-Roth (1979, pp.275–276) a plan is the "predetermination of a course of action aimed at achieving some goal." According to Battman (1987, p.4), a plan is "an ordered set of control statements to support the efficiency of actions and the preparation of alternative actions for the case of failure." In everyday life, people spend a lot of time planning how to do things. This is particularly true when a prospective task is a novel or complex one involving a sequence of actions, and when decisions have to be taken as to which actions will produce the best results. People plan journeys and holidays; what to buy for dinner and what to plant in the garden; how to play a hand of bridge or behave at a job interview. Those actions which are unplanned are very simple or very routine ones; automatic, unconscious actions or purely impulsive actions. For most people a high proportion of their daily activities involves some degree of planning.

Planning has been described as mental simulation, envisaging the circumstances and running through possible actions, evaluating the consequences and selecting the optimal actions and the optimal order for executing them. Planning depends on memory. Knowledge derived from past experience and stored in long-term memory must be retrieved and used in formulating possible plans, and in constructing representations of hypothetical events. A working memory buffer store is needed to hold tentative or incomplete plans while these are being evaluated or revised. These important functions of memory have been relatively neglected by psychologists.

Individual Differences in Planning

It is common knowledge that people differ in the amount of planning they habitually do. We all know people who rush into things without stopping to think at all, and others who obsessively think through every detail before embarking on a course of action. There has been little formal investigation of these differences. Giambra (1979) analysed the content of daydreams (defined as thought unrelated to the current task), and found that for all age groups the majority of daydreams were of the type he called "problem solving" and involved planning future activities. Young males were the exception to this generalisation; they had more daydreams of love and sex than of problem solving. Females of all ages had more problem-solving daydreams than males. This finding has also emerged from a questionnaire used in a pilot study by Cohen and Faulkner (unpublished). Females reported spending more time on mental planning, planning in more detail, and formulating more alternative plans in case of difficulties. Elderly people also reported more planning than young people. The reasons underlying these differences are not clear, but probably include personality, level of anxiety, work load, and the importance of efficient performance.

Planning Meals

A detailed study of planning by Byrne (1977) f%cused on the everyday task of planning meals. Six experienced cooks were taken as subjects, and were asked to plan a three-course meal for a dinner party, and subsequently to plan five further meals for the same guests. They were encouraged to "think aloud" as they planned, and their speech was recorded and later transcribed and analysed. This method of asking people to think aloud while they perform a task yields what is called a *verbal protocol*. The use of verbal protocols was discussed on pp.8–9.

In analysing the protocols, the researcher searches for patterns that can be classified. In Fig. 2.4, the protocol of one of Byrne's subjects (given in

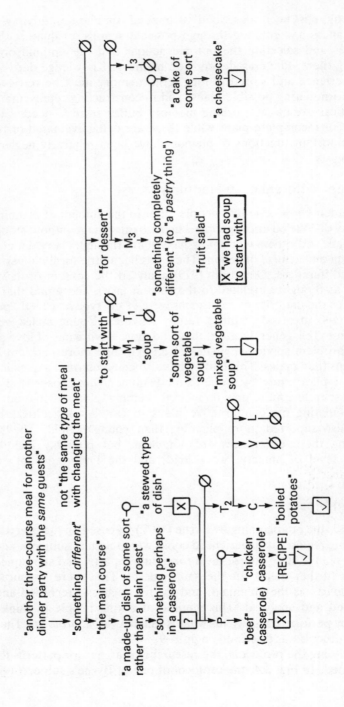

FIG. 2.4   The flow of decisions in the planning of a dinner-party menu (from Bryne, 1977).

---

1. Another three-course meal for another dinner party with the same guests – I see
2. Right. So now we have to change things
3. well if we're going to be original we won't just use the same type of meal with changing the meat, we'll have something different
4. so perhaps as the main course we'll have a made-up dish of some sort rather than just a plain roast [5 sec]
5. something perhaps in a casserole
6. or even a stewed type of dish [3 sec]
7. not beef, perhaps a chicken casserole, that would be nice
8. have a chicken casserole with lots of veg in the casserole, like onions and carrots and leeks and mushrooms
9. and, er, boiled potatoes would go with that, as the main dish
10. then
11. soup, to start with, be nice change, can always do that
12. and you have to specify a kind of soup [3 sec]
13. I should think some sort of vegetable soup
14. mixed vegetable soup [4 sec]
15. and then
16. for dessert [3 sec]
17. if we gave them a pastry thing last time, we're going to want something completely different
18. which could perhaps be [3 sec]
19. not a fruit salad, if we had soup to start with, we want something a bit more solid than that, I think [6 sec]
20. perhaps a cake of some sort
21. like cheesecake
22. to finish with

(*Pause times are shown in brackets: total planning time was 110 seconds.*)

---

the extract above) is represented as a transition graph, showing the flow of decision making.

In Fig. 2.4, stages marked X indicate a dish has been rejected. A question mark signals judgement is deferred, and a tick shows a dish has been accepted. The symbol $\varnothing$ is used to show a goal or sub-goal is satisfied.

The protocols showed a number of general characteristics. Subjects set up a list of goals (main course, starter, dessert). Goals such as the main course were subdivided into separate subgoals for P (protein), V (vegetables), and C (carbohydrate). Different subjects ordered the goals consistently. For example, the main course was selected before the starter, and the P component of the main course was chosen before C and V. Certain common processes could be identified. Subjects generated a category (e.g. a cake) and then an instance (a cheesecake). Each choice imposed new restrictions on subsequent processes (e.g. a wet starter like soup rules out a wet dessert like fruit salad). Byrne concluded that people generate abstract descriptions of meals which set out goals they must satisfy, e.g. constraints of costs, seasonal availability, or creating contrasts within and between meals. The memory structures involved in the meal-planning task appear to include abstract descriptions of this kind, as well as a domain-specific knowledge base in semantic memory which stores long-term knowledge of cookery in the form of sets and subsets representing categories and instances of dishes and their properties. In addition, Byrne concluded that a short-term memory store was needed to hold an ordered stack of current goals, as well as a buffer store for evaluation and comparison of candidates.

This detailed analysis of a planning task makes explicit the mental processes that are involved in a natural everyday task. Even so, the generality of the observed patterns cannot be taken for granted. Other types of planning activity, such as planning journeys, are subject to different kinds of constraints such as time and distance, and are determined more by externally imposed factors like transport availability than by internally imposed preferences. Also the meal-planning task involves selection of items to satisfy goals, whereas other tasks involve selection of actions as a means toward attaining goals.

Planning Errands

Another detailed study of planning by Hayes-Roth and Hayes-Roth (1979) also used verbal protocols to study the way people plan a day's errands. The subjects' task was to produce a plan for completing as many as possible of the errands listed in the following extract, moving around the hypothetical town shown in the map (Fig. 2.5).

> You have just finished working out at the health club. It is 11.00 and you can plan the rest of your day as you like. However, you must pick up your car from the Maple Street parking garage by 5.30 and then head home. You'd also like to see a movie today, if possible. Show times at both movie theatres are 1.00, 3.00 and 5.00. Both movies are on your 'must see' list, but go to whichever one fits most conveniently into your plan. Your other errands are as follows:
> pick up medicine for your dog at the vet
> buy a fan belt for your refrigerator at the appliance store
> check out two of the three luxury apartments
> meet a friend for lunch at one of the restaurants
> buy a toy for your dog at the pet store
> pick up your watch at the watch repair
> special order a book at the bookstore
> buy fresh vegetables at the grocery
> buy a gardening magazine at the newsstand
> go to the florist to send flowers to a friend in hospital

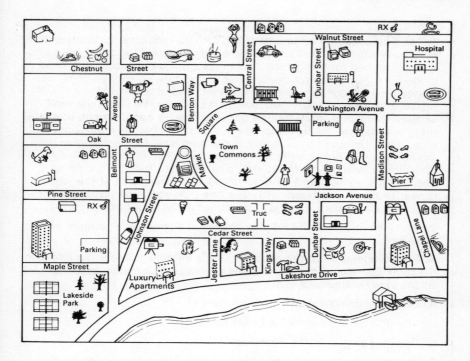

FIG. 2.5   The town map for the errand-planning task (Hayes-Roth & Hayes-Roth, 1979)

Figure 2.6 reproduces one of the verbal protocols. This typical subject started by defining the goal and tasks and classifying errands as high priority or low priority. He begins sequencing the errands from the start point, forming clusters of errands based on priority and on adjacency. There are frequent revisions of the plan, and at a later stage, some sequencing backward in time from the final errand (picking up the car at 5.30). The mental simulation of one stage of the plan guides the later stages, and consists in mentally timing the actions and inferring the consequences. Planning occurs at different levels of abstraction, sometimes involving specific items and sometimes higher-order clusters.

Hayes-Roth and Hayes-Roth noted that planning was opportunistic. The subject did not formulate an overall global plan and then proceed to fill in the stages by successive refinements, but jumped about between levels with many shifts and changes. Instead of being controlled in a top-down direction by higher-order principles and pre-set goals, the plan was under multi-directional control, many decisions being influenced on a moment-to-moment basis by new facts that came to light as planning proceeded.

1. Let's go back down the errand list. Pick up medicine for the dog at veterinary supplies. That's definitely a primary, anything taking care of health. Fan belt for refrigerator. Definitely a primary because you need to keep the refrigerator. Checking out two of three luxury apartments. Its got to be a secondary, another browser. Meet the friend at one of the restaurants for lunch. All right. Now, that's going to be able to be varied I hope. That's a primary though because it is an appointment, something you have to do. Buy a toy for the dog at pet store. If you pass it, sure. If not, the dog can play with something else. Movie in one of the movie theaters. Better write that down, those movie times, 1, 3, or 5. Write that down on my sheet just to remember. And that's a primary because it's something I have to do. Pick up the watch at the watch repair. That's one of those borderline ones. Do you need your watch or not? Give it a primary. Special order a book at the bookstore.

2. We're having an awful lot of primaries in this one. It's going to be a busy day.

3. Fresh vegetables at the grocery. That's another primary. You need the food. Gardening magazine at the newsstand. Definitely secondary. All the many obligations of life.

4. Geez, can you believe all these primaries?

5. All right. We are now at the health club.

6. What is going to be the closest one?

7. The appliance store is a few blocks away. The medicine for the dog at the vet's office isn't too far away. Movie theaters – let's hold off on that for a little while. Pick up the watch. That's all the way across town. Special order a book at the bookstore.

8. Probably it would be best if we headed in a southeasterly direction. Start heading this way. I can see later on there are a million things I want to do in that part of town.

9. No we're not. We could end up with a movie just before we get the car. I had thought at first that I might head in a southeasterly direction because there's a grocery store, a watch repair, a movie theater all in that general area. Also a luxury apartment. However, near my parking lot also is a movie, which would make it convenient to get out of the movie and go to the car. But I think we can still end up that way.

10. All right. Apparently the closest one to the health club is going to the vet's shop. So I might as well get that out of the way. It's a primary and is the closest. We'll start . . .
   [The experimenter mentions that he has overlooked the nearby restaurant and flower shop.]

11. Oh, how foolish of me. You're right. I can still do that and still head in the general direction.

12. But, then again, that puts a whole new light on things. We do have

a bookstore. We do have. OK. Break up town into sections. We'll call them northwest and southeast. See how many primaries are in that section. Down there in the southeast section, we have the grocery store, the watch repair and the movie theater. In the northwest section we have the grocery store, the bookstore, the flower shop, the vet's shop, and the restaurant.

13. And since we are leaving at 11.00, we might be able to get these chores done so that some time when I'm in the area, hit that restaurant. Let's try for that. Get as many of those out of the way as possible. We really could have a nice day here.

14. OK. First choose number one. At 11.00 we leave the health club. Easily, no doubt about it, we can be right across the street in 5 minutes to the flower shop. here we go. Flower shop at 11.05. Let's give ourselves 10 minutes to browse through some bouquets and different floral arrangements.

FIG. 2.6   Thinking aloud protocol from the errand-planning task. (From Hayes-Roth & Hayes-Roth, 1979).

Planning was incremental, with tentative decisions becoming gradually firmer, and alternative plans were considered in parallel.

The cognitive model they formulated to represent these aspects of the planning process included a working memory buffer, which they call the *blackboard*, where different forms of knowledge interact. The different kinds of knowledge include:

1. Knowledge of the overall task (the metaplan).
2. A set of possible actions, procedures for implementing them and outcomes (plans).
3. A list of desirable attributes (such as quick, adjacent) for these plans (plan-abstractions).
4. A knowledge base of specific data about errand routes and locations.

The model also has an executive for taking decisions and for allocation of resources. A computer simulation of this model of errand planning produced a protocol broadly similar to that produced by a human subject, but the computer's plan was more feasible. It sacrificed more of the low-priority errands and, unlike the human subject's plan, it could have been completed in the available time.

The errand-planning task is clearly different in many respects from the meal-planning task. The problem lies in selecting and ordering actions, not items. The constraints are mainly of time and distance, and the structure of the task is less hierarchical. However, some common features do emerge from the two studies. Both tasks involve a number of goals that are interdependent. Both models of the planning process include a knowledge base. Byrne's abstract descriptions are roughly equivalent to the Hayes-Roths' plan-abstractions, and his buffer store for carrying out evaluations and decision processes is like the Hayes-Roths' blackboard.

The Travelling Salesman Problem

A rather different approach is reflected in Battman's (1987) study of the planning involved in the travelling salesman problem. He is interested primarily in the function of planning and in individual differences in planning. Battman argues that planning entails an investment of time and effort. It is therefore only cost effective if it improves efficiency and/or reduces anxiety in the execution phase. But planning is not always helpful. If the plan is inadequate, or if circumstances change, it may be a positive disadvantage.

Battman compared the performance of two groups of subjects in a version of the travelling salesman task. Subjects had to act as chain-store supervisors, visiting 10 stores in one day. Three of the visits had to be made at pre-arranged times, plus or minus 10 minutes. They had to make decisions about marketing or finance at each store. They had access to a map and information about average between-store travel times and the average time needed to handle a problem within a store. In addition, they could change any of the appointment times, provided this was done at least 25 minutes beforehand. Arriving early for an appointment meant wasting time; arriving late entailed making a second visit. One group of subjects were instructed to plan before beginning the task. They could fix intermediate goals and write out a schedule of visits. The other group were not instructed to plan ahead.

The planning subjects performed more efficiently. They kept more appointments punctually, completed more visits, spent less time driving between stores, and made more use of the ability to change appointments. As well as these indices of efficiency, level of stress was monitored during performance. The findings differed according to the intelligence of the subjects. High I.Q. subjects who planned were more stressed on the first trial, but benefited on later trials. Planning was cost effective for them since it improved efficiency and reduced anxiety. For low I.Q. subjects planning brought no reduction in anxiety. Planning did increase their efficiency, but sticking to the plan was effortful, and a high level of stress was maintained. Battman concluded that generating and executing a plan can, in some circumstances, be more demanding than simply responding in an *ad hoc* way and "making it up as you go along". Most of us can probably think of people we know who are meticulous planners, but who clearly suffer a good deal of agitation in trying to execute these plans.

Memory Representations in Planning

Types of Representation

The types of representational system that are current in cognitive psychology fall into three basic types: propositional, analogical, and procedural (Rumelhart & Norman, 1985). In propositional systems knowledge is represented as a set of symbols arranged to constitute statements of facts or rules. Much of the factual knowledge used in planning is represented as propositions. For example, the knowledge that a cheesecake is a dessert and a chicken casserole is a meat dish, or that restaurants serve lunch between 12.30 and 2 p.m. can all be represented propositionally.

Procedural representations encode knowledge about how to perform actions like cooking or ordering a book, and this knowledge is stored in the form of a set of procedures. Procedural knowledge must necessarily be involved at the stage when planned actions are executed.

Analogue representational systems are ones in which the objects and events being represented map directly onto the representation. An analogue representation is more like a copy of the real thing. Some kinds of information involved in planning might be better represented analogically. The same information could be represented propositionally, but the analogical form has certain advantages. An analogical representation of the spatial layout of a town allows relations like *next to*, *nearest to*, to be read off directly, and hypothetical moves can be evaluated in terms of locations and distances. Analogical representations are dynamic. They are readily transformed, rotated, dismantled. They can be constructed from different viewpoints; they can represent change and movement; and they are specific and determinate. Whereas propositions are truth functional (i.e. they are either true or false), analogical models can be hypothetical. These characteristics of analogical representations are well suited to mental planning tasks, but they also have some shortcomings. It is not easy to see how some kinds of information can be represented in an analogue form. Temporal and causal factors, quantifiers like *all, some, several*, and relations like negation are easier to represent propositionally.

It is important to note that these different forms of representation are not mutually exclusive. Different aspects of the real world may be represented in different ways, and a particular object or event may be represented in different ways at different times. It is a reasonable assumption that the memory representations used in planning are of more than one kind.

Difficulties may be solved by adopting a hybrid model combining both kinds of representation. Kosslyn (1981) incorporates both propositions and analogue imagery in his model. He postulates a "deep representation" which stores propositional knowledge in long-term memory. Also in long-term memory, there is what Kosslyn calls a "literal representation ", consisting of sets of co-ordinate points. From the deep and literal representations, a "surface representation" in the form of an analogue spatial image can be generated as a temporary display, and there are processes that can scan the image, and can expand, contract, or rotate it. This kind of multiple representation model is well suited to the demands of planning, especially plans that involve spatial judgements.

Another form of multiple representation has been proposed by Johnson-Laird (1983, p.447): "What we remember consists of images, models, propositions and procedures for carrying out actions." The central component in this set of representations is the mental model. Mental models "play a central and unifying role in representing objects, states of affairs, sequences of events, the way the world is, and the social and psychological actions of daily life. They enable individuals to make inferences and predictions, to understand phenomena, to decide what action to take and to control its execution, and, above all, to experience events by proxy." (P.397.)

According to Johnson-Laird, mental models are representations that constitute a working model of the real world, although they may be incomplete or simplified. They are derived from perception and from verbal information. Mental models may be physical or conceptual. Physical mental models are analogue in form and can represent relations, space and time, change, and movement. Conceptual mental models can represent more abstract features such as negation. Mental models are specific, but can be used to represent hypothetical states of affairs. They are intermediate between propositions and images because they represent a mapping, or interpretation, of propositional representations and can be used to generate images. Mental models, as described by Johnson-Laird, are not fixed structures, but dynamic models which can be constructed as and when they are required, and this makes them peculiarly well suited to planning since they are able to simulate dynamic actions and events. In this they appear to have the advantage over the images in Kosslyn's model which only represent scenes and objects, and are limited in the kind of transformations they can undergo.

However, critics of Johnson-Laird's proposals have objected that there is no compelling evidence for the existence or use of mental models. Gentner and Gentner (1983) conducted an experiment in which subjects were asked to simulate mentally a state of affairs with a closed room in which certain conditions of temperature, air pressure, and humidity were specified. They were required to decide how changes in one condition would affect the other conditions. Gentner interpreted their responses as evidence for mental modelling, but Rips (1987) considered that subjects could not have been using mental models to work out their decisions because their judgements were inconsistent. He argued that if they had based their judgements on a mental model, they would have produced responses which were consistent, even if they were not correct. Rips concluded that there is no evidence to constrain us to believe in the existence of mental models, and doubts whether they are either functionally or conceptually distinct from other forms of representation. However, it is quite possible that people cannot construct a mental model for the Gentners' problem because it is too difficult and they do not have the requisite knowledge. Mental models may still be used to represent situations that are more familiar. Moreover, cognitive processes like planning appear to require a hybrid form of representation which is dynamic and which can represent hypothetical states of affairs. Mental models fulfil these criteria better than other systems of representation.

In this chapter we have considered several aspects of memory for plans and actions, including the ability to execute plans, and the slips that occur when actions are not executed according to plan; the ability to remember to implement prospective plans; and the ability to determine whether or not a plan has been already implemented; as well as how and why people make plans. All these topics relate to naturally occurring behaviour in everyday life, but each has been illuminated and interpreted by the application of formal theories of cognition developed in the context of traditional laboratory experiments.

3 Memory for Places, Objects, and Events

Visual experience and visual memory play a pervasive and dominant role in everyday activities. This chapter reviews some of the most interesting and important functions of visual memory in daily life. These functions are very varied and seem to have little in common with each other except the fact that the information stored in memory is originally acquired visually. They include memory for routes and maps, spatial layouts, and landmarks; memory for the appearance of objects and their location; and memory for complex events which have been witnessed. Memory for faces is another important aspect of visual memory in everyday life, but this is deferred to Chapter 4 and treated as part of memory for people.

One common feature of the different functions of visual memory is selectivity. Walking around with our eyes open for 16 hours a day supplies us with far more visual information than we could possibly store efficiently and far more than we could ever need. People lead complex lives in a very complex physical environment, and, because we spend a lot of time moving around and travelling to new places, the proportion of novel elements to familiar elements in our daily experience is high. It is arguable that the memory system can only cope with this massive load of novel information by being highly selective. A great deal of visual information is never stored in memory or is stored in a very partial or fragmentary way. You remember the route to the town centre but not the buildings that lie along it; you remember the faces of 3 people you met at a party but not the other 30. You remember the location of some of the objects in a complex scene but not all of them, and you may have witnessed a mugging in the street and seen the mugger running away, but be unable to give an accurate description of him. We remember only a small part of what we see. How do we select what to remember? Examples in this chapter indicate that numerous factors influence the selection process. We remember what is useful and important; we remember what is bizarre and surprising but we also remember what we expect to see. Sometimes, as the eyewitness testimony studies show, we remember what other people tell us we have seen. This chapter may seem to emphasise the errors and shortcomings of visual memory, but we have to remember that, in everyday life, the visual memory system is severely overloaded.

MEMORY FOR PLACES

Spatial memory encodes information about location, orientation, and direction. Although this information can be represented in other sensory modalities, such as touch and movement, it is most commonly associated with the visual modality. Spatial memory has two main functions in everyday life: It is used in remembering places and in remembering how to find our way around; and it is used for locating objects, for remembering where to find things. Both these functions involve knowledge of the spatial layout of the environment. In the first case, the problem is to locate oneself within this spatial layout, and in the second to locate some specific object. In this section we begin by considering spatial memory in relation to remembering places and navigating around the environment.

Navigating in the Environment

In everyday life people have to find their way about within buildings, within cities, or across country. They may be pedestrians or they may be using various forms of transport. They may be equipped with maps or instructions or be relying on memories of previous experience. The most important variables in navigation tasks are scale, complexity, and familiarity. In finding your way around your own home, or following a daily route to shops in the next street, the environment is familiar, small scale, and relatively simple. These are very different problems from finding your way when driving through a strange city or walking through mountainous country, where the environment is large scale, unfamiliar, and complex.

In a simple, small-scale, familiar environment, navigation is a matter of following routes that are remembered as a set of paths, with specific directions and specific distances, linking known landmarks. It is unlikely that you will get lost. Problems only arise if you emerge from a building or a shopping centre by an unfamiliar exit and have difficulty re-orienting yourself with respect to the known routes. Or, if you have learned a route in one direction only, it will be unfamiliar if you need to traverse it in the reverse direction. In this case, landmarks must be recognised from different viewpoints and changes of direction transposed.

In a less familar, larger-scale urban environment, navigation becomes more complex. It may involve finding short-cuts or new routes. In this case, the kind of spatial ability required includes orientation and making spatial inferences. To figure out a quick way to the station, or to re-orient yourself after your known route is blocked by a newly imposed one-way restriction, you have to be able to orient yourself with respect to your destination: To remember the spatial relationships that hold between alternative routes and to infer, for example, that if the station is at two o'clock from your present position, a sequence of turns such as right–left–right will bring you approximately to its location. In this situation, you can get lost if your spatial inferences are based on inaccurate estimates of distances and directions.

Following directions in an unfamiliar environment presents different problems. You may be given route instructions such as "Go past the post office, take the first right and then turn left at the town centre." To map this description onto the scene in front of you requires that you be able to recognise the landmarks that are described. You have to match the buildings you encounter against your mental representation of a post office. You can get into difficulties deciding whether a particular configuration of roads and buildings answers the description "town centre", or whether a narrow entry should be counted as a turning or not.

Navigating in a strange environment may involve following a map instead of following route instructions. To match the actual environment to the mapped representation you have to abstract and simplify in order to extract the essential skeleton of the road layout from the cluttered scene in front of you. Of course, if the map you are following is in memory, you may get lost because your memory is inaccurate. If the map is available in front of you, you may still make navigation errors if you cannot match it to the area you are travelling through, as, for example, when the map omits minor roads.

Methods of Studying Navigation

Observations of naturally occurring navigation behaviour are too haphazard to yield much insight into the mental representations and mental processes that underlie memory for places. To gain greater understanding, psychologists have used a variety of methods including experiments that range from naturalistic, ecologically valid situations to more artificial tasks; self-assessment questionnaires and psychometric testing.

Different measures of spatial ability are not necessarily testing the same thing. Psychometric tests, such as object assembly and block design, essentially test memory for configurations of objects and have traditionally been used as indices of spatial ability. However, Kirasic and Allen (1985) reported that these tests failed to predict performance on an experimental task that mimicked everyday demands on memory for places. In this experiment, subjects had to plan and execute the most efficient route for collecting designated items on a shopping list within a familiar supermarket and an unfamiliar supermarket. Performance on this task was related, though not very systematically, to memory for the supermarket layout, but was not related to the psychometric tests of spatial ability.

Experimental tests of spatial ability which stay fairly close to natural situations include memorising maps, estimating distances and directions, and recognising landmarks from unfamiliar viewpoints. Other experimental tests of spatial ability are not so directly related to navigation in everyday life. These include mental rotation tasks which test ability to determine whether two stimuli (letters, numbers, or three-dimensional shapes), presented at different orientations, are identical. Although the abilities tested in such tasks may well be similar to those used in everyday situations, the results are unlikely to be predictive of real-world navigation because this is determined by so many different processes.

Individual Differences in Memory for Places

Most people would agree intuitively that individuals vary very considerably in navigational ability. Some have a poor sense of direction: Put them in a maze or an unfamiliar town and they have little idea which direction they have come from, or which direction they should be heading for. Some are notoriously poor map readers and car drivers are tempted to risk trying to study a map while driving, rather than rely on their guidance. Other people have a good sense of direction and a good track record as successful navigators.

One study that attempted to analyse these differences was carried out by Kozlowski and Bryant (1977). They examined the relationship between self-assessed "sense of direction" and a variety of performance measures. They asked students to rate their own sense of direction on a seven-point scale from very poor to very good. The performance measures included pointing to the location of buildings on the campus when these buildings could not be seen from the room where testing took place; estimating distances; pointing to the location of nearby cities; and filling in the location of six buildings on an incomplete map of the campus. Self-assessed sense of direction correlated significantly ($r=0.49$) with the accuracy of pointing to campus buildings, and with the accuracy of distance estimates ($r=0.65$), but was not related to accuracy of pointing to cities.

Kozlowski and Bryant considered the possibility that the subjects with a good sense of direction might be performing better because they were more familiar with the campus environment, rather than because they had superior spatial ability. To test this, they walked subjects through a maze of underground service tunnels beneath the campus from a start point to an end point and back again. Subjects were divided on the basis of their self-assessed sense of direction into good and poor groups. On return to the start, they had to point to the location of the end point. In this unfamilar environment, there was no difference between good and poor groups on the first trial, but on later trials those with a good sense of direction improved more than the poor group. Kozlowski and Bryant concluded that this kind of directional orientation is not automatic but requires effort, attention, and repeated exposures. Those with a "good sense of direction" are those who are able to benefit from experience and acquire an accurate cognitive map.

Besides performing better on these tasks, those with a good sense of direction also rated themselves as better at giving and following directions; at remembering routes experienced as a passenger in a car; at remembering written directions; and as liking to read maps and to find new routes to places. It is not clear, however, whether a sense of direction can be regarded as a unitary ability which mediates performance in a variety of spatial tasks, or a constellation of different abilities (such as visuospatial memory, ability to estimate angular relations and distances, ability to visualise, and spatial reasoning) that reinforce each other.

A study by Thorndyke and Stasz (1980) focused on individual differences in ability to acquire knowledge of an environment by studying maps. In this task, subjects studied a map and had to memorise the absolute and relative positions of the named objects and places shown, so that they could draw the map from memory in a recall test. After six study-test trials, they were also asked to solve some route-finding problems from memory. The two maps used, a town map and a country map, are shown in Figs. 3.1 and 3.2, respectively.

Three of the subjects were experienced in the use of maps. DW was a retired army officer who had taught recruits to use field maps. FK was a retired air force pilot experienced with military maps, and NN was a scientist who worked with geographical data and cartography. Five other subjects were inexperienced with maps. Both expert and novice subjects were asked to verbalise the strategies they used while studying the maps and their verbal protocols were recorded and analysed. An extract from one of the protocols is shown in Fig. 3.3.

The task revealed large individual differences. On trial 5, the best subject (DW) scored 100% and the poorest scored 19%. Surprisingly, the expert subjects did not necessarily outperform the novices. Although DW was

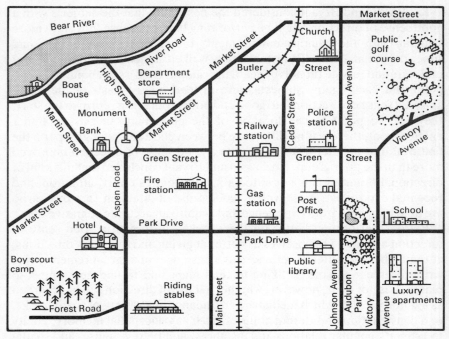

FIG. 3.1   The town map (from Thorndyke & Stasz, 1980).

outstandingly good, FK was sixth out of the eight subjects and NN was the poorest of all. The verbal protocols revealed that different acquisition strategies were associated with good map learning. Good and poor learners differed in three ways:

1. *Allocation of attention:* Good learners partitioned the map into areas and focused attention on one area at a time before shifting to a fresh one. The protocol in Fig. 3.3 exemplifies this homing-in strategy. Poor learners adopted a more diffuse global approach, trying to learn the whole map at once.

2. *Encoding strategies:* Good learners reported using visuospatial imagery to encode patterns and spatial relations. Poor learners used no imagery, and relied on verbal rehearsal of named elements or verbal mnemonics.

3. *Evaluation:* Good learners tested their own memory to find out how they were doing and then focused on areas they had not learned. Poor learners did not do this efficiently.

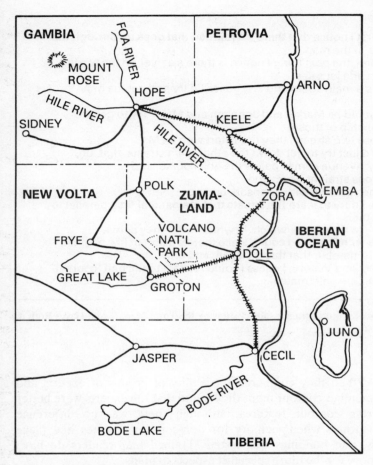

FIG. 3.2 The country map (from Thorndyke & Stasz, 1980).

In a second experiment Thorndyke and Stasz tested the effects of instructing subjects to use the more effective techniques. Those subjects who had high scores on tests of visual memory benefited from the training, but those with poor visual memory failed to improve. Neither the greater experience of the expert subjects, nor training in optimal strategies, was sufficient to guarantee efficient map learning. A good visual memory appeared to be a prerequisite. However, Gilhooly, Wood, Kinnear, and Green (1988) suspected that the failure of the experts to show superior skill might be due to the fact that the maps used in these tests were simplified planimetric maps without contours, which gave little scope for the exercise

1. Um. First I notice that there's a railroad that goes up through the middle of the map.
2. And then, the next thing I notice is there's a river on the top left corner, and let's see.
3. There's a main street and . . . I guess I'd try and get the main streets first.
4. That would be Market and Johnson and Main. Try to get the relationship of those.
5. On these two streets, they both start with an M.
6. Then I'd just try to get down the other main streets, that, uh,
7. Victory Avenue comes below the golf course, and
8. then goes straight down and
9. becomes parallel with Johnson, and . . .
10. I guess I'd try to learn the streets that are parallel first, parallel to each other.
11. Just try to remember which, in which order they come.
12. I guess with this one I could, since there's a sort of like a forest, I could remember that this is Aspen, and um,
13. let's see, and Victory, I guess I could relate it to the golf [course], winning the golf [match].

FIG. 3.3   A verbal protocol from a subject studying the Town Map. (From Hayes-Roth & Stasz, 1980, p. 146).

of expertise. When they compared the ability of groups of experts and novices to remember contour maps they found that the experts were better at remembering contour features, although there was no difference between the groups when memory for non-contour features like place names, roads, and buildings was tested. Trained map-readers do have superior memory for the more specialist aspects of maps.

Map Knowledge and Route Knowledge

It is fortunate, perhaps, for those who are no good at it, that studying a map is not the only way to acquire knowledge of the environment. It can also be learned directly from the experience of moving around. Thorndyke and Hayes-Roth (1982) set out to compare the kind of spatial knowledge that results from these two modes of learning. They tested two groups of subjects for their knowledge of a large complex building. The map-knowledge group learned from floor plans. The navigational, or route-knowledge, group was composed of people who worked in the building. Each group included people at two different levels of experience. A series of tests were administered:

1. *Distance:* (a) estimate the straight-line distance between two named locations, and (b) estimate the route distance (walking from one location to the other).
2. *Orientation:* (a) point to the location of one place when standing at another location, and (b) point to the location of one place while imagining yourself standing at some other location.
3. *Location:* mark designated locations on an incomplete plan.

Route-knowledge subjects were better at estimating route distances and at orientation. Map-knowledge subjects were better at estimating straight line distances and marking locations. Thorndyke and Hayes-Roth concluded that map knowledge (sometimes called survey knowledge) is good for representing global relationships and gives direct access to distance and location information. It provides a bird's-eye view, but this is difficult to transform into a different view. Navigational route knowledge is based on sequentially organised procedural knowledge acquired by traversing the routes, and results in a ground-based view. However, the results suggested that route knowledge can be used to generate map knowledge. Mental simulation of navigation (i.e. imagining yourself walking around) yields information about routes, distances, and locations, and information about orientation and straight-line distances can be computed from route knowledge. Comparison of subjects with high and low experience suggested that with increasing experience, navigationally acquired route knowledge undergoes qualitative changes, becoming more flexible. Thorndyke and Hayes-Roth claim that this ground-based view becomes effectively translucent, so relationships between points can be "seen" in spite of intervening obstructions. The best all-round performance in this experiment was achieved by the highly experienced navigators.

Types of Representation

The way that spatial knowledge is represented mentally appears to depend on two factors: One is its function (i.e. how it is used), and the other is the amount of experience. Bartram and Smith (1984) have described some of the characteristics of different types of representation, and these characteristics fall into two main groups as shown in Table 3.1.

These distinctions are not hard and fast. If Thorndyke and Hayes-Roth are correct in claiming that route knowledge is transformed into map knowledge with experience, there must be transitional stages in between, and experience confirms that one kind of spatial knowledge can be converted into the other. You can derive a route from studying a map, and you can construct a map from knowledge of routes. However, it is possible to

TABLE 3.1
Characteristics of Map Knowledge and Route Knowledge

Map Knowledge	Route Knowledge
Global	Local
Macro	Micro
Semantic	Episodic
Bird's-eye	Ground-based
Topological	Egocentric
Propositional	Procedural
Schematic/abstract	Concrete/detailed
Hierarchical levels	–
Flexible, reversible and transitive	Sequential

distinguish between the two kinds of knowledge. Route knowledge is typically small-scale knowledge of local areas, acquired episodically from personal navigational experiences. It is represented from a ground-based, egocentric point of view in terms of sequentially organised procedures for getting from one point to another. Map knowledge is larger scale, and represents global spatial relations topologically from a bird's-eye point of view.

Although maps are sometimes precise and detailed, they may also be abstract and schematic, like maps of the London Underground, preserving simplified spatial relations, but distorting distances. Real maps are ana- logue in form, but, according to Bartram and Smith, map knowledge is represented mentally in the form of a network of propositions rather than as a pictorial image. We can assess the evidence for these ideas about how spatial information is stored by looking more closely at the processes that operate on it.

Spatial Information Processing

Stored and Computable Knowledge

Propositions about spatial locations may be hierarchically arranged, so, for example, the proposition "Scotland is north of England" is super- ordinate to "Edinburgh is in Scotland" or "Newcastle is in England." Both representations and processes are important in accessing spatial know- ledge. This is because spatial information comes in two forms: stored and computable. The information that Edinburgh is in Scotland is, in our example, already stored as a proposition and can be accessed directly. The information that Edinburgh is north of Newcastle is not stored directly, but is computable by logical deduction from this set of propositions. New information can also be derived by goal-directed analysis of existing knowledge. For example, new routes to a given destination can be found by means–ends analysis of a propositional network. This process consists of selecting moves so as to reduce progressively the difference between the current location and the goal or subgoal.

Spatial inferences

Stevens and Coupe (1978) asked subjects to judge the relative positions of one city from another (e.g. Reno from San Diego). The errors that were made showed that subjects derived their answers by inferences from superordinate propositions which express the spatial relationship between Nevada and California. Because Nevada lies east of California, they assume (wrongly) that Reno lies east of San Diego. Similarly, in the U.K., if people are asked whether Bristol lies east or west of Edinburgh, they tend to infer (again wrongly) that Bristol must be west because it lies on the west coast and Edinburgh lies on the east coast.

Wilton (1979) showed that the time taken to make spatial inferences could reveal the nature of the representation on which the inferences were based. He measured reaction times to questions about the relative position of pairs of towns. When subjects were asked whether one town was north of another town, response times were faster if one was in Scotland and the other was in England. This finding suggests that people are deducing the answer from the superordinate proposition that Scotland is north of England. If both towns were in England, a more precisely specified and detailed mental map had to be consulted, and this was reflected in a longer response time. Wilton also found that the greater the distance between the towns, the faster the response. This latter finding is more consistent with consulting an analogue type of mental map rather than inferencing from propositional information. If the judgement were based on "looking" at a mental map, it would be easier to see that one town was north of another if they were far apart, but if the judgement were based on propositions stating their positions, the distance between them should not make any difference.

Estimation of Distance and Orientation

Information about distance and orientation is also computable when it is not stored directly. Byrne (1979) asked subjects to estimate walking distances between pairs of locations in and around the town of St. Andrews. These included short routes and longer routes; routes in the town centre and routes in the suburbs; straight routes and routes with changes of direction. People tended to overestimate the short routes, those with more changes of direction, and the town-centre routes where there were more landmarks. Byrne concluded that distance estimation was based on the number of identifiable segments in the route. The larger the number of segments, the greater the estimated distance.

Byrne also tested subjects' ability to draw from memory the angles between the roads at familiar junctions. The results showed that all types of angles were normalised towards the right angle. Inaccurate estimates of angles would necessarily distort inferences about direction and orientation; so this tendency would explain why it is that short cuts do not always take you to your intended destination. Memory for places, and being able to find your way around, depends on the accuracy and completeness of the mental representation of spatial knowledge and, also, on the processes employed to read out or compute the required information.

Propositions, Analogues, Procedures, or Mental Models?

Some of these findings have suggested that both map knowledge and route knowledge can be represented in different ways. Whereas Bartram and Smith considered that map knowledge is propositional and route knowledge is procedural, both introspective and experimental evidence suggests a role for analogue representations. The subjective experience of consulting a mental map seems more like looking at a pictorial or graphic representation than reviewing a set of propositions. Remembered routes are experienced as a series of pictorial images. Remembered maps are a mental analogue of real maps. Kosslyn's (1981) theory of mental imagery (outlined in Chapter 2, p.48) allows us to reconcile the evidence of our own experience and the evidence from experiments. According to his model, long-term spatial knowledge is stored as propositions, and as sets of co-ordinate points, and these representations can be used to generate a temporary analogue visual display. The analogue display represents orientation, direction, and distance in a form that allows judgements of relative position and relative distance to be read off directly from the display.

Some of the experimental findings are consistent with this model. For example, Wilton's finding that the time taken to judge the relative position of two towns varied with distance between them mirrors the findings from an experiment by Kosslyn, Ball, and Reiser (1978). They asked subjects to memorise a pictorial map of an island (similar to the one shown in Fig. 3.4). The subjects then had to form a mental image of the map and focus their attention on a named object (e.g. the tree). When a second object (e.g. the hut) was named, they had to scan mentally to the location of this second object, and press a button on reaching it. Scan times were recorded, and increased linearly with the distance between points. The

FIG. 3.4   Pictorial map of an island similar to the one in the experiment of Kosslyn, Ball, and Reiser (1978). Copyright (1978) by the American Psychological Association. Reprinted by permission of the author.

mental scan from the tree to the hut took longer than that from the tree to the lake. These results have been interpreted as evidence that the subjects had an analogue representation of the island. The influence of distance on response time is difficult to account for in terms of propositions. However, it has been argued that the reaction times are not really reflecting the time taken to scan a mental representation. Instead it is claimed that the subject, acting on the assumption that it "ought" to take longer to respond when distance is greater, adjusts his reaction times accordingly. This interpretation seems unsatisfactory but is impossible to disprove.

Another group of classic laboratory experiments (e.g. Metzler & Shepard, 1974) has demonstrated the processes of mental rotation that allow us to recognise routes and landmarks seen from novel viewpoints. Subjects could decide that the objects shown in Fig. 3.5, panels A and B, were identical by mentally rotating one object through 80° into alignment with the other. Similarly, the objects in panel C could be recognised as non-identical when mentally aligned. Response time varied systematically with the amount of rotation that had to be carried out in order to bring the objects into alignment. This fact has been interpreted as evidence that the objects are represented analogically, and that mentally rotating an object is analogical to the process of actually rotating a real object. This interpretation has been the subject of considerable controversy (e.g. Pylyshyn, 1981). However, if it is accepted, it suggests that recognising landmarks from a novel point of view might involve the mental rotation of analogical representations. So, for example, in order to recognise the building you are

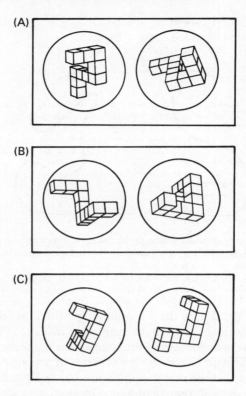

FIG. 3.5   Three-dimensional objects at different rotations (from Metzler & Shepard, 1974).

looking at as the unfamiliar back view of the town hall, you might mentally rotate your mental representation of the familiar front view, and see whether this fits your current perception.

Just as map knowledge can be represented both propositionally and also, temporarily, in picture-like analogue displays, so route knowledge may also have multiple forms of representation. You may have a set of procedures that, if executed, will enable you to walk from home to the station. This knowledge can also be represented visually as a series of mental pictures showing the roads and landmarks. If you were asked to describe the route, you could convert your knowledge into a verbal description, and there is no reason why this route knowledge should not also be stored as propositions.

The representation of spatial knowledge, like the representation of plans, discussed in Chapter 2, can also be characterised in terms of mental models. Johnson-Laird (1983) offers this demonstration of the way people can construct a mental model of spatial layouts from descriptions. The extract is from Conan Doyle's story *Charles Augustus Milverton* (quoted from Johnson-Laird, 1983, pp.158-159).

With our black silk face-coverings, which turned us into two of the most truculent figures in London, we stole up to the silent, gloomy house. A sort of tiled veranda extended along one side of it, lined by several windows and two doors.

'That's his bedroom', Holmes whispered. 'This door opens straight into the study. It would suit us best, but it is bolted as well as locked, and we should make too much noise getting in. Come round here. There's a greenhouse which opens into the drawing room'.

The place was locked, but Holmes removed a circle of glass and turned the key from the inside. An instant afterwards he had closed the door behind us, and we had become felons in the eyes of the law. The thick, warm air of the conservatory and the rich, choking fragrance of exotic plants took us by the throat. He seized my hand in the darkness and led me swiftly past banks of shrubs which brushed against our faces. Holmes had remarkable powers, carefully cultivated, of seeing in the dark. [!] Still holding my hand in one of his, he opened a door, and I was vaguely conscious that we had entered a large room in which a cigar had been smoked not long before. He felt his way among the furniture, opened another door, and closed it behind us. Putting out my hand I felt several coats hanging from the wall, and I understood that I was in a passage. We passed along it, and Holmes very gently opened a door upon the right-hand side. Something rushed out at us and my heart sprang into my mouth, but I could have laughed when I realized that it was the cat. A fire was burning in this new room, and again the air was heavy with tobacco smoke. Holmes entered on tiptoe, waited for me to follow, and then very gently closed the door. We were in Milverton's study, and a portière at the farther side showed the entrance to his bedroom.

It was a good fire, and the room was illuminated by it. Near the door I saw the gleam of an electric switch, but it was unnecessary, even if it had been safe, to turn it on. At one side of the fireplace was a heavy curtain which covered the bay window we had seen from outside. On the other side was the door which communicated with the veranda. A desk stood in the centre, with a turning-chair of shining red leather. Opposite was a large bookcase, with a marble bust of Athene on the top. In the corner, between the bookcase and the wall, there stood a tall, green safe, the firelight flashing back from the polished brass knobs upon its face.

Here is a simple plan of the house with the veranda running down one side of it:

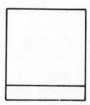

The question is: which way did Holmes and Watson make their way along the veranda – from right to left, or from left to right?

FIG. 3.6a   A spatial problem from a story by Conan Doyle (from Johnson-Laird, 1983). Copyright 1983 AAAS.

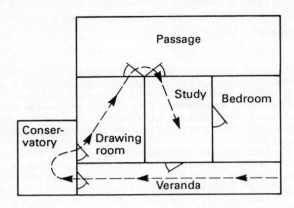

FIG. 3.6b   The solution showing Holmes's and Watson's route.

The solution is shown in Fig. 3.6b. As in Chapter 2, it is doubtful whether it is necessary to assume the existence of mental models to explain how people solve this problem, or whether a mixture of propositions and images would suffice. Whatever the status of mental models, it seems safe to assume that spatial knowledge can be instantiated in several different types of representation.

MEMORY FOR OBJECTS

In everyday life memory for objects has two main functions. The first involves object identification. We rely on memory representations to identify and classify objects, to recognise what they are and what category of objects they belong to. The second function involves memory for the location of objects. Because we are moving around in our environment we need to remember where objects are, as well as what they are. The role of memory in object recognition will not be discussed here. The main reason for this omission is that this topic has received detailed treatment elsewhere (e.g. Smith & Medin, 1981). So this section will be concerned with memory for object location.

Memory for Object Location

Losing Objects

Forgetting where you put something, misplacing or losing objects, is a common and frustrating experience in everyday life. The lapse of memory may be only temporary. The moment when you realise you cannot remember where you parked the car is usually short-lived and the memory is recovered quite soon. In other cases, forgetting is complete, the memory is never recovered and the missing object may never be located. The questions of interest are why we sometimes forget an object's location, and how we set about trying to find missing objects. Several different causes of error in object location can be distinguished:

1. *Absent-mindedness:* The object has been put in an unusual, unintended place by mistake, and the subject does not remember putting it there.
2. *Updating errors:* The object has been put in one of several familiar places. The subject has memories of putting it in all of these places on different occasions, but cannot remember which memory is the most recent one.
3. *Detection failures:* The object has been put in its proper place. The subject looks there, but fails to detect it.

In trying to locate missing objects there are also several different kinds of search strategy that can be employed:

1. *Action replay strategy:* The subject tries mentally to reconstruct the sequence of actions, and so retrieve the memory of placing the object.
2. *Mental walk strategy:* The subject can generate visual images of locations in which the object might be placed and mentally inspect these locations to see if the object is present.
3. *Reality monitoring strategy:* The subject can generate images of putting the object in various possible locations, and employ the reality-monitoring criteria described on pp.33–34 to judge whether any of these correspond to reality.

4. *Physical search:* Instead of mentally searching for the object, the subject can physically search possible locations.

Tenney (1984) administered a "lost and found" questionnaire to young and elderly subjects. She expected to find that elderly people misplaced objects more often than the young, and she generated two preliminary hypotheses about why we lose things. The first hypothesis attributed such incidents to memory problems. Tenney suggested that elderly people might be more absent-minded than the young, and lack of attention to ongoing activities would cause them to put objects down inadvertently in unintended places. Tenney's second hypothesis attributed object loss to detection failures. She suggested that elderly people might have more difficulty in finding objects because of perceptual difficulties caused by sensory handicaps, or poor search strategies. Subjects were asked to report any incidents of losing objects occurring within a two-week period. Approximately 30% of the subjects experienced such an incident, but young and elderly subjects did not differ in the number of incidents reported.

The Absent-minded Hypothesis.   Subjects were also asked to supply self-ratings on an absent-mindedness scale. Although there was again no age difference, object losers rated themselves as more absent-minded than those who had not lost any objects. The absent-minded hypothesis received further support from the fact that in 62% of the incidents the objects were left in unintended places and in 58% of these cases the subject had no recollection of ever having put the object there. Tenney divided the misplaced objects into common objects (misplaced by more than one subject) and unique objects (misplaced by only one subject). Common objects included pen, pencil, chequebook, keys, money, glasses, watch, and jewellery. Although it is not clear from her data exactly how many incidents involved common objects, it does seem as if a substantial number of incidents occurred in the course of routine activities handling routine objects. In these circumstances, failures of memory for object location can be interpreted in the same way as slips of action (Chapter 2, p.18). They occur during routine activities that are under automatic control. Because of the lack of conscious attentional monitoring, the action of misplacing the object is not adequately encoded in memory, and the object's location cannot be recollected later. This kind of explanation fits those cases when the subject has no memory of putting the object in the place where it is eventually found.

The Memory-updating Hypothesis.   Another explanation also rests on the fact that many misplaced objects are those that are handled very frequently. This hypothesis suggests that, when you try to recall an object's location, the problem is one of correctly dating the memory that is retrieved. You may remember putting the car keys on the hall table, or the chequebook in the desk drawer, but is this the memory from the last, most recent time you used the keys or chequebook, or is it derived from some previous occasion?

Bjork (1978) has indicated the importance of updating in every sphere of everyday life. You need to remember where you parked the car today, not last week. You need to know your current car's registration number, not the number of the car you had before. You need to know what are trumps in the hand of bridge you are playing now. Bjork also points out that very many jobs, from short-order cook to air traffic controller, require continual memory updating. Effective management of any enterprise requires accurate updating of information about supplies, orders, personnel, etc. There is a very general need to forget, erase, or override information that is no longer current, and replace it with the most recent version. When we make mistakes about object locations, it is often because this updating process has failed and we retrieve an outdated memory.

Bjork distinguished two mechanisms of updating: *destructive updating* whereby earlier versions are completely destroyed, and *structural updating* whereby earlier versions are preserved but order and recency information is built into the series by some structural principle. In his experiment, the task tested memory for paired associates . The stimulus word remained the same, but was paired with a different response word on each trial (e.g. *frog–rope*; *frog–plum*, etc.). As well as testing total recall of all the response words, the task tested updating by asking subjects to recall the most recent response word. Subjects were given different instructions. In the *destructive updating condition* they were told to imagine writing the words on a blackboard, erasing the previous response word and filling in the new one on each trial. In the *ordered rehearsal condition* they were told to rote rehearse the items in order of presentation. In the *structural updating condition* they were given a story line to connect the items, and in the *imagery condition* they had to form a mental picture relating the items (e.g. a frog with a rope), then undo the picture and replace the old item with the new one on each trial (e.g. replace the rope with a plum). Subjects reported that they were unable to carry out the destructive instructions. The structural condition produced the best updated recall of the most recent item, but total recall was poor in this condition, indicating that some destruction of earlier items may have occurred.

These findings fit well with common-sense observations. Although it is often useless in everyday life to remember outdated information, we do not seem to be able to erase it at will. And when we are having updating problems, we may use action replay as a structural principle. When I cannot remember where I parked the car today I trace back through a sequence of activities (which direction did I come from as I approached the building I work in? Did I arrive early, when the nearest parking slots would have been vacant?) In effect, I supply a story line in order to identify the most recent of my parking memories. By elaborating the memory in this way I can place it in the right temporal context.

The Perceptual Hypothesis. Tenney found that some of the object-losing incidents fitted the perceptual hypothesis. Elderly subjects reported a higher incidence of cases where object misplacing involved defective search or failure of detection, but even young subjects reported some occasions when they found the object in plain sight (6.8%), in a place where it was usually kept (21.5%), or in a place where they had already looked (23.75%). Although it seems odd that people should fail to find an object when it is in its usual place, this is obviously quite a common experience. Sometimes, of course, the object may be partly concealed or obscured by other objects, but when an object is in plain sight it may be undetected if memory for the object's appearance is incomplete, inaccurate, or based on an inappropriate orientation.

Memory for a Common Object

Nickerson and Adams (1982) produced evidence that people have surprisingly poor memory for the visual appearance of common objects. They asked 20 subjects to draw each side of a U.S. one cent coin. Out of a total of 8 features (4 on each side), the mean number of features correctly reproduced was only 3, and nearly half of these were mislocated. Nickerson and Adams considered the possibility that performance was poor because, although people often need to recognise coins, recall is rarely required. However, on a recognition test, where subjects had to select the correct version from 15 drawings of different versions, only half the subjects were correct. They concluded that people only remember enough of the visual properties of objects to be able to make the quite gross discriminations required in everyday life. In the case of coins, knowing the size and colour is sufficient and it is unnecessary to know anything about the inscriptions and symbols on the coin faces. If memory for the visual appearance of other common objects is similarly vague, it is not so surprising that people sometimes fail to find an object that is in its proper place. A further contributing factor in failures of object detection may relate to the process of mental rotation described on p.64. When searching for an object, the searcher generates a visual image of the missing object in the expected location and looks for a match. If the target object is at an unusual orientation (fallen over, lying askew) it will not match the visual image unless either image or stimulus is mentally rotated into alignment. Failure to carry out the appropriate mental rotations could account for cases when objects in plain view are not found.

Another aspect of memory for object location is invoked when instead of having to remember the location of a particular object, you are asked to remember all the objects present in a particular location. Brewer and Treyens (1981) tested people's ability to remember objects in a room. The rationale and interpretation of this experiment were based on schema theory, so it is necessary to outline the main principles of schema theory first.

Schema Theory

Schema theory is able to provide a theoretical explanation of considerable generality for many phenomena in everyday memory. It can account for the fact that many of our experiences are forgotten, or are reconstructed in a way that is incomplete, inaccurate, generalised, or distorted. Schema theory emphasises the role of prior knowledge and past experience, claiming that what we remember is influenced by what we already know. According to this theory, the knowledge we have stored in memory is organised as a set of schemas, or knowledge structures, which represent the general knowledge about objects, situations, events, or actions that has been acquired from past experience.

Bartlett (1932) introduced the idea of schemas to explain why, when people remember stories, they typically omit some details, introduce rationalisations and distortions, and reconstruct the story so as to make more sense in terms of their own knowledge and experience. According to Bartlett, the story is "assimilated" to pre-stored schemas based on prior knowledge. These processes are described in more detail in Chapter 6, pp.207–208. Although for many years Bartlett's ideas were neglected, in recent years schemas have been given a central role in theories of memory.

Schemas represent all kinds of knowledge from simple knowledge such as the shape of the letter A, for example, to more complex knowledge such as knowledge about political ideologies or astrophysics. Like the action schemas described on p.21, knowledge schemas may be linked together into related sets, with superordinate and subordinate schemas. So, for example, the schema for *table* would be linked to schemas for *furniture*, *rooms*, and *houses*. A schema has slots which may be filled with fixed compulsory values, or with variable optional values. A schema for a boat would have *floats* as a fixed value, but has *oars* and *engine* as variable values. Schemas also supply default values. These are the most probable or typical values. If you are thinking about some particular boat, and you cannot remember the colour of the sails, the boat schema might supply the default value *white* as being the most probable value to fill the colour slot.

Pre-existing schemas operate in a top-down direction influencing the way we encode, interpret, and store the new information coming in. According to schema theory, new experiences are not just passively "copied" or recorded in memory. A memory representation is actively constructed by processes that are strongly influenced by schemas in a variety of ways, as outlined by Alba and Hasher (1983):

1. *Selection:* The schema guides the selection of what is encoded and stored in memory. Information that is relevant to whichever schema is currently activated is more likely to be remembered than information that is irrelevant.

2. *Storage:* A schema provides a framework within which current information relevant to that schema can be stored.

3. *Abstraction:* Information may undergo transformation from the specific form in which it was perceived to a more general form. Specific details of a particular experience tend to drop out, whereas those aspects that are common to other similar experiences are incorporated into a general schema and retained.

4. *Normalisation:* Memories of events also tend to be distorted so as to fit in with prior expectations and to be consistent with the schema. They are sometimes transformed toward the most probable or most typical event of that kind. People may remember what they expected to see rather than what they actually saw.

5. *Integration:* According to schema theory, an integrated memory representation is formed which includes information derived from the current experience, prior knowledge relating to it, and default values supplied by the schema.

6. *Retrieval:* Schemas may also aid retrieval. People may search through the schema in order to retrieve a particular memory. When the information that is sought is not represented directly, it can be retrieved by schema-based inferences. (If you know that John has measles, you can infer, from your measles schema, that he won't come to the party.)

"Schema" is used as a general term to cover all kinds of general knowledge. More closely specified versions of schemas are called *scripts*, which consist of general knowledge about particular kinds of *events*; or *frames* which consist of knowledge about the properties of particular *objects* or *locations*.

The most important prediction from schema theory is that what is normal, typical, relevant, or consistent with pre-existing knowledge will be remembered better than what is unexpected, bizarre, or irrelevant. Intuitively, this prediction is not entirely convincing. Often it seems that what is odd or unusual tends to stick in memory.

Memory for Objects in a Room

Brewer and Treyens (1981) set up an experiment to test the predictions from schema theory. Subjects were called one at a time to serve in an experiment. When they arrived they were asked to wait in a room and left there alone for 35 seconds. They were then called in to another room and given the unexpected task of recalling everything they had seen in the first room. This first room was arranged to look like a graduate student's office, and contained 61 objects. Some of the objects were schema-relevant, i.e. they were objects people would expect to find in such a room, such as a table, typewriter, coffee pot, calendar, posters, etc. Other objects were schema-irrelevant (e.g. a skull, a toy top, a piece of bark). A different set of subjects were asked to rate all the objects on two scales, a schema-expectancy scale and a saliency scale. For the schema-expectancy scale, they rated "how likely the object would be to appear in a room of this kind". For the saliency scale, they rated how noticeable the object was.

The mean number of items correctly recalled was 13.5 per subject. Responses included some items such as books and telephone, which had not actually been present, but were probable in the context. These had been inferred from the schema. Recall correlated with both schema-expectancy ratings and with saliency ratings. That is, the most probable items and the most noticeable items were most often remembered. Items that formed part of the room itself, like walls and doors, were also frequently recalled. Brewer and Treyens refer to these as *frame objects*. Table 3.2 lists the items that were most frequently recalled. It is clear that bizarre objects, with low schema expectancy, like the toy top and the skull, were also recalled quite frequently. The results also demonstrated the normalising influence of schemas on memory for location. When subjects were asked to recall the exact location of objects in the room, they tended to shift the objects toward a canonical location. For example, a note pad was remembered as being on the desk when it was really lying on the seat of a chair.

Brewer and Treyens' experiment shows that people remember objects that are typical, normal, and consistent with the currently active schema, better than objects that do not fit the schema. Schema-consistent objects are more likely to be encoded; they are better retained because they are stored in a permanent framework, and they are more likely to be retrieved by schema-guided search processes. The experiment also provided evidence of schema-induced errors. People remembered the expected objects whether they actually saw them or not, and they remembered things in their expected places when they were elsewhere.

However, the experiment also shows that schemas are not the only factor at work. Saliency also affected what was remembered. Very noticeable objects were more likely to be recalled. Brewer and Treyens did not

TABLE 3.2
Items Recalled in an Experiment Testing Memory for Objects in a Room

Object	No. Subjects[a]	Object	No. Subjects
Chair (next to desk)	29	Filing cabinet[c]	3
Desk	29	Frisbee	3
Wall[b]	29	Jar of coffee	3
Chair (in front of desk)	24	Poster (in addition to those in room)[c]	3
Poster (of chimp)	23		
Door[b]	22	Screwdriver	3
Table (worktable)	22	Snoopy picture	3
Shelves	21	Rotary switches	3
Ceiling[b]	16	Cactus	2
Table (with coffee)	15	Cardboard boxes	2
Skinner box	14	Coffee cup[c]	2
Child's chair	12	Computer cards	2
Door[b]	12	Papers on bulletin board	2
Light switch[b]	12	Pens[c]	2
Toy top	12	Pot (for cactus)	2
Brain	11	Solder	2
Parts, gadgets (on worktable)	11	Vacuum tube	2
		Window[c]	2
Swivel chair	11	Wires	2
		Ball[c]	1
Poster on ceiling	10	Brain (in addition to that in room)[c]	1
Books[c]	9		
Ceiling lights[b]	9	Brick	1
Poster (of food)	9	Computer surveys (on floor)	1
Typewriter	9		
Bulletin board	8	Curtains[c]	1
Clown light switch	8	Decals on walls[c]	1
Coffee pot	8	Desk (in addition to those in room)[c]	1
Skull	8		
Mobile	7	Doorknob[b]	1
Road sign	7	Eraser	1
Calendar	6	Fan	1
Wine bottle	6	Glass plate (covering desk)[c]	1
Football-player doll	5		
Jar of creamer	5	Globe	1
Pipe (cord)	5	Hole in wall (for pipe)	1
Postcards	5	Homecoming button	1
Tennis racket	5	Lamp[c]	1
Blower fan	4	Magazines	1
		Nails[c]	1
Coloured patterns on ceiling lights	4	Packets of sugar	1
Piece of bark	4	Paper (on desk chair)	1

Table 3.2 (cont.)

Object	No. Subjects[a]	Object	No. Subjects
Papers on shelf	1	Scissors	1
Pencil holder[c]	1	Screws[c]	1
Pencils[c]	1	Teaspoon	1
Picnic basket	1	Telephone[c]	1
Pliers[c]	1	Umbrella	1
Saucer	1	Wrench	1

[a] Maximum number of subjects = 30.
[b] Frame object.
[c] Inferred object, i.e. an object not in the office.

From Brewer and Treyens (1981).

distinguish between perceptual saliency and the kind of distinctiveness conferred by incongruity, but the results suggested that some objects, such as the skull, were remembered because they were bizarre and incongruent in that setting. In everyday life, if you ask someone to recall the contents of a kitchen or a garage which they have just seen, you would probably find that they remember both the highly probable, schema-consistent objects, and also any very distinctive, surprising, or peculiar objects.

Brewer and Treyens' finding that memory for the *position* of items in a room was influenced by stored knowledge about where things ought to be has also been noted by Mandler and Parker (1976). They showed people pictures of organised scenes and unorganised scenes as shown in Fig. 3.7, and asked them to reconstruct these scenes from memory, either immediately afterwards or one week later. The organised scene was reconstructed much more accurately, but, when testing was delayed for a week, there was an interesting difference in the accuracy of placement on the vertical dimension and the horizontal dimension. Vertical positions were better remembered. Mandler and Parker suggested that vertical placement is predictable from stored knowledge of spatial relations. We know that pictures go on walls, and are higher than chairs, which go on floors, but horizontal placement is not predictable and there is no way of guessing whether the flower-pot should be on the left or right of the television set.

These studies give clear evidence that memory for object location is strongly influenced by stored schemas which have been constructed by generalising over past experience about what kinds of objects are found in which locations.

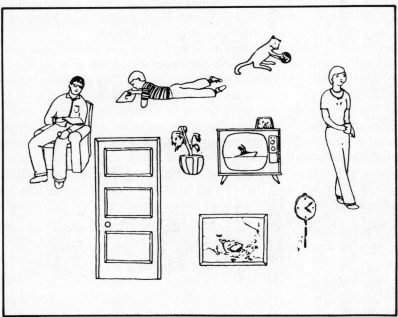

FIG. 3.7   Examples of an organised scene (top) and an unorganised scene (bottom) (from Mandler & Parker, 1976).

MEMORY FOR EVENTS: EYEWITNESS TESTIMONY

How Accurate are Eyewitnesses?

This section is concerned with memory for events that have been witnessed. How accurately can people recall these events? Failures of reality monitoring (p.30) show that people are sometimes unable to distinguish in memory between what they have actually perceived and what they have only heard about or imagined. Brewer and Treyens' experiment showed that the influence of schemas sometimes induces people to "remember" nonexistent objects, and List (1986) showed similar effects of pre-existing schemas on memory for events. Subjects in her experiment watched a video showing eight different acts of shop-lifting being carried out. Each of the sequences contained some elements people had previously rated as high in probability in a shop-lifting scenario, and some rated as low in probability. When the viewers' memory for these events was tested one week later, the influence of a shop-lifting schema was clearly evident because they remembered more high-probability elements than low-probability ones, and they also made more high-probability errors. That is, they falsely remembered events which had not actually occurred, but which were rated as highly likely to occur during shop-lifting.

As well as containing schema-induced inaccuracies and distortions, memory for events also tends to be very incomplete. In everyday life situations, if an event is not very remarkable people may not pay much attention to it, and may simply fail to see what is going on. If the event is highly dramatic, observers are more likely to pay attention, but stress induced by frightening or emotional events can make their subsequent recall less reliable (Buckhout, 1982).

Eyewitness Testimony

Elizabeth Loftus and her colleagues have carried out a detailed examination of eyewitness testimony in an extensive series of experiments. The main thrust of their research has been to demonstrate that memory for an event which has been witnessed is highly malleable. If someone is exposed to new information during the interval between witnessing the event and recalling it, this new information may have marked effects on what they recall. Loftus has interpreted the results as showing that the original memory can be modified, changed, or supplemented.

These findings are of great practical importance in a legal context, when the credibility of a witness is at issue. Loftus has claimed that the witness's memory can be altered by the type of questions posed during police questioning. Leading questions, misinformation, or even quite subtle implications, can introduce errors into the witness's subsequent recall of the event. There is considerable controversy, however, about exactly what happens to the original memory in these circumstances. For example, McCloskey and Zaragoza (1985) have disputed Loftus's claim that the memory is changed, and have argued that misinformation biases the way that people respond to questions, but does not affect the original memory.

Effects of Misleading Information

Eyewitness research relies on naturalistic experiments. These experiments typically consist of three phases. In the first phase, the subjects are asked to view a film or a series of slides depicting an event such as a car accident. Of course, this is rather different from the real-life situation, when witnessed events are not necessarily the focus of deliberate and sustained attention, and people do not usually know, or even guess, that they will be asked to recall the event later. In the second phase, the subjects are exposed to post-event verbal information about the event they have seen. This might take the form of being asked questions or being asked to read a narrative description of the event. In the third phase of the experiment, memory for the original event is tested by further questions, or, if phase 1 consisted of a slide sequence, then the memory test in phase 3 may be a forced-choice picture recognition test in which pairs of slides are shown. One member of each pair is "old" i.e. it occurred in the original phase 1 presentation, and one of the pair is new. The subjects have to pick out the picture which is old.

The critical factor in these experiments is the nature of the post-event information presented in phase 2. At this stage the subjects are divided into two groups. For the control group, the post-event information is *consistent* with the witnessed event (i.e. true). For the other group (the misled group) the post-event information is *misleading* (i.e. false). For example, in one experiment (Loftus, 1975), after all the subjects had witnessed a film of a car accident, post-event information for the control group included the question "How fast was the white sports car going when it passed the Stop sign?" The misled group were asked "How fast was the white sports car going when it passed the barn while travelling along the country road?" In the original film, the car did pass a stop sign, but there was no barn. Hence the mention of a barn was misleading because it implies its existence. In phase 3, when all the subjects were questioned about the accident seen in the film, 17% of the subjects who had been exposed to the false information in the misled condition reported seeing a barn. Less than 3% of those in the control condition made this mistake. According to the Loftus interpretation of these results, the original memory of the event is supplemented with the false post-event information. The

FIG. 3.8   The red Datsun at a Stop sign (left) and at a Yield sign (right) (from Loftus, Miller, & Burns, 1978).

nonexistent barn is added to and integrated with the original memory representation of the event.

Further experiments have demonstrated that, as well as inserting non-existent items into a memory representation, false information may transform the memory, deleting some elements and replacing them with others. In an experiment by Loftus, Miller, and Burns (1978) subjects viewed a set of 30 colour slides of a car accident. One group of subjects saw a version with a red Datsun stopped at a Stop sign, and the other group saw a version with the Datsun stopped at a Yield sign, as shown in Fig. 3.8. In phase 2, subjects answered 20 questions about the accident. Half the subjects in each group were asked "Did another car pass the red Datsun while it was stopped at the Stop sign?" and half were asked "Did another car pass the red Datsun when it was stopped at the Yield sign?" So, overall, for half the subjects the post-event information was consistent with what they had seen and for half it was conflicting. Twenty minutes later, both groups received a forced-choice recognition test. Fifteen pairs of slides were presented, and subjects had to choose which one of each pair corresponded to the original version they had seen. Of the subjects who had received consistent information in phase 2, 75% made the correct choice. Only 41% of those who received conflicting post-event information were correct. Loftus interpreted this result as showing that a witness's memory of an event can be transformed by false post-event information.

Leading Questions

In other studies (e.g. Loftus, 1974) Loftus demonstrated that quite subtle differences in the wording of questions can influence the responses of a witness. After seeing a film of a multiple-car accident, subjects were asked either "Did you see *a* broken headlight?" or "Did you see *the* broken headlight?" The question with the definite article "the" (implying that there was a broken headlight) elicited more positive answers. In a study by Loftus and Palmer (1974) subjects were asked "About how fast were the cars going when they smashed into each other?" Alternative versions of the question used the verbs "collided", "bumped", "contacted" or "hit". Subjects who received the "smashed" version estimated a higher speed, and were more likely to answer "yes" to the question "Did you see any broken glass?", even though no broken glass was shown. These effects show that people are sensitive to the presuppositions and implications underlying the questions they are asked, and that their responses can be manipulated by the wording of the questions.

Resistance to Distortion

Witnesses are not always easily misled. In some cases, their memory for the original event resists distortion. Further experiments have revealed some of the conditions that make witnesses more, or less, suggestible. One factor is public commitment. Subjects who make a public statement of what they recall before being exposed to false information are much less likely to change their recollection. Whether this is because verbalisation "fixes" the original memory and makes it more resistant, or because they are unwilling to contradict themselves, is not clear.

Another factor is the plausibility of the false information. People resist attempts to mislead them more successfully if the false information is "blatantly incorrect". Loftus (1979b) showed subjects a series of slides showing a man stealing a large, bright red wallet from a woman's bag. When accuracy of perception was tested by an initial set of questions immediately afterwards, 98% of subjects had perceived the colour of the wallet correctly. They then read a narrative description of the event (allegedly generated by a psychology professor to enhance its credibility). One version of the narrative contained "subtle" errors such as errors about the colour of items that were only peripheral in the original event and not important. Another version contained, in addition, the "blatantly incorrect" statement that the wallet was brown. The final test showed that all but two of the subjects resisted this blatantly incorrect information, and continued to remember the wallet as red, but many subjects were misled by the false information about peripheral items. Thus, memory for obviously important information, which is accurately perceived at the time, is not easily distorted. The colour of the wallet was correctly remembered because the wallet was the focus of the event, not just a peripheral detail, and because its colour was correctly noted at the initial viewing. The experiment also demonstrated that, once witnesses recognise one piece of misleading information as false, they become more distrustful and are less likely to be misled by other false information.

Loftus and Greene (1980) tested memory for a staged event, rather than a film. This involved a man entering a classroom, picking up a book and arguing with the professor. Misleading versions of the questions in phase 2 incorporated a critical question with the false presupposition that the man had a moustache. When the false presupposition was embedded in a subordinate clause ("Did the intruder, who was tall and had a moustache, say anything to the professor?") more subjects were misled and subsequently remembered the intruder as having a moustache than when the false presupposition was contained in a simpler sentence ("Was the moustache worn by the intruder light or dark brown?"). In the first version, the nonexistent moustache is tacked onto the question "by the way". In the second sentence, where it is the main point of the question, the attempt to mislead is too obvious and is less successful. To be effective, misleading information must be plausible, not too obvious, and come from an authoritative source that has not been previously discredited.

Time factors also influence the effects of false information. In the Loftus, Miller, and Burns study, the final test was given one week after the viewing, but the interval between the original viewing and the false information in phase 2 was varied. The number of subjects who resisted the misleading information fell from 50% when the false version followed immediately after viewing the accident, to 20% when the false information was delayed for one week and presented just before the final test. False information has more effect if the original memory has had time to fade.

The Fate of the Original Memory

When people are misled by false post-event information, what has happened to the original memory? There are several possibilities:

1. *The vacant-slot hypothesis* claims that the original information was never stored at all, so the false post-event information is simply inserted into a vacant slot in the memory representation. Loftus and Loftus (1980) reject this possibility on the grounds that 90% of subjects who are tested immediately after witnessing the event, and are not exposed to any post-event information, are correct.

2. *The co-existence hypothesis* states that both the original version and the false post-event version co-exist as two competing alternatives. When tested, subjects usually respond with the false version because it has been presented more recently, and is therefore more accessible. This hypothesis implies that even if subjects produce the false version when memory is tested, the original correct version is, in principle, recoverable.

3. *The demand characteristics hypothesis* also claims that both memories co-exist, but argues that they are equally accessible. According to this

hypothesis, people respond with the misleading information because they think this is what is demanded of them, not because it is more accessible. Loftus, et al. (1978) tested this hypothesis by asking subjects in a final de-briefing to recall *both* the original and the false versions, but very few could do so.

4. *The substitution hypothesis* states that the false post-event information displaces or transforms the original memory representation, which is then irrecoverably lost. This hypothesis is the one favoured by Loftus. It assumes a destructive updating mechanism (see p.69). Both the co-existence and the substitution hypotheses contain the "would-have-remembered" assumption, that is, they assume that subjects would have remembered the original version correctly if their memory had not been interfered with by the false post-event information.

5. *The response-bias hypothesis* put forward by McCloskey and Zaragoza (1985) claims that misleading post-event information has no effect on the original memory, but simply biases the response. They argue that, in most of the experimental paradigms, people have forgotten the original information by the time it is tested. When people respond with the false information, they are not *remembering* wrongly, they are just choosing the wrong response.

The evidence for and against these hypotheses is reviewed next. On the co-existence hypothesis, the original memory should be recoverable, but both the substitution hypothesis and the response-bias hypothesis claim that the original memory is not recoverable. This issue about the recoverability of the original memory has been investigated by studying the effects of warnings. If people are given false information, and then warned that this information was inaccurate, are they able to disregard it and reinstate the original memory? In addition to the theoretical issue about the fate of the original memory, this question also has important practical implications. For example, can jurors discount the evidence given by a witness who is subsequently discredited? Greene, Flynn, and Loftus (1982) found that a warning given after the false information produced no significant improvement in the memory of the misled subjects relative to those who were not warned. The warned subjects seemed unable to disregard the discredited false information and recover the original memory.

Bekerian and Bowers (1983) produced evidence favouring the co-existence hypothesis. They presented slides of a car accident (as in Loftus et al., 1978) showing either the Stop or the Yield sign. Half the subjects received misleading information in phase 2. In the recognition test, pairs of slides were either presented in the original sequence, or, as was done in the Loftus et al. experiment, the slides were presented in a random order. The random order produced the typical misled effect. In this experiment 94%

of the control subjects made the correct choice on the critical pair, but only 60% of the misled subjects were correct. However, presentation in the correct sequence elicited as many correct responses from the misled subjects (87%) as from the controls (85%). Bekerian and Bowers argued that the original information had not been lost, and going through the slides in the correct sequence provided enough cues to make it accessible. However, McCloskey and Zaragoza (1985) failed to replicate this result, so the status of this finding is in doubt. It is worth noting, however, that when the original and misleading alternatives are in direct contradiction, the co-existence hypothesis is, in common-sense terms, rather implausible, since it suggests that people go around believing two contradictory things at the same time.

If the original memory is still intact and recoverable, it is certainly not very easily reinstated. Loftus gave her subjects a $25 incentive to respond correctly, but the percentage of misled subjects who chose the correct alternative did not increase. Another way to test whether the original memory is intact is to offer subjects a second guess. On the co-existence hypothesis, people whose first response was the misleading information should be able to make the correct choice from among the remaining alternatives on their second guess. Loftus (1979a) reported an experiment in which subjects saw, in phase 1, a man reading a green book. The misleading information in phase 2 described the book as yellow. On test, the alternatives offered were green, yellow, or blue. Misled subjects whose first choice was yellow were only at chance level on their second choice, showing that their memory of the original colour could not be recovered. On the whole, the evidence for recoverability of the original memory is too slight to give much support to the co-existence hypothesis.

McCloskey and Zaragoza (1985) and Zaragoza, McCloskey, and Jamis (1987) have challenged the substitution hypothesis. Re-assessing the experimental findings to take account of the probabilities of choosing different responses by pure guessing, they see no reason to conclude that the misleading information has any effect whatever on the original memory. They argue for the response-bias hypothesis, claiming that a high proportion of subjects in both control and misled groups forget the original item. In a two-choice test, suppose that 50% of the control group remember the original item and choose correctly. The other 50% have forgotten and are forced to guess. Half of these will make the correct choice by chance, so, altogether, 75% of the control group will be correct. In the misled group, 50% will also remember the original item and be correct. But the 50% who have forgotten will be biased to choose the false alternative because it was mentioned in the misleading information. Because of this bias, fewer than half will choose correctly, so the total number of subjects who are correct in the misled group will necessarily be smaller than in the control group.

McCloskey and Zaragoza demonstrated that, if the response biasing factor is removed, misled subjects perform as well as controls. In their procedure, control and misled subjects both witnessed an event with a man using a hammer. Misled subjects read a narrative account describing the tool as a screwdriver, while controls were given a narrative which did not mention the tool. In the test phase, the choice was between a hammer and a wrench. The misleading false alternative was not offered as a choice, so no response bias could operate. If the false mention of a screwdriver had impaired or altered the original memory of the hammer, fewer misled subjects would choose "hammer". In fact, misled and control groups did not differ. Both were about 70% correct. From this result, McCloskey and Zaragoza concluded that misleading information does not affect the original memory. However, Loftus remains unconvinced by their arguments.

The fate of the original memory therefore remains controversial. It may be transformed or rendered inaccessible or lost altogether. It may be replaced with a false memory or a false response bias. There is, in fact, no good reason to suppose that original memories should always suffer the same fate. Given that Loftus has shown that susceptibility to misleading information varies with different circumstances, it is a reasonable conclusion that the fate of the original memory might also vary, being sometimes lost and sometimes changed. It is also arguable that the issues would be clearer if researchers distinguished more carefully between the effects of misleading information on memories, and its effects on beliefs and on reports. Whatever may be its effect on memory, it is undeniable that misleading information changes what witnesses report.

If this chapter has seemed to emphasise the fallibility and weaknesses of memory for places, faces, objects, and events, this is partly a reflection of research techniques rather than an objective evaluation. Researchers deliberately contrive tasks with a level of difficulty that ensures a substantial proportion of errors simply because the nature of the errors and the pattern of incidence yield more information about the underlying mechanism than successful performance can reveal. These experiments do not give much idea of how well memory functions in the real world. Memory efficiency in everyday life needs to be judged in the street, not in the laboratory. In ordinary circumstances, efficiency is determined by values and costs, by the trade-off between effort and accuracy. Destructive updating is economical in storage and makes for easier retrieval than keeping superseded or falsified memories in store, but it carries penalties in that old versions cannot be reinstated if new ones are discredited. Schemas are a powerful device for making the most of what we remember. They supply information that is missing, and allow us to make inferences and to reconstruct what has been forgotten. These benefits are also accompanied by some disadvantages. Mistakes and distortions occur. Reconstructions may be inaccurate, particular details may be lost, and the unexpected may be disregarded. The way memory functions in everyday life is in the nature of a working compromise between the conflicting demands that are made on the system.

4 Memory for People

Memory for people is such a crucial element in everyday life, both in social interaction and in work and family life, that it merits a chapter of its own. Although memory for faces and memory for names form separate sections in this chapter, remembering people in everyday life involves different kinds of information about their physical appearance, names, and biographical details, and it makes more sense to think of memory for people as a single system in which all this information is integrated.

MEMORY FOR FACES

Remembering Faces in Everyday Life

Remembering Faces or Remembering People?

Remembering faces is a skill that is in daily use, but in real life we are not often called on to recognise people by their faces alone. Faces are rarely seen in isolation, even in photographs. We recognise people, not faces. Information about a person's identity is supplied by body build, clothes, gait, voice, and the context in which the person is encountered, as well as the face. We know very little about the relative contribution of these different aspects of personal identity to the recognition process, but mistakes and difficulties of identification suggest they are important cues. Clothes and context are both liable to change, and therefore ought to be less reliable as cues, but experience suggests that we do rely on them to a

considerable extent. It is hard to recognise your bank manager at the disco
or your dentist in evening dress.

In contrast to the real-life situation, almost all the experiments that test
face recognition ability use still photographs of isolated faces, taken out of
context, and stripped of all the additional information that normally
accompanies a face. In real life we are rarely required to recognise isolated
faces in this way. Although you may sometimes be asked to identify a
person whose photograph or portrait is shown to you, there would usually
be some visible background or contextual information.

Face Identification, Face Recognition, and Face Recall

How good is our memory for faces? In everyday life, this ability is tested
in different ways, by face identification, face recognition, or face recall.

Face identification entails being able to look at a person's face and say
who it is; being able to remember the person's name or some details about
the person, or the circumstances in which the person was previously
encountered. In the case of full identification, all this information is
remembered, but sometimes you may remember only some of it. For
instance, you may remember many details of a person but be unable to
recall the name.

Face recognition, as distinguished from identification, occurs when you
recognise a face as one that you have seen before. Familiar faces are
usually identified as well as recognised, but recognition may sometimes
occur without identification, as when you know that a face is familiar but
cannot recall who it is. Recognition without identification is a form of face
memory that is very commonly tested in experiments. Subjects are shown a
set of photographs, and are later required to recognise these as familiar,
discriminating them from novel, unfamiliar faces. In everyday life, however, this type of face memory is relatively useless. To behave appropri-
ately toward someone, it is necessary to know more about them than just
that they seem vaguely familiar.

Face recall occurs in everyday life when you try to describe a face
verbally to someone else, when you try to draw a face from memory, or
when you try to "picture" a face by forming a mental image of it.

We know from our own experience that people seem to vary in face-
memory ability quite considerably, so that it is difficult to say what level of
performance should be considered normal. The incidence of errors varies
with the degree of familiarity. Identification failures for faces that are well
known do occur, but they are usually temporary mistakes due to misleading circumstances, such as changes of appearance, seeing someone in
an unusual context, or poor visibility. Confusions may happen if a person is
very similar in appearance to someone else, but such errors do not usually

persist with prolonged inspection. With less well-known faces, identification failures are more common. It is quite easy to forget the face of someone you have met only casually, seldom, or a long time ago. Recognition is affected by familiarity in the same way as identification. Although it is relatively rare for someone to fail to recognise a well-known face, it is not so unusual when the face is unfamiliar. Face recall is not so often required of us in everyday life. When we need to describe a person to someone else, with the intention of enabling the hearer to identify that person, we do not usually supply much detail about the face. We generally describe age, height, build, and any very distinctive features (e.g. "curly red hair", "beard" or "glasses") rather than giving a comprehensive description of the face. The accuracy and completeness of face recall, as opposed to person recall, is largely untested by the demands of everyday life.

Ecological Validity in Studies of Memory for Faces

Experience and Experiment Contrasted

Studies by Bahrick (reported by Bahrick, 1984a) highlight the differences between the traditional laboratory experimental test and more realistic assessment of memory for faces. In his study, the same students were used as subjects in both types of test. In a traditional type of paradigm, they were first shown photographs of 20 target faces for 5 seconds each, and later tested for ability to recognise them. In the recognition test, the faces were presented in sets of 10, with each set containing 2 target faces and 8 distractors (new faces that had not been seen before). The mean percentage of correct recognitions was 29%. In the realistic assessment, the target faces were those of classmates on a course which had met 40–45 times over a 10-week period. The distractor faces were those of students at the same university who were not classmates. Subjects had to pick out the photographs of their classmates. Recognition accuracy was 38%. Performance on the realistic task was significantly better and performance on the two tasks was not significantly correlated.

Bahrick noted that the tasks differed mainly in the degree of control over motivation and attention. In the laboratory version, subjects studied the faces for a fixed time, learning was intentional, and the amount of interference was controlled. In these conditions, performance reflects learning capacity and encoding strategies. In the realistic situation learning was incidental and there was no control over the amount of exposure or the degree of attention paid to the classmates' faces. Even though the overall duration and type of interaction were to some extent standardised by the classroom situation, some of the target faces might have acquired social or emotional significance for some of the subjects. In ordinary everyday circumstances, the frequency of encounter and the nature of the interaction must be powerful factors in determining how well a face is remembered. Another difference between the studies was that the faces of fellow students were seen from many different angles and with different expressions, whereas the faces in the laboratory experiment lacked dynamic information.

In another realistic study of memory for faces, Bahrick tested the ability of college teachers to recognise photographs of their students and former students. The amount and duration of contact was constant (3–5 times a week for 10 weeks), but the time elapsed since the last encounter was varied. In a face recognition task, the teachers had to pick out each of the target students' faces from four distractors, and in a face identification task they had to name the faces. The percentages of correct responses were as follows:

	11 days	1 year	4 years	8 years
Recognition (%)	69.0	47.5	31.0	26.0
Identification (%)	35.5	6.0	2.5	0.0

After eight years recognition was scarcely above chance. When face identification was tested, and teachers had to name the faces, scores were, predictably, much lower. Memory for faces, even ones that are well known at some period, fades if time passes without further encounters. No doubt the continuing waves of new faces that teachers experience contribute to this effect.

Naturally Occurring Errors

In the same way that Reason and Mycielska (1982) collected slips of action and attempted to infer the underlying mechanism, Young, Hay, and Ellis (1985) studied naturally occurring errors in recognising people and developed a model of person recognition based on an analysis of the types of error that were reported. In their study, 22 people kept diaries of the errors they made and the difficulties they experienced over an 8-week period. The most common types of error were:

1. *Failure to recognise a person* (114 cases). Most of these incidents involved people who were not very familiar, but in a few cases the person was well known and these lapses are difficult to account for.

2. *Mistaking one person for another* (314 cases). Most of these misidentifications were very quickly corrected and involved mistaking an unfamiliar person for a familiar one on the basis of similarities of hair, build, or clothing.

3. *Failure to remember who someone was* (233 cases). In these cases the person seemed familiar but the diarist could not remember who it was. Most of these incidents involved meeting people who were not very well known in an unexpected context (e.g. "I was walking along the streets when I saw a person who looked familiar. At first I thought she was an assistant in the library, but I wasn't sure. Gradually I became convinced she was. I would have recognized her instantly in the library.")

4. *Incomplete recall* (109 cases). Another common type of error was failure to remember some details about the person (usually the person's name), although enough information was remembered for an identification to be made. In most of these cases, the diarist could recall the person's occupation.

Other, less frequent, errors included being unsure who a person was; giving the wrong name to a person; and various combinations of different types of error. Diarists also reported incidents in which they noted the resemblance of one person to another, although no error was made. The subjects in this study reported that, although many different kinds of information were used in person recognition, they relied mostly on facial features. Incomplete recall and mistaken identification were types of error that often involved people known through the media, rather than from personal acquaintance.

From these data, Young et al. concluded that person recognition is a graded process with levels of recognition varying from "seeming familiar" to full identificaiton. They proposed a model in which there is a recognition unit for each known person that stores information about physical features, a person identity node that stores biographical information, and a further store holding additional information and the person's name. This model is diagrammed in Fig. 4.1.

Person recognition may succeed at one level, but fail to reach a higher level. Mistakes occur if the physical information causes the wrong recognition unit or the wrong person identity node to be activated. The model is designed to preclude the types of error that have not been found to occur. For example, it does not seem to happen that you recognise someone as familiar, and know the name but do not know any details of their identity. In the model, because name information is only accessed via the person identity node, this could not occur.

Theories of Face Recognition

Several theories of face recognition have been proposed. It has been suggested that there is a specific mechanism for face recognition, but most research attempts to explain face recognition in terms of general theories of perception and memory.

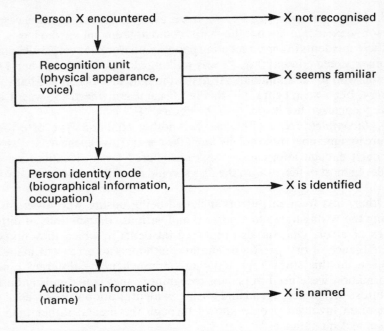

FIG. 4.1   Levels of person recognition (adapted from Young, Hay, & Ellis, 1985).

Feature Testing

According to this theory, faces are analysed into component features and recognition is by a process of feature matching. Some experimental findings fit with this account but others do not.

Feature Saliency.   In support of the theory, there is evidence that some features are more salient than others. Subjects spend more time looking at some features when memorising a face; recognition is more disrupted by changing some features than by changing others; and a face with a highly distinctive feature is more easily recognised. Experiments (Ellis, 1975) suggest that features in the upper part of the face (hair, forehead, eyes, and nose) are more important than features in the lower part (chin and mouth).

Harmon (1973) developed a computer simulation of face recognition using weighted feature testing. First, 10 observers examined 256 face photographs and rated each for 21 features as shown in the chart in Fig. 4.2. Using this feature rating information the computer searched for a specified target face, listing all the faces in order of closeness to the target face. The target was in the top 4% on 99% of occasions, showing that feature testing can produce good identification.

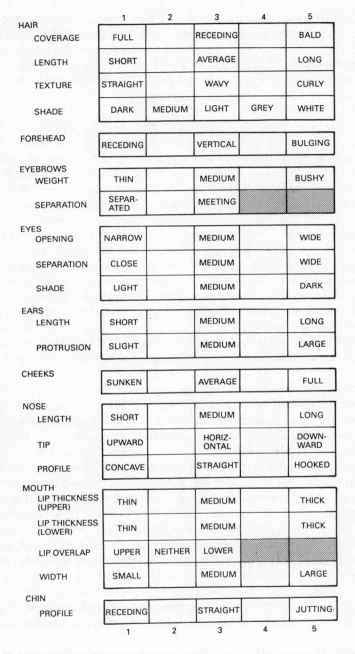

	1	2	3	4	5
HAIR					
COVERAGE	FULL		RECEDING		BALD
LENGTH	SHORT		AVERAGE		LONG
TEXTURE	STRAIGHT		WAVY		CURLY
SHADE	DARK	MEDIUM	LIGHT	GREY	WHITE
FOREHEAD	RECEDING		VERTICAL		BULGING
EYEBROWS					
WEIGHT	THIN		MEDIUM		BUSHY
SEPARATION	SEPAR-ATED		MEETING		
EYES					
OPENING	NARROW		MEDIUM		WIDE
SEPARATION	CLOSE		MEDIUM		WIDE
SHADE	LIGHT		MEDIUM		DARK
EARS					
LENGTH	SHORT		MEDIUM		LONG
PROTRUSION	SLIGHT		MEDIUM		LARGE
CHEEKS	SUNKEN		AVERAGE		FULL
NOSE					
LENGTH	SHORT		MEDIUM		LONG
TIP	UPWARD		HORIZ-ONTAL		DOWN-WARD
PROFILE	CONCAVE		STRAIGHT		HOOKED
MOUTH					
LIP THICKNESS (UPPER)	THIN		MEDIUM		THICK
LIP THICKNESS (LOWER)	THIN		MEDIUM		THICK
LIP OVERLAP	UPPER	NEITHER	LOWER		
WIDTH	SMALL		MEDIUM		LARGE
CHIN					
PROFILE	RECEDING		STRAIGHT		JUTTING
	1	2	3	4	5

FIG. 4.2 The feature-rating system used in Harmon's computer simulation of face recognition (from Harmon, 1973). (From 'The recognition of faces', copyright ©1973 by Scientific American Inc., all rights reserved.)

93

Evidence against a feature-testing theory comes from a study by Woodhead, Baddeley, and Simmonds (1979), who found that an intensive three days of training in analysing facial features produced no significant improvement in face-recognition scores. Indeed, in a search task where subjects had to pick out a "wanted criminal" face from 240 others, the trained subjects did worse than an untrained group.

The Difference Between Recognition and Recall. Further evidence against a feature-testing theory comes from studies of face recall. One of the most striking aspects of memory for faces is the huge gap between ability to recognise and ability to recall. Why should this be so? Tests of recognition typically require subjects to discriminate photographs of faces they have seen before from others they have not seen. Tests of recall require subjects to produce verbal descriptions, or to construct photofit representations from memory. These can be evaluated by judged likeness to the original target face, or by how well other people can recognise the target face from the description or photofit. Experiments of this kind sometimes mimic the situation in which witnesses are asked to describe suspects to the police.

Scores on recognition tests range from 60–90% correct, but scores on recall tests are much lower. Immediately after 10 seconds' viewing, Ellis, Shepherd, and Davies (1975) asked subjects to reconstruct from memory the 6 photofits shown in the left-hand column of Fig. 4.3. Judges who tried to pick out the target face from the reconstructions achieved on average 12.5% correct.

This poor performance on tests of face recall has been attributed to production, or output constraints. Phillips (1978) argued that we lack a sufficiently rich and precise vocabulary for verbal descriptions to be an effective way to represent or communicate information about faces. He found that face-recognition ability correlated with self-rated ability to image a face, and concluded that faces are represented visually in memory. On his view, recall is difficult because it involves recoding the visual memory to a verbal form and the verbal form is impoverished. This explanation is not very convincing since Christie and Ellis (1981) found that verbal descriptions were a better basis for target recognition than photofits. Another explanation of the discrepancy between recognition and recall is that recall is feature analytic whereas recognition is not necessarily so. Whether recall is tested by verbal description or by photofit or identikit construction, the output is feature by feature. If the memory representation is a holistic one and recognition is generally a holistic matching process, this might explain why it is hard to recode the memory representation into a piecemeal form for recall.

Shepherd, Davies, and Ellis (1978) devised a more realistic test of face recall. From among people who all worked in the same university department and knew each other well, they recruited subjects, targets, and judges. For the eight targets, subjects had to generate verbal descriptions of their facial features. Judges attempting to match the descriptions to the targets achieved 47% correct identifications. However, identification based on a second-hand verbal description still does not approach the kind of accuracy that is achieved when it is based on internal representations acquired first hand. The inferiority of recognition when it is based on feature lists suggests that recognition normally works in a different way.

The Inversion Effect.   Another argument that has been brought against the feature-testing theory is based on the effects of inversion: It is almost five times as difficult to recognise a face when it is upside-down (Yin, 1969). This is much greater than the increase in errors produced by inverting pictures of objects. Yin has argued that this difference shows that there is a specific face-analysing mechanism which is distinct from general visual pattern analysis. It is claimed that faces are particularly sensitive to inversion because they are normally recognised holistically, and inversion destroys the global pattern relationships between features. It makes more sense, however, to interpret the inversion effect in the context of other studies looking at the effects of change of pose. Baddeley and Woodhead (1983) reported that recognition performance deteriorated systematically as the degree of rotation between the originally learned pose and the test pose increased. Best performance was obtained with the same pose; a 45° shift (e.g. full face to three-quarter) was next best; a 90° shift (e.g. full face to profile) was poorest. Inversion represents a 180° rotation in the picture plane. It requires a mental rotation of the kind described on p.64, and, as faces are rarely seen upside-down in the normal course of events, this is an unpractised task, so it is not surprising that it causes difficulty. It does not seem necessary to conclude that a feature-testing mechanism is used and is disrupted by inversion.

Levels of Processing

Face recognition has also been explained in terms of the levels of processing theory developed by Craik and Lockhart (1972). They suggested that the probability of recalling or recognising something increases with the "depth" to which it has been processed at the encoding stage. According to this theory, processing of physical characteristics is classed as "shallow", and processing of meaningful semantic characteristics is classified as "deep". Depth of encoding can be manipulated experimentally by instructing subjects to make deep or shallow judgements about stimuli as they are displayed, and later testing recognition memory unexpectedly. The theory has been applied mainly to memory for verbal material. Level

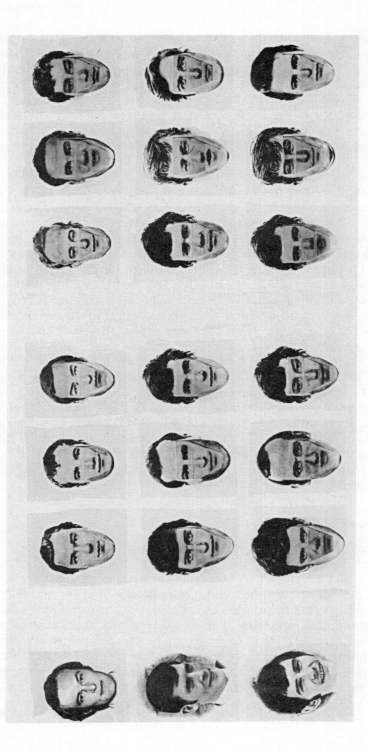

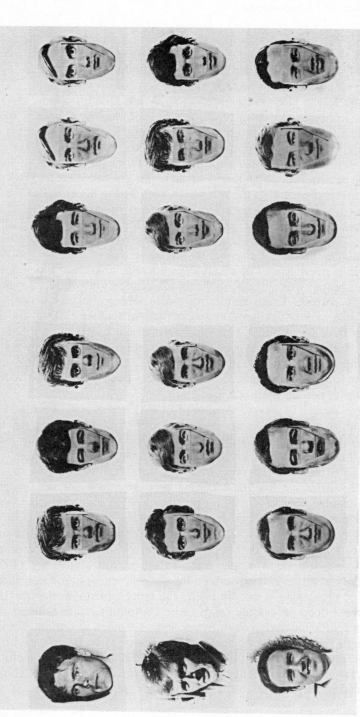

FIG. 4.3   The use of Photofit for recalling faces. The six target faces are shown in the left-hand column. Reconstructions in columns 2, 3, and 4 were made by good subjects; those in columns 5, 6, and 7 by poor subjects (from Ellis, Shepherd, & Davis, 1975).

of processing is typically manipulated by instructing subjects to make deep judgements about the meaning of the words or shallow judgements about the physical appearance of the print, or about the spelling. Deep-level judgements usually produce better memory than shallow judgements.

Bower and Karlin (1974) attempted to apply levels of processing theory to memory for faces. In their study, a group of shallow encoders were asked to classify each of 72 target faces as male or female. Judgements of sex are based on physical appearance and so are classed as shallow. A group of deep encoders were asked to judge either how honest or how likeable the person was. Judgements of character are considered to rest on deep semantic processing. In the test phase, they had to discriminate the 72 target faces from 72 distractors. Both the deep processing judgements produced better recognition scores than the shallow condition. In a similar experiment, Winograd (1976) also found a clear advantage for deep processing. Judgements about physical features like size of nose or straightness of hair yielded scores of about 62% correct; character judgements about intelligence, friendliness, or probable occupation produced scores around 75% correct. These results were also interpreted as favouring a holistic theory of face recognition as opposed to feature testing, on the assumption that deep judgements of character are based on whole-face properties. Deep and shallow processing of faces can also be seen in terms of the Young, Hay, and Ellis model in Fig. 4.1. Shallow processing only involves the low-level recognition units, whereas deep processing involves the higher-level person identity nodes.

In a later study, however, Winograd (1978) compared two kinds of shallow feature processing with deep character trait processing. In the *distinctive feature condition,* subjects had to decide which was the most distinctive feature in each face. In the *constrained feature condition,* the subjects had to make a judgement about a specified feature (e.g. is the nose big?). Distinctive feature encoding produced 78% correct recognitions; constrained feature encoding produced 64%; and character traits 73%. Winograd concluded that feature processing can be as effective as personality judgements if, as in the distinctive feature condition, the subject is forced to make a thorough inspection of all the facial features instead of focusing on a single one. Patterson and Baddeley (1977) obtained only a very small advantage for deep processing and concluded that level of processing is not, in itself, the crucial factor in memory for faces. Rather, deep processing tends to be confounded with holistic processing, and with more thorough inspection and more attention. Similar doubts about the influence of depth of processing have been raised in a study by Intraub and Nicklos (1985). They found that recognition memory for pictures of objects was better after shallow processing. They concluded that processing physical features can produce superior memory if the features are distinctive ones. The distinctiveness of the encoding, therefore, emerged as a more powerful determinant of memorability than the depth of processing. The general conclusions that emerge from these experiments do not go much beyond our everyday intuitions. We remember faces better if we pay attention, inspect them thoroughly, and pick out the features that best distinguish them from other faces.

A Multicode Model

Bruce and Young (1986) have put forward a detailed theoretical model of face recognition which includes a number of different codes. The model includes pictorial codes, which are static and highly specific. These may be derived from pictures or photographs but natural viewing conditions produce multiple view-specific representations of the same face. These are integrated in a structural code which is a more abstract form of representation capable of mediating recognition across transformations of viewpoint. The structural code comprises sets of structural descriptions representing both configurational properties and detailed features, and provides the information for face-recognition units to operate. Other codes also represent personal identity information, facial expression, and the information which underlies the analysis of the facial movements made during speech. This multicode model gives a more comprehensive account linking face recognition to person recognition. The inclusion of a more abstract level of representation has the advantage of being able to explain how we can recognise faces in spite of changes of viewpoint, expression, and accessories like hair-styles, beards, or glasses.

Individual Differences in Memory for Faces

Many researchers have commented on the wide spread of individual differences in face-memory tasks, and this conforms with our everyday experience. However, Baddeley and Woodhead (1983) found that people's self-ratings of their own ability to recognise faces in everyday situations bore no relationship ($r=-0.05$) to their performance in a laboratory face-recognition experiment. Either people are very bad at assessing their own ability or the formal face-recognition experiment tests quite different abilities from those exercised in everyday life. However, people who do well at one laboratory task perform consistently well across a variety of other experimental tests of face memory, and are also good at other tests of visual memory, such as picture recognition. It has proved difficult, however, to obtain clear and consistent results to show what characteristics define a good face recogniser. Face memory is poorer in childhood and in old age (Winograd, 1978); women are sometimes superior, but only at recognising women's faces (Goldstein & Chance, 1971); and good face recognition has sometimes been found to correlate with measures of field dependence (field-dependent individuals are those who find it difficult to pick out target objects or shapes embedded in a confusing background) (Ellis, 1975). On the whole, however, research has little to say about why some people are better than others at remembering faces and little to offer in the way of suggestions as to how we could train people to improve their face-recognition skills. Laboratory experiments using artificial material like photographs, presenting disembodied faces divorced from any social or situational context for observation lasting only a few seconds, are posing very different problems from those encountered in the real world.

MEMORY FOR NAMES

When people are recounting their personal experiences, or when they are quizzed about things that have happened to them, it is noticeable that memory seems to be particularly fallible for the recall of people's names, and it is quite common to hear people complaining that they have a poor memory for names. Everyday experience suggests that, although we seldom forget the names of objects, we often forget the names of people or places, so that memory for proper names appears to differ from memory for common nouns.

Studies of memory for names can be divided into two kinds. Some studies have asked subjects to recall the names of people they have known in the past, and have probed the retrieval strategies used in this situation. Other studies have focused on naturally occurring lapses of name recall, and have analysed the failures of name recall that occur in everyday life when you meet someone, or want to talk about someone, but cannot remember their name.

Recalling Names from Long-term Memory

Names of Classmates

Williams and Hollan (1981) asked four subjects between the ages of 22 and 37 to recall as many names of their schoolfellows as possible. Over a series of test sessions, spread over 2 weeks and amounting to up to 10 hours, the number of names retrieved ranged from 83 (the poorest subject's score) to 214 (the best subject's score). Recall was cumulative and new names were still being retrieved in the final session, even though subjects had earlier been convinced that they could not recall any more. Persistent searching produced names that had seemed inaccessible. Verbal protocols were recorded so that the retrieval processes could be analysed.

Several different kinds of retrieval process could be identified. Subjects first tried to narrow down the search context by concentrating on a particular location, activity, or time. For example, they searched within contexts like the general science class, the lunch queue, school dances, or neighbourhood friends, often using pictorial imagery as they searched. Contextual information was used to construct and enrich a description of the target person, as in: "I'm trying to remember the name of this guy who used to—Art—He was in our 10th grade art class—He would also bring a whole lot of people to—At his house was the first time I heard a Jefferson Airplane album." "I remember this girl who used to play the oboe, and it was junior year, she was our age—or was she older?"

In these examples, the subject is constructing a description, or target specification. General knowledge schemas about school activities and customs and what clothes were worn, etc., are used to define the context and to enrich the description. The more complete the description, the greater the chance of retrieving the name. Subjects sometimes recalled only fragments of a name such as the first letter or syllable, and then generated a list of candidate names with these characteristics. One of these might then be recognised as the target name. Groups of names from within the same context were sometimes recalled in batches.

In line with a model outlined by Norman and Bobrow (1979), there was evidence for three stages of retrieval: formation of the initial specification; matching a retrieved name against this specification; and evaluating the match (deciding whether the name was correct). It is an obvious, but significant, point that in this task, when the subjects were simply asked to recall names, what they actually recalled was primarily the people, and only secondarily the names. Apparently, names are not accessed directly, but only indirectly, via the contextual and personal identity information.

Names of Teachers

Whitten and Leonard (1981) carried out a similar study, asking people to recall the names of their teachers, one from each of the 12 school grades. They were particularly interested in studying the effects of order of retrieval. If past experiences are chronologically organised in memory, then retrieval might be best achieved by searching along the temporal dimension. Whitten and Leonard set out to compare the efficacy of forward-ordered search (beginning with the first year at school); backward-ordered search (beginning with the last year); and randomly ordered search. They reasoned that forward-ordered search might be most efficient because it would benefit from a primacy advantage and from the coincidence of order of retrieval with order of experience. Backward-ordered search, however, would have the advantage of recency effects. They found that subjects who were instructed to recall in backward order were more successful, recalling more names correctly, and recalling them more rapidly, than subjects in either the forward or the random conditions. From these results, Whitten and Leonard concluded that event memories are not accessed independently. If they were stored and accessed as separate and independent units then a random order of search would have been equally successful. Instead, memories are interdependent, with memories that are adjacent in time sharing the same context of occurrence and being retrieved together. In backward search, the starting point is the most recent period (the last year in school) and is therefore most easily recalled. Once this is accessed it aids recall of the next-to-last item which shares some of the same context, and so on, in a reverse chain.

The verbal protocols recorded during retrieval showed a variety of other strategies in addition to chronological search. As in the Williams and Hollan study, subjects focused their search on particular locations or particular academic subjects. Some teachers were remembered for distinctive physical attributes ("she was a gigantic woman with a scar on her neck"); some were linked to landmark events in the pupil's own life such as changing schools or moving house; and some were associated with the emotional responses they evoked.

Although Whitten and Leonard's findings demonstrated the superiority of backward search, this result may be specific to this kind of task. Teachers' names, and the order in which they occur, are arbitrary, but many autobiograpical episodes are sequentially determined, each being causally related to a prior episode. It is a reasonable assumption that a "begin at the beginning" strategy would be better for recall of these causally related events. Recall of the different jobs I have held, for example, might be more easily accomplished in a forward order because the nature of the later jobs was determined by the nature of the earlier ones.

Names of Entertainers

Read and Bruce (1982) analysed the memory blocks that occur when attempts at name recall are initially unsuccessful. Their subjects were tested repeatedly for the recall of names of entertainers from theatre, film, and television. Recall was cued by either a photograph of the entertainer, or an identifying description, such as "He created the role of Charley's Aunt on Broadway". A total of 497 memory blocks occurred, which were ultimately resolved either by remembering the name, or by recognising it when four alternatives were presented.

When each cue was initially presented the subjects were asked to give a "feeling of knowing" (FOK) rating of 1 (the name has come to me immediately); 2 (it is on the tip of my tongue); 3 (it is not on the tip of my tongue, but I feel I know it and can get it after some thought); 4 (it is not on the tip of my tongue, and though I feel I know it I don't think I can get it); or 5 (I simply do not know the name). Read and Bruce examined the relationship between these FOK judgements, and the time actually taken to resolve the name blocks. They found that the stronger the FOK, the sooner the name was likely to be recalled, and the more likely it was to be recalled by the subject's own unaided search.

Subjects' reports indicated that 21.5% of the blocks were accompanied by partial recall of the name (e.g. length, component letters, or component sounds). Retrieval processes included generating additional contextual information, using visual and auditory imagery, and running through lists of plausible names. Memory blocks are occasionally resolved when the forgotten name suddenly comes to mind at a time when no conscious attempts at retrieval are being made, and the subject is thinking of something quite different. Spontaneous pop-up retrievals of this kind were relatively rare in Read and Bruce's study (5.3%), and the mechanism underlying pop-up recall is disputed. Norman and Bobrow (1976) argue that pop-ups are the product of continuing unconscious search processes, the hunt for the missing name being continued without conscious awareness. Read and Bruce disagree with this interpretation, and believe that pop-ups occur as a result of search processes that were originally conscious, but have been forgotten, and so cannot be reported. Alternatively, the pop-up may be triggered by an environmental cue. An example of this kind occurred in a study by Cohen and Faulkner (1986). A subject had forgotten the surname "Bell". Hours later, having consciously abandoned the search, she heard the clock strike and the name popped up. Sometimes an internally generated cue may induce a pop-up, as when a train of thought on a completely different topic fortuitously provides an association which triggers the missing name. However, pop-up often seems to happen without any identifiable external cue. Whatever the underlying process, the subjective experience of pop-up as a spontaneous event is a compelling one when it occurs.

Naturally Occurring Name Blocks

Reason and Lucas (1984) carried out a diary study designed to investigate naturally occurring occasions when memory for a word is blocked and people experience a "tip-of-the-tongue" (TOT) state. When this kind of incident occurs, people are temporarily unable to remember a word, although it is one they know and feel they ought to be able to remember, but for the moment it is tantalisingly out of reach. In these cases, the direct automatic retrieval process fails and a laborious attentional search must be instituted. The corpus of data collected by Reason and Lucas included blocking of both common words and proper names, but the high proportion of proper names (77%) confirms that blocks are particularly likely to occur for names.

In a similar study, Cohen and Faulkner (1986) asked subjects to record details of any name blocks they experienced during a two-week period. There were large individual differences in the frequency of blocks. The incidence was higher in elderly people, and subjects also reported that more blocks occurred when they were feeling tired, stressed, or ill. The majority (68%) of blocks were for names of friends or acquaintances, and most of these were rated as well-known names, which were usually easy to retrieve. Although this seems counterintuitive, the same finding also emerged from the Reason and Lucas study. It is perhaps partly due to the fact that there are more opportunities to forget names that are in frequent use. This fluctuating availability of well-known names suggests that retrieval failure results from dynamic variations in the retrieval process, rather than defective encoding or storage. In Cohen and Faulkner's data, names of famous people accounted for 17% of the blocks; only 7% were names of places, and 8% were other proper names such as brand names, book titles, names of pop groups, etc.

Most of the blocked names were eventually remembered without recourse to external aids like looking it up, or asking someone else, although 62% took more than an hour to recall, and in some cases several days elapsed before the name came to mind. When name recall was blocked, subjects were almost invariably able to remember all the personal identity information they had ever known about the target person such as biographical details, physical appearance, and the nature of previous encounters. Partial information about the name itself was also recalled in 56% of cases. Typically, this consisted of phonological or orthographic features or name fragments, such as the first letter, first syllable, or name length. Occasionally attributes of the names such as "pretty", "uncommon" or "foreign" were also remembered.

When elderly people suffered name blocks they tended to report that they experienced a complete mental blank, with no names at all coming to mind. However, when younger subjects attempted to retrieve a blocked name, they often found that other names came to mind instead of the target. These non-target candidates were nearly always recognised as being incorrect, but were persistent and difficult to set aside. They were often phonologically similar to the target name (for example, *Sylvia* instead of *Cynthia*, or *Ken* instead of *Kevin*). Sometimes the non-target candidates were contextually related to the target name (*Carter* instead of *Reagan*). Reason and Lucas also recorded that candidate names were elicited on 59% of blocks. They describe these non-target items as "blockers" which impede access to the target, but Cohen and Faulkner's subjects reported that, in the process of rejecting non-target candidates they sometimes retrieved additional information about the target name. When several non-target candidates were elicited, these could be graded as more or less similar to the target. In one example, the target name was *Kepler*. The first letter and first vowel sound were retrieved. Candidates, in order of occurrence, were *Keller, Klemperer, Kellet,* and *Kendler*. All of these were rejected, but *Keller* was recognised as being closest to the target, and the additional information that the target name was foreign came to light during evaluation of the candidates. Non-target candidates may sometimes be stepping stones toward recall, rather than blockers. Jones (in press) has reported an experiment specifically designed to test whether these non-target candidate words (he calls them "interlopers") obstruct or facilitate target retrieval. He presented word definitions (e.g. for the target word *anachronism*, "something out of keeping with the times in which it exists") and each definition was accompanied by an interloper. Interlopers were related to the target word in either sound or meaning or both or neither. Because more TOT states resulted when the interloper was similar in sound to the target than when it was not, Jones argued that these phonologically similar interlopers obstructed target retrieval. However, interlopers supplied by the experimenter may not have the same effect as candidates which emerge spontaneously within the subject's own memory.

When people were trying to resolve name blocks they used a variety of different kinds of retrieval strategies. These included:

1. Generating names to fit partial information. If you know that the target name is a short name for a female beginning with *A*, you can search through all the names you know which fit that specification (*Ann, Alice,* etc.).
2. Generating candidates from the relevant context. If the target name is of a politician, you can search through all the names of politicians you can remember.
3. Trying to enrich the target description by re-living past encounters with the target person.
4. Trying to induce a pop-up. This strategy was rare, but one subject described trying to "force up" the name of the author John Braine by rapidly repeating aloud the title of his book, "Room at the Top by ????".

It is not clear which strategies have the best success rate. Reason and Lucas reported 30.4% spontaneous pop-up recalls in their study, but Cohen and Faulkner identified only 17%. However, elderly people frequently said they found that conscious search was self-defeating and it was more effective to abandon it and hope for some serendipitous external cueing or spontaneous pop-up.

Why are Proper Names Difficult to Recall?

Is it true that proper names are actually harder to remember than other words or other kinds of information? Or do we just notice these memory lapses more because they are more socially embarrassing and more difficult to circumvent by choosing other words for what we want to say? McKenna and Warrington (1980) constructed a clinical test for nominal dysphasia which distinguished object names from proper names. Subjects had to name pictures of objects (e.g. *thimble, sundial*) or pictures of the referents of proper names (e.g. *Napoleon, Taj Mahal*). Both normal and clinical subjects did better at object naming. McKenna and Warrington also reported a single-case study that showed a specific impairment of proper naming. This finding indicates that memory for proper names is functionally distinct from memory for other words.

There seems to be an asymmetry in the process of retrieval such that, although we can almost always recall personal identity information when the name is known, it is much harder to go in the opposite direction from the description to the name. Cohen and Faulkner, in their 1986 study, tested recall of information from fictional minibiographies. Subjects heard, for example, "James Gibson is a policeman who lives in Glasgow and wins prizes for ballroom dancing," and later attempted to fill in blanks in a written version of this "biography". Recall of first names and surnames was poorer than recall of place names, occupations, and hobbies.

McWeeny, Young, Hay, and Ellis (1987) also confirmed experimentally that names are harder to remember than occupations. They were concerned to test possible explanations for the difficulty of retrieving names. The following explanations were considered:

1. *Arbitrariness:* Occupations might be easier to recall than names because context and visual appearance can give clues to a person's occupation, but not to his or her name. This is because names are only arbitrarily related to their referents. There are no characteristics (other than sex and nationality) that are necessarily related to an Ann or a John, and the person I know as Ann might equally well have been called by another name.
2. *Frequency:* Names may be retrieved less frequently than other information about a person.
3. *Imageability:* Names are often not easily imageable, and are also less meaningful than occupations.

All these factors, which might favour recall of occupations, were systematically eliminated in an experiment by McWeeny et al. Subjects viewed 16 photos of middle-aged men's faces one at a time and were told each man's name and occupation. The faces were presented without visible background or clothing to eliminate any contextual cues; frequency of names and occupations was matched and, in some examples, the same word (e.g. *Baker* or *Potter*) was interchanged so that it sometimes functioned as a surname and sometimes as an occupation. When this was done, imageability and meaningfulness were equated. Even when these factors were controlled there was a massive difference betwen memory for names and memory for occupations. The percentage of trials on which subjects recalled occupation but not name (75%) far exceeded the trials on which they recalled name but not occupation (5%).

Modelling Name Retrieval

McWeeny et al. argued that the explanation lies in the model shown in Fig 4.1, in which access to name information can only be achieved via the person identity node. Thus there is no way of knowing the name without also knowing the biographical information. This model received some confirmation from the results of an experiment by Young, McWeeny, Ellis, and Hay (1986) which showed that response times to name photographed faces were consistently slower than times to categorise them as familiar/unfamiliar, or as politicians/non-politicians. The personal identity information was accessed earlier than the name information. However, when this model is applied to the naturally occurring name blocks it is apparent that it cannot account for all the observations without some modification. There are three kinds of blocks which require explanation: (1) total blocks in which nothing can be recalled; (2) partial blocks when contextually related wrong names are recalled; (3) partial blocks when phonologically related wrong names are recalled. The model can account for total blocks since these may occur if the activation of the person identity node is too weak to trigger the name node effectively. Blocks when contextually related wrong names are recalled can also be explained since these might occur if the target and the non-target candidate share the same context or the same personal identity attributes, so that activation of the personal identity node triggers more than one name node. This is what may happen when you block on the name of someone's current girl friend, and recall the name of his former girl friend instead. However, in order to explain how phonologically similar non-target candidates are elicited instead of the target name (*Sylvia* instead of *Cynthia*), the model needs to be extended to include associations between similar sounding names. Then, if the target name node is only weakly activated, so that there is only partial recall of name fragments, these might activate other non-target names which share the same fragments.

In its present form, the model is also unable to account for the cases when you can name a face, but cannot remember any contextual or biographical information about the person. This occurred on a small number of trials in McWeeny et al.'s experiment and may also happen occasionally in everyday life. According to the model, it should be impossible to access the name without going through the personal identity information. The model also fails to explain why there is a cueing asymmetry between the name node and the person identity node, so that it is easier to remember the personal details when you are given the name than it is to remember the name when you are given the personal details.

Headed Records

Morton, Hammersley, and Bekerian (1985) developed their headed records model to account for this phenomenon as well as other aspects of memory. They proposed memory units, or records, storing related information, each of which is accessed via its own particular index or heading. Personal identity information about someone would be stored in a record. The person's name might function as the heading, and so give access to all the information in the record, but, according to the model, the content of the heading itself cannot be retrieved. A name can therefore only be retrieved if it is stored in the record as well as in the heading. If it is stored only as part of the heading it is inaccessible, and it will then be necessary to search through other records to find one where the name is represented within the body of the record. This model accounts, though in a rather *ad hoc* fashion, for failures of name recall, and for the asymmetry of recall whereby personal identity information can be recalled from names, but names cannot always be recalled from personal identity information. However, since recall of information from a record is said to be all-or-none, it does not account for partial recall of name fragments or recall of wrong names. It also fails to explain why a particular name can sometimes be recalled and sometimes not.

Many other aspects of memory for names are still extremely puzzling. It is not clear why proper names are organised differently from object names or why they are particularly susceptible to age and stress. In everyday life, memory for names is often poor because we don't make enough effort to learn them in the first place, but even well-learned names elude and desert us from time to time. In some ways names behave more like the vocabulary of a foreign language than the words of our mother tongue.

5 Memory for Personal Experiences

This chapter is concerned with how we remember the events and experiences that form our own personal history. Aspects of everyday memory that have already been discussed, such as memory for places and faces, objects and actions, are components within this broader framework. Memory for personal experiences comprises many different kinds of specific memories which together form the stuff of daily life. Many of the experiences of everyday life involve people and places, and objects as well as events. Memory for our own personal history is of great importance since it is an essential element of personal identity. To a considerable extent we are what we remember. If someone suffers, through trauma or disease, from loss of memory and cannot recall their own personal history, in a very real sense they lose their identity. This is why the practice of reminiscence therapy, whereby elderly people are induced to revive their own memories of the past and to reminisce about their youth, is found to be helpful in preserving a sense of identity.

Memory for personal experiences has other functions besides that of reinforcing personal identity. It provides us with a store of "recipes" for handling current problems and current situations. We know how to behave in social and professional contexts, how to cope with practical problems like changing the wheel on a car or booking tickets for the theatre because we remember how it worked out last time we had a similar experience. Likes and dislikes, enthusiasms and prejudices are also the product of

remembered experiences. This chapter deals with memory for autobiographical experiences in adult life and in childhood and with theoretical
models of how such experiences are stored in memory.

MEMORY FOR EXPERIENCES: SCRIPTS AND MOPS

Theoretical ideas developed in the course of computer modelling have
provided a useful and illuminating approach to understanding how people
represent experiences in memory. Schank and Abelson (1977) and Schank
(1982a) introduced the concept of a *script*, which is a particular kind of
schema (see Chapter 2, p.29, and Chapter 3, p.71) representing knowledge
about events and experiences.

Scripts

A script is a general knowledge structure which represents the knowledge
abstracted from a class of similar events, rather than knowledge of any one
specific episode. So, people have scripts for familiar experiences like eating
in restaurants, going shopping, visiting the dentist, and so on. Through
everyday experience everyone acquires hundreds of such scripts. An
example is shown in Fig. 5.1. A script consists of a sequence of actions
which are temporally and causally ordered and which are goal-directed. So
you sit down *before* ordering; the waitress brings the food *because* you
ordered it; you go to the cashier *in order* to pay; and the *goal* of the whole
activity is to satisfy your hunger. Notice the script does not contain details
about the kind of food, the decor, the company, or the size of the bill.
These details belong to specific episodes. When you remember a particular
occasion, specific details can be inserted into the relevant slots in this
general script. Scripts are broken up into subscripts, or scenes, which are
hierarchically organised with a main action and subordinate action.

The concept of a script was originally designed to explain comprehension
processes, so that, for example, when we hear that John went to a restaurant and had an omelette, we can fill out this brief account from the stored
knowledge in our restaurant script. Script elements function as default
values, so that, unless told otherwise, we would infer from the underlying
script that John sat down and that he paid a bill. The scripts allows us to
supply missing elements and infer what is not explicitly stated. As well as
guiding and enriching our understanding of events, scripts also provide an
organising framework for remembering events. They explain the common
observation that in remembering routine, familiar, often-repeated events
we seem to have a generic memory in which individual occasions, or
episodes, have fused into a composite. Looking back on schooldays, or
bus-rides, or trips to the library, you may find that you cannot remember

Script:	Restaurant (the script header)
Roles:	Customer, waitress, chef, cashier
Goal:	To obtain food to eat
Subscript 1:	Entering
	move self into restaurant
	look for empty tables
	decide where to sit
	move to table
	sit down
Subscript 2:	Ordering
	receive menu
	read menu
	decide what you want
	give order to waitress
Subscript 3:	Eating
	receive food
	ingest food
Subscript 4:	Exiting
	ask for check
	receive check
	give tip to waitress
	move self to cashier
	move self out of restaurant

FIG. 5.1   The restaurant script (from Schank & Abelson, 1977).

any specific occasion, but have a generalised memory of what typically happened.

The psychological reality of scripts has been demonstrated in a study by Bower, Black, and Turner (1979). They asked students to generate the component actions that comprise an event, and list them in order of occurrence. The events they asked about were attending a lecture; visiting a doctor; shopping at a grocery store; eating at a fancy restaurant; and getting up in the morning. There was very substantial agreement about the component actions and their sequence, as can be seen in Fig. 5.2. Subjects also agreed on how a given script was subdivided into scenes, and there was also evidence that they recognised that scripts were hierarchically structured with superordinate goals and subordinate goals. Bower et al. went on to study memory for written texts based on the scripts that had been generated. Subjects read either one, two, or three different versions of a script. For example, the "visit to a health professional" script had a doctor version, a dentist version, and a chiropractor version. Twenty minutes later the subjects were asked to write down as much as they could remember of

Attending a lecture	Visiting a doctor
ENTER ROOM	*Enter office*
Look for friends	CHECK IN WITH RECEPTIONIST
FIND SEAT	SIT DOWN
SIT DOWN	Wait
Settle belongings	Look at other people
TAKE OUT NOTEBOOK	READ MAGAZINE
Look at other students	*Name called*
Talk	Follow nurse
Look at professor	*Enter examination room*
LISTEN TO PROFESSOR	Undress
TAKE NOTES	*Sit on table*
CHECK TIME	Talk to nurse
Ask questions	NURSE TESTS
Change position in seat	Wait
Daydream	Doctor enters
Look at other students	Doctor greets
Take more notes	Talk to doctor about problem
Close notebook	Doctor asks questions
Gather belongings	DOCTOR EXAMINES
Stand up	Get dressed
Talk	Get medicine
LEAVE	Make another appointment
	LEAVE OFFICE

Note: Events in capital letters were mentioned by most subjects, items in italics by fewer subjects, and items in ordinary print by fewest subjects.

FIG. 5.2   Script actions listed by subjects in the experiment of Bower, Black, and Turner (1979).

each one. Each action they recalled was classified as stated (i.e. had been in the original text) or unstated (i.e. had been in the underlying script but had not been mentioned in the text). Of the actions recalled, 26% were unstated script actions. The different versions were confused and actions from one version were transposed to another. Moreover, when the actions in the text were in a disordered sequence there was a tendency to recall them in the familiar canonical order. These findings confirm the psychological reality of scripts and demonstrate their influence on memory.

The Schema-plus-tag Model

In real life events are not always routine repeated ones, and memories are not always generalised. Many events are unique one-off experiences. Some events are first times, never experienced before, or novel deviations from more familiar experiences. It is clearly nonsense to suppose that these events are not memorable, and common-sense observations suggest the contrary. The day you won the 100 metres sprint; the day little Johnny was sick in the doctor's waiting-room; the time you hadn't enough money to pay the restaurant bill; these are the occasions that stand out in your memory. The unusual or atypical event seems to be more memorable than the ordinary run-of-the-mill occasions.

Experiments have confirmed these intuitions. Just as in Chapter 3, p.73, in Brewer and Treyens' experiment, the objects in a room were rated according to their schema relevance, so actions can be graded as being more or less relevant to the current script. Sitting in a chair is a relevant action in the restaurant script, but standing on the table is not. Nakamura, Graesser, Zimmerman, and Riha (1985) compared ability to remember script-relevant and script-irrelevant actions. Students attended a 15-minute lecture which was specially staged. During the lecture, the lecturer performed a number of actions that varied in relevancy to the lecture script. Examples are shown in Fig. 5.3.

After the lecture, the students were given a recognition test in which they had to work through a list of actions, and identify those which had been performed by the lecturer. Irrelevant actions were recognised better than relevant actions, and the "false-alarm" rate was three times higher for relevant actions than for irrelevant actions, i.e. subjects were much more likely to falsely claim that relevant actions had been performed when they had not.

These results have been interpreted in terms of the schema-plus-tag model. According to this model, the memory representation for a specific event consists of the instantiated script, which includes both script-relevant actions that actually occurred, script-relevant actions that were inferred,

---

Relevant Actions
Pointing to information on the blackboard
Opening and closing a book
Moving an eraser to the blackboard
Handing a student a piece of paper

Irrelevant actions
Scratching head
Wiping glasses
Bending a coffee stirrer
Picking up a pencil off the floor

FIG. 5.3 Some of the relevant and irrelevant actions incorporated in the lecture (from Nakamura, Graesser, Zimmerman, & Riha, 1985).

plus tags which correspond to the irrelevant, unexpected, or deviant aspects of the event. These distinctive tags are highly memorable, and serve as markers, or indices, for the retrieval of specific episodes. This modification of the original script model accounts for the way that novel or atypical occasions (like Johnny being sick on the doctor's carpet) seem to stick in memory.

Episodic and Semantic Memory

Tulving (1972) distinguished between memory for personal experience and general world knowledge and considered these as two separate and distinct memory systems. According to this distinction *episodic memory* consists of personal experiences, and the specific objects, people, and events that have been experienced at a particular time and place. *Semantic memory* consists of general knowledge and facts about the world. Table 5.1 shows the main features of the episodic–semantic distinction.

Tulving developed this distinction to clarify the difference between long-term semantic knowledge and the kind of knowledge acquired in verbal learning experiments where learning a specific list of words constitutes an "episode". The distinction has since been extended to autobiographical memory where memories of personal experiences are classed as episodic. However, further consideration has blurred the edges of this distinction. The two forms of knowledge are not separate compartmentalised structures but are in an interactive and interdependent relationship. Semantic knowledge is derived from episodic memories by a process

TABLE 5.1
The Episodic–semantic Distinction

	Episodic	*Semantic*
Type of information represented	Specific events, objects, people	General knowledge facts about the world
Type of organisation in memory	Chronological (by time) or spatial (by place)	In schemas or in categories
Source of information	Personal experience	Abstraction from repeated experience or generalisations learned from others
Focus	Subjective reality: the self	Objective reality: the world

of abstraction and generalisation. Episodic memories are interpreted and classified in terms of general semantic knowledge in the form of schemas and scripts.

Levels of Memory: Scripts, MOPs, and TOPs

More recent developments, and modifications of the script model (Schank, 1982a; 1982b) have focused on this relationship between generalised event knowledge and memory for specific episodes. In Bower et al.'s (1979) experiment they noted that people tended to confuse elements from different scripts in memory. The existence of confusions between actions occurring during the visit to the doctor, and actions that occurred during the visit to the dentist, suggested that there exists some memory structure that is common to both scripts. To account for this finding, Schank (1982a) proposed that memories can be organised at many different levels of generality. He also confronted another weakness of the original script model. He recognised the fact that people can understand and remember an enormous range and variety of different situations. The original model, in which each situation is interpreted by means of pre-stored knowledge about a pre-set sequence of actions is at once too rigid and too cumbersome to cope with this fact. The number of scripts that would be required would be highly uneconomical to store and pre-compiled scripts would be too rigid to handle novel situations. Moreover, life experiences do not conform so neatly to categorised and compartmentalised units as script theory implies. An experience of a picnic, for example, may involve eating and drinking, games, quarrels, minor injuries, thunderstorms, and many other elements that cannot be fitted into a single pre-compiled picnic script.

These observations led Schank to revise the original version of scripts and develop a model that is more dynamic, more flexible, and more economical. The main features of this version are:

1. Memory structures are constantly re-organised in the light of new experiences and repetitions of previous experiences, and links between structures reflect similarities between different experiences.

2. The new system is dynamic. Instead of using pre-stored, precompiled scripts to understand experiences and organise memories, memory structures are assembled as and when required. Different kinds of knowledge can be activated and linked up to create an appropriate representation for a particular occasion.

3. Instead of replicating elements that are common to many scripts (like entering a building, paying, taking a seat, etc., which belong to the cinema script, the restaurant script, the doctor script, and so on) these common

elements are each represented separately at a higher, more general level, and can be called in and incorporated into the current script when required. So the generalised actions like entering and paying can be activated when a memory structure for a visit to a restaurant is being created, but the restaurant script itself now contains only the actions that are specific to restaurants like calling a waitress, reading the menu, etc. This organisation, whereby generalised actions are common to different scripts, is more economical in storage and can account for the way people sometimes make confusions between related scripts.

4. The higher-level generalised event representations have been called MOPs, short for memory organisation packets. A MOP is a kind of high-level script which is linked to related MOPs. In the picnic example, the memory of this particular picnic would involve weather MOPs, friendship MOPs, sports activities MOPs, and first-aid MOPs. The memory representation for this event would invoke general knowledge from all these MOPs as well as the standard picnic MOP.

5. Non-standard aspects of a particular occasion are stored as specific pointers, tags or indices, which serve to retrieve the memory of a particular occasion. Standard occasions, or standard aspects of novel occasions, are absorbed into the relevant generalised event representations (the MOPs). The specific pointers provide the mechanism for the process Schank calls "reminding". You may be reminded of a particular episode by a friend who says: "Do you remember the time David fell in the river? You know, the day we got caught in a thunderstorm. You must remember, we played frisbee in a field of cows." The friend is *reminding* you of the event by activating successively the tags he thinks you are most likely to have used as indices.

6. Within this new dynamic memory system a particular episode, like going to a party, can therefore be stored at several different levels of generality, such as:

Going to David's party last Saturday evening; *or*
Going to parties; *or*
Social interactions.

The system also allows for even more general, higher-level representations, which Schank (1982a) has called TOPs, or thematic organisation points. Themes like *Getting what you want, Achieving power*, or *Failing to achieve a goal* are examples and their existence is evident in conversational exchanges like the following:

"I just heard I didn't get the job."
"Bad luck. And I've failed my driving test again. Let's go and have a drink to cheer ourselves up."

The conversation illustrates how two disparate events can be organised under the high-level theme of *Failures*. These high-level structures allow us to recognise similarities and analogies between superficially quite different events. In Schanks' own example of the Steak and the Hair-Cut a friend's complaint that his wife will not cook his steak rare enough reminds the listener of occasions when a barber would not cut his hair short enough. The events are related to the common theme of failing to get a service performed in a sufficiently extreme form.

The details of this model are still in course of evolution. Schank's theories were originally developed in the process of writing programs for computer modelling of language understanding, rather than being designed to account for human memory in everyday life, but they have been modified and adapted so as to explain experimental findings and observations. Some aspects, such as the emphasis on the need for economy of storage, may be more appropriate for the computer than for the human brain. However, the later versions of the model provide what is, on the whole, a convincing account of how people remember the events they experience in daily life.

AUTOBIOGRAPHICAL MEMORY

Autobiographical memories are episodes recollected from an individual's past life. The study of autobiographical memory has undergone a marked change in the last decade. Before then, the approach was almost exclusively psychoanalytic or clinical in orientation and diagnostic or therapeutic in aim. Recent studies, however, have adopted a cognitive approach and seek to interpret autobiographical memory within the theoretical framework of mainstream memory research. This undertaking is fraught with difficulty because of the great quantity and variability of the data. It is a daunting task to try to discover the general principles that govern the encoding, storage, and retrieval of personal experiences accumulated over their lifetimes by different individuals with different personal histories. Nevertheless, some progress has been made, at least in defining the questions that are of most interest, and in exploring methods of gathering the data.

What is Autobiographical Memory?

Personal experiences are usually stored without conscious intention to memorise them and give rise to memories which can be of several different kinds. Autobiographical memories may be *declarative* or *experiential*. I may have a declarative memory of the fact that I went to school in Wales or I may have an experiential memory, re-living the experience with associated imagery and emotions. Autobiographical memories may be *specific* or *generic,* so, for example, I may remember eating lunch at a particular restaurant on a particular occasion, or I may have a generic memory of family dinners. Neisser (1986) has also noted that a personal memory may be one that is representative of a series of similar events and has termed this type of memory "repisodic".

Brewer (1986) argues that memories vary in the extent to which they are *copies* or *reconstructions* of the original event. Some personal memories seem like copies because they are vivid and contain a considerable amount of irrelevant detail. However, some personal memories are not accurate, and, rather than being raw experiences, they incorporate the interpretations which are made with hindsight, which suggests they are reconstructed.

Autobiographical memories are strongly linked to the concept of self, since the self is both the experiencer and the product of the experiences. Nigro and Neisser (1983) found that when people examined their own memories, some were remembered from the original viewpoint of the experiencer, but a larger number of memories seemed like viewing the event from the outside, from the point of view of an external observer. These "observer" memories cannot be copies of the original perception and must have been reconstructed. Nigro and Neisser reported that recent memories were more likely to be copy-type memories re-experienced from the original viewpoint but older memories were more likely to be reconstructed ones seen from the observer's viewpoint.

It has been argued that memory for specific episodes has no real function in everyday life, and that behaviour is guided entirely by procedural and semantic knowledge. However, specific episodic memories can have a role in problem solving. When we are confronted with a current problem, the general knowledge that has been abstracted from past experiences may not always be relevant, and it may be more useful to search back through autobiographical memory and review specific experiences with analogous problems.

Issues in Autobiographical Memory

It is possible to discern a number of different issues in the study of autobiographical memory, but all these issues are highly interrelated.

The Contents of Autobiographical Memory

An obvious question to ask is what kind of experiences people are most likely to remember from their past lives, and, conversely, what kinds of experiences they are most likely to forget. In the ordinary language of everyday, we often speak of an experience as "unforgettable", and, in fact, we probably do have quite accurate intuitions about what kinds of events someone ought to be able to remember. If a person could not remember his or her own wedding, we would consider this abnormal; if he could not remember going to a party ten years ago we would not think this very unusual.

Determinants of Memorability

Recall of personal experiences is influenced by many different factors. Some of the factors which tend to make an event memorable are characteristics of the event itself, and operate at the time of encoding. Events which are personally important, consequential, unique, emotional, or surprising are liable to be better remembered. These variables tend to co-occur so that it is difficult to assess the relative contribution of each. Recall is also affected by variables that operate during retention, such as how frequently the event is talked about or thought about, and by age and time variables such as the length of time elapsed since the event, the age at which it was experienced, and the age of the person at the time of recall.

The Distribution of Autobiographical Memories

Some researchers have addressed this issue in terms of quantity, i.e. the number of memories that are recalled from different parts of the life span. Others have been concerned with differences in the quality of memories from different parts of the life span and have asked questions about the relative vividness of early memories and later memories.

The Organisation and Retrieval of Autobiographical Memories

Some memories come unbidden into consciousness. Salaman (1982) has described examples of these involuntary memories which are peculiarly vivid and emotional and have a strong feeling of immediacy. More often, however, personal memories are deliberately sought and retrieved in response to a query, or for comparison with a current experience. Personal memories may be organised chronologically, like the memories of school-teachers in Whitten and Leonard's study (p.101), but they may also be organised in categories, or schemas such as illnesses, holidays, parties; or in lifetime periods, sometimes called "extendures" (schooldays, retirement, etc.). Specific episodes, it is claimed, are nested in a rough hierarchy within these general categories, and can be accessed for retrieval via the super-ordinate categories.

The Dating of Autobiographical Memories

The ability to date memories is crucial to chronological organisation. Memories are stored within a temporal frame of reference, and are linked to landmark events in public life and in personal life. Studies have focused on the accuracy of dating and on the kind of temporal inferences used in date estimation.

The Accuracy of Autobiographical Memory

Research in autobiographical memory is complicated by the fact that most of the methods used are highly subjective, and rely on self-reports. There is usually no way of checking whether the memories reported are veridical, but a study by Field (1981) provides some indication of the reliability of personal memories. Field analysed interviews carried out on people at age 30 and again at 47 and at 70, asking questions about family, education, occupation, and relationships with spouses and children. The average correlation for factual questions over this 40-year span was 0.88. For questions about emotions and attitudes it was 0.43.

These issues are addressed in the studies described in the following sections. However, because they are so interrelated they are difficult to disentangle from each other.

Diary Studies of Autobiographical Memory

Linton (1982) undertook a systematic six-year study of her own memory for the events of her daily life. Every day she wrote on cards a brief description of at least two events that occurred on that day. Every month she re-read two of these descriptions, which were selected at random from the accumulating pool, so that the retention period was varied. She then tried to remember the events described, to estimate the temporal order in which they occurred and the date of each event. She also rated each memory for saliency (importance) and for emotionality both at the time of writing the description, and again at the time of recall.

Linton noted two types of forgetting. One form was associated with repeated events, such as regular trips to attend a committee meeting in another town. Over time, memories of particular trips became indistinguishable from each other, and she found she had only retained a generic composite memory. The specific memory of a particular occasion had been absorbed into a generalised event memory. She had acquired a script for these events. This finding conforms to most people's own experience. Unique occasions are usually better remembered than repeated events which blend into each other. A second type of forgetting also occurred: When she re-read descriptions of some events she simply could not remember the event at all. Here it was not the case that similar events had been confused and amalgamated in memory, but that a single event had been forgotten. The number of events forgotten in this way increased steadily with each year of the study, and after six years had elapsed 30% of the events recorded had been totally forgotten.

A surprising feature of Linton's study was her failure to find any strong relationship between rated importance and emotionality, and subsequent recall. Common-sense experience suggests that we remember important events, and those that roused strong passions better than those that were trivial or left us unmoved. However, Linton found that the emotionality and importance ratings she initially gave to an event did not correspond closely with those she gave later on with hindsight. It appears that the characteristics of an event at the time of encoding only affect memorability if the same qualities are still present at the time of recall.

To gain insight into the way events are organised in memory Linton also studied strategies of recall. She tried to recall all the events that occurred in a designated month. Introspective monitoring of her own attempts at recall showed that many events were organised chronologically and were recalled by temporally ordered search. Some were organised in categories and were retrieved by working through named categories like parties or sporting activities. For events that were more than two years old, there was a shift away from chronological search toward a greater use of categorical search, reflecting a change in memory organisation. Recall attempts also revealed that events may be organised in terms of lifetime periods (extendures) which are continuing situations like a job, a marriage, or living in a particular place. Within these extendures, specific events are embedded and can be accessed via the relevant extendure.

Wagenaar (1986) employed similar methods in recording 2400 events of his daily life over a period of 6 years. He specifically recorded each event in terms of *who, what, where,* and *when* plus some critical identifying detail. This format had two advantages: He was able to determine which of these facts about an event were best retained, and also which facts provided the best cues for retrieving the rest of the information. He also rated the pleasantness, emotionality, and saliency of each event. Saliency was defined as how often such an event might be expected to recur, so unique events were rated as highly salient, and routine events were rated low. Figure 5.4 shows the pro forma for recording the events. When memory was tested, each cue was presented in turn. For example, on Trial 1 Leonardo da Vinci (the *who* cue) was supplied and Wagenaar had to try to recall *what* happened, *where,* and *when.* On Trial 2, two cues were given; on Trial 3, three cues; and on Trial 4 all four cues were given and the question about the critical detail was posed. Cue order was varied systematically.

The retention function showed that the percentage of questions answered correctly dropped over a four-year period from 70% to 35%.

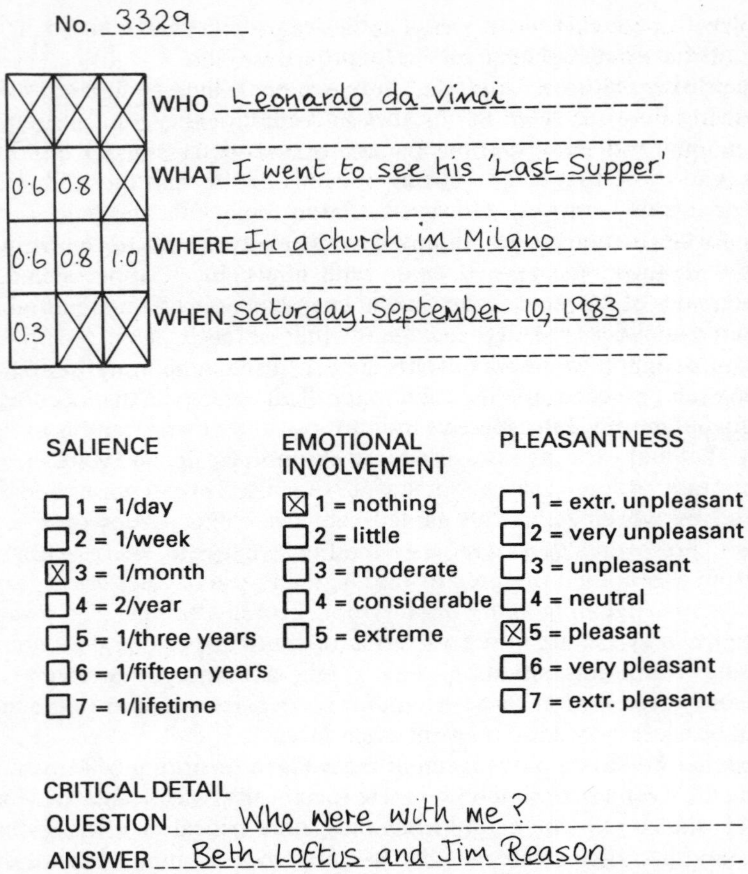

No. _3329____

WHO _Leonardo da Vinci_____

WHAT _I went to see his 'Last Supper'_

WHERE _In a church in Milano_____

WHEN _Saturday, September 10, 1983___

0.6 0.8

0.6 0.8 1.0

0.3

SALIENCE	EMOTIONAL INVOLVEMENT	PLEASANTNESS
☐ 1 = 1/day	☒ 1 = nothing	☐ 1 = extr. unpleasant
☐ 2 = 1/week	☐ 2 = little	☐ 2 = very unpleasant
☒ 3 = 1/month	☐ 3 = moderate	☐ 3 = unpleasant
☐ 4 = 2/year	☐ 4 = considerable	☐ 4 = neutral
☐ 5 = 1/three years	☐ 5 = extreme	☒ 5 = pleasant
☐ 6 = 1/fifteen years		☐ 6 = very pleasant
☐ 7 = 1/lifetime		☐ 7 = extr. pleasant

CRITICAL DETAIL
QUESTION____ _Who were with me ?_____
ANSWER ___ _Beth Loftus and Jim Reason_____

FIG. 5.4   An example of a recorded event from Wagenaar's diary study (1986).

Recall increased with the number of cues provided. Pleasant events were remembered better than unpleasant or neutral ones, but retention was also related to the other rated dimensions of salience and emotionality. The order of efficacy of the retrieval cues when presented singly was *what, where, who, when*. *What* was by far the most powerful cue and *when* was almost useless. Chronological information was often missing from the memory of the event, and could not be used as a search criterion. Wagenaar concluded that only a few landmark events were precisely dated in memory, and events were, on the whole, not filed in memory by dates. In everyday terms, it is unlikely that you will remember if I ask you what happened on 17th July four years ago, but, if I tell you that you went to watch a tennis match you would probably remember who played, where it took place, at roughly what period of the year, and what happened. The power of the *what* cue suggests that autobiographical memories are predominantly organised in categories. Wagenaar concluded that the information coded under the *what* heading was a better recall cue because it was more unique and more specific than information filed under the other headings.

The use of the diary method appears to provide a built-in check on the accuracy of recall, but in practice it is difficult to know how far answers are recalled and how far they are the product of inferential reconstruction or of guesses based on past experience. For instance, I know what time of year tennis tournaments are most likely to be held and which of my friends are most likely to enjoy watching, so I could answer these questions without actually remembering the event.

Studies of Distribution and Retention

Studies that focus on the retention of autobiographical memories over time and on the distribution of memories across the life span have used different methods, and addressed different issues. Rubin, Wetzler, and Nebes (1986) have collated the results of a number of studies (e.g. Rubin, 1982; Crovitz & Schiffman, 1974) which used a method known as word-cueing and investigated the incidence of memories across the life span. With this method, subjects are presented with a list of cue words. For each cue word they report the first autobiographical memory that comes to mind, and, after completing the list, they supply the date of each reported memory. So, given the cue word *plum*, a subject may respond "I remember making plum jam" and identify that this occurred 10 years ago. In these studies, the number of memories elicited from each period of the life span is then plotted. Rubin et al. reported that the data fitted a retention function with a linear relationship between the log of memory frequency and the log of recency of occurrence. That is, the mean number of memories elicited declined as a function of the age of the memories; there were lots of recent memories and fewer remote ones. Superimposed on this retention function, Rubin et al. noted a "reminiscence peak" consisting of a disproportionate number of memories recalled from the period when the subjects were between 10 and 30 years old. This finding was replicated in data collected by Cohen and Faulkner (1988a), who pointed out that this peak was composed of highly significant life events which tended to occur at this period in life. Fitzgerald and Lawrence (1984) reported another discrepancy in the retention function. Using older people as subjects, they found that the rate of decline in the number of memories elicited levelled off, so that the incidence of memories over 20 years old was roughly the same as the incidence of memories that were 60 years old. Again the same result was echoed in the data from Cohen and Faulkner's elderly subjects.

Further research has shown that the distribution of elicited memories across the life span is extremely sensitive to the method used. The recency effect observed by Rubin et al. was evident when subjects were asked to supply a memory for each of the word cues, and then go back through the memories they had produced and date them. Holding, Noonan, Pfau, and Holding (1986) asked their subjects to date each memory as it was produced, and found that this method produced a primacy effect, with memories being more numerous from the early part of the life span. They concluded that the dating process induced a chronological search. Cohen and Faulkner did not use word cueing, but simply asked subjects to produce and describe their most vivid memories. This technique also induced a forward-order chronological search through the life span and resulted in a preponderance of early memories. Thus the incidence of memories from different parts of the life span varies according to the retrieval process being used. These methods do not test whether recent memories are better retained, or more easily elicited, than remote ones. They simply reflect the fact that when people retrieve memories by searching backwards through their past lives they produce more recent memories; and when they begin at the beginning and search forwards they produce more remote memories.

The accuracy and quality (as opposed to the incidence) of autobiographical memories is more consistently found to deteriorate with time elapsed. As in the studies already cited by Linton and by Wagenaar, and in Bahrick's data on teachers' memory for their students (p.89), information is lost over time, and Cohen and Faulkner also found that the self-rated vividness of autobiographical memories declined over time, with older memories being less vivid than recent ones.

Determinants of Memorability

Rubin and Kozin (1984) asked a group of students to describe three of their clearest memories, and to rate them for national importance, personal importance, surprise, vividness, emotionality, and how often they had discussed the event. The most commonly reported events concerned injuries or accidents, sports, and encounters with the opposite sex. Memories which were more vivid also received higher ratings for importance, surprise, and emotionality. Cohen and Faulkner also reported that memory vividness correlated significantly with emotion, importance, and the amount of rehearsal. In their study, the relative power of these factors shifted with the age of the person who was remembering. For younger people, characteristics of the event itself, such as emotionality and importance, were the best predictors of memory vividness, but for elderly people the amount of rehearsal was the most powerful factor. The vividness of their remote memories was preserved because the events were often thought about and talked about. The events that were most often remembered were: births, marriages and deaths (22.2%); holidays (11.8%); trivia (8.2%); illness/ injury (8%); education (8%); family (7.5%); war (6.1%); love affairs (5.1%); recreations/sports (4.9%). Events in which the subjects were actors were remembered better than events in which they were only bystanders, and unique occasions and first times were remembered more often than generic events or last times.

Organisation and Retrieval Processes

Instead of relying on verbal protocols, or self-reports, to reveal retrieval strategies, as in some of the name-recall studies, researchers have attempted to infer organisation and retrieval processes in autobiographical memory by comparing the response times taken to retrieve personal memories to different cues. For example, Robinson (1976) compared the time taken to recall experiences involving an activity (e.g. *throwing*) or an object (e.g. *car*) with those involving an emotion (e.g. *happy*). He found that retrieval was slowest with emotion cues. This result indicates that people do not organise their memories in terms of the associated emotions. Robinson argued that this would be an inefficient form of organisation because many different experiences share the same emotions.

Reiser, Black, and Abelson (1985) investigated how script-like knowledge structures function in the organisation and retrieval of experiences. They compared the effectiveness of two different kinds of knowledge structure as a means of accessing personal memories. One kind of knowledge structure they called *activities*. These are script-like structures consisting of knowledge about sequences of actions undertaken to achieve a goal such as eating in restaurants, shopping in department stores, going to libraries, etc. The other kind of knowledge structure they termed *general actions*. These are MOP-like structures which represent higher-level knowledge about actions which can be components in many different specific activities. So paying, sitting down, buying tickets are examples of general actions.

Reiser et al. predicted that activities would be better retrieval cues than general actions because accessing specific activities, such as eating in restaurants, generates many inferences about food, decor, and service which can serve as further cues for retrieval of specific experiences. General actions are not "inference-rich" structures in this way. They do not constrain the area of search sufficiently and are too abstract to generate useful cues. To test their predictions, Reiser et al. asked subjects to recall specific personal experiences to fit an activity cue such as *went out drinking*, or *had your hair cut* and a general action cue such as *paid at the cash register*. They varied the order in which these two cues were presented. More experiences were successfully recalled and responses were faster when the activity cue was first. In everyday terms, you would find it easier to remember an occasion when you had your hair cut than an occasion when you bought a ticket. Reiser et al. concluded that retrieval involves two stages: first, establishing a context, like hair cuts, and, second, finding an index or tag which identifies a particular experience within that context. Activities are knowledge structures at the optimal level of specificity. This is the level at which experiences are originally encoded, and is the level which provides the optimal context for search. This context-plus-index model is similar to the schema-plus-tag model (p.112) and to the account of retrieval processes given by Williams and Hollan (p.101).

Although the idea that there is an optimal level of specificity for search contexts is convincing, Reiser et al. only tested the efficacy of actions as retrieval cues, and did not compare actions with other cues such as locations or lifetime extendures, or the names of objects or emotions. Conway and Bekerian (1987) found that retrieval was facilitated when cued by lifetime period (e.g. schooldays, time at college), and suggested that people's memories of their own personal history are organised in terms of such periods. However, Wagenaar's finding that *what* cues (i.e. what happened or what action took place) were more effective than *who, when,* or *where* tends to confirm that memories of personal experiences are organised around actions. It is doubtful, though, whether it make sense to look for a single system of organisation. Different kinds of memories are likely to be organised in different ways, and recalled in different ways. Remembering personal experiences is not always the result of effortful search through a context. Memories are sometimes spontaneously elicited by some cue such as a phrase, a smell, a tune, or when we are reminded of them by a similar current experience.

Dating Autobiographical Memories

The idea that memories are organised and retrieved by some form of chronological search raises questions about the accuracy of subjective dating. Rubin (1982) checked a sample of events that subjects had recalled and dated against their own diary records, and found that 74% were correct to within a month. Brown, Rips, and Shevell (1985) pointed out that people seldom have a precise memory record of the dates of public events, so that dates are estimated rather than remembered. They suggested that estimation is based on the amount of information about the event that can be recalled. That is, people work on the assumption that information is progressively lost from memory over time, so the less that is remembered, the older the memory must be. Brown et al. asked subjects to date the month of 50 news events from 1977 to mid-1982. They selected some events that subjects would know a lot about, and some events they would know little about, and predicted that dates of high-knowledge events (like *President Reagan shot*) would be shifted toward the present, and dates of low-knowledge events (like *25 die in California mud slides*) would be shifted toward the past. The results conformed to the prediction. Dates of high-knowledge events were too recent by an average of 0.28 years, and dates of low-knowledge events were too remote by an average of 0.17 years. The number of propositions a subject could recall about an event was systematically related to the judged recency of the event.

People also estimate dates of public events using the strategy of relating the target event to autobiographical events or to some other, more easily dated public event. If a landmark event can be dated, and the temporal relationship of landmark to target is known, the target date can be estimated. For example, I can estimate the date of the Prince of Wales's wedding because I remember being on holiday in Switzerland at the time and seeing it on television in a hotel in the mountains, and I know the date of this holiday.

Loftus and Marburger (1983) confirmed that events are dated more accurately if a landmark is supplied as a temporal reference point. They noted that people usually overestimate the recency of events, especially ones that are very emotional and salient, a phenomenon known as *forward telescoping*, but this tendency was reduced by using landmarks. They compared responses to questions preceded by landmarks with responses to the same questions preceded by no landmark. In the no landmark condition the questions were:

During the last six months did anyone try to rob you?
did anyone attack you with a weapon?
did you report a crime to the police?
did the failure to rescue the hostages in Iran occur?
did you have a birthday?
did you eat lobster?

In the with landmark condition, the same questions were preceded by

Since the eruption of Mount St. Helens did you . . . , *or*
Since last New Year's Day did you . . . ,

or the subject was instructed to supply a personal landmark to use as a reference point when answering the question. Forward telescoping was reduced by the use of all of these landmarks.

Questions about the date of events may be important when medical histories are elicited. The patient's ability to recall the dates and ordering of episodes and symptoms and their frequency and intensity is crucial for diagnosis. Means, Mingay, Nigam, and Zarrow (1988) have pointed out that in chronic health conditions, recurring events blend into a generic memory and are difficult to decompose. Their study showed that when people were trained to link events to personal landmarks, like birthdays or holidays, recall improved. They also showed that generic memories could be decomposed by detailed questioning. Loftus, Smith, Johnson, and Fiedler (Note 4) have noted that accuracy of dating improves when two time-frames are interrogated instead of one. Asking whether X occurred (1) in the last six months, and (2) in the last two months, forces patients to be more accurate and precise than simply asking whether X occurred in the last six months.

Brown, Shevell, and Rips (1986) collected verbal protocols from subjects during date estimation. In this study, both political events (*Cyrus Vance resigns*) and non-political events (*Mount St.Helens erupts*) were dated after lags of up to five years. Overall, 70% of the protocols contained temporal inferences of the kind "I know X happened just before Y and Y was about last autumn"; 61% of political events were related in this way to other political events and 31% to personal history. For non-political events, 25% were related to public events and 50% to personal history. It was easier to "place" non-political events within personally defined periods, like college terms, and to place political events within publicly defined periods, such as the Reagan administration, but public and personal event histories were clearly interwoven and each provided a reference system for the other.

Although many aspects of autobiographical memory are still obscure, these studies have had considerable success, particularly in revealing the organisation and retrieval processes. The concensus of the findings indicates that organisation is predominantly categorical, with types of events or actions being represented at different levels of generality/specificity. When people try to recall a particular episode from the past, retrieval processes access the level of categorisation that provides the optimum context for search. This optimum level of categorisation is one that is rich and specific enough to generate useful cues and reminders. Particular episodes that are sufficiently distinctive, novel, deviant, or recent are not absorbed into generalised representations but are represented at the most specific level where they can be identified by specific tags.

FLASHBULB MEMORY

Flashbulb memory is the term given to the kind of vivid and detailed recollection people often have of the occasion when they first heard about some very dramatic, surprising, important, and emotionally arousing event. Hearing the news that President John Kennedy had been shot is the example that is usually cited. It is claimed that almost everyone can remember with unusual clarity where they were when they heard of this event, what they were doing at the time, who told them and what happened next.

Brown and Kulik (1982) suggested that there is a special neural mechanism triggered by dramatic events of this kind. This mechanism, they claimed, causes the whole scene to be "printed" on the memory. Neisser (1982b) has questioned this account of flashbulb memories. He believes that their preservation results from frequent rehearsal and re-telling after the event, rather than special processes activated at the moment itself. He pointed out that the importance of such events is not always apparent at the time, but is only established later. He also cited cases where flashbulb memories recounted in great detail and good faith turned out to be inaccurate when independently checked. In his own recollection of hearing the news of the bombing of Pearl Harbour in December 1941, he remembered that he was listening to a baseball game on the radio when the programme was interrupted by a newsflash. Neisser believed this memory must have been a fabrication because no baseball games are broadcast in December. However, Thompson and Cowan (1986) have discovered that a football game was actually broadcast at the relevant time, so Neisser's memory was inaccurate, but not completely wrong. It is not clear whether the peculiar vividness and long-lasting quality of these memories should be attributed to some special mechanism, or whether they are just ordinary memories that survive because they are often reactivated.

Brown and Kulik based their claim that a special mechanism exists for flashbulb memories on the fact that they have a canonical structure. People remember *location* (where they were); *activity* (what they were doing); *source* (who told them); *affect* (what they felt) and *aftermath* (what happened next). However, according to Neisser there is no need to postulate a special mechanism to explain these uniformities, since they are the product of "narrative conventions", the traditional schemas that govern the format for story telling. If schema theory can explain the canonical form of flashbulb memories and frequency of rehearsal can explain why they are selectively well preserved, there is no need to invoke a special "print" mechanism.

Winograd and Killinger (1983) were interested in the development of flashbulb memories, and in whether dramatic events experienced by young children would be remembered in the same way as these events appear to be remembered by adults. They used subjects who were between the ages of 1 and 7 at the time of John Kennedy's assassination and testing took place 16 or 17 years after this event. The subjects were asked questions about location, activity, the effect on those around them, the aftermath, how often it was discussed, and any additional details. They plotted recall as a function of age at the time of the event using two different criteria for recall. The lenient criterion was satisfied if the subject claimed to be able to recall the event and could supply information in answer to one of the questions. The stricter criterion was satisfied only when four questions could be answered. It is clear from Fig. 5.5 that older children were more likely to remember the event and to recall more details about it. The information most frequently recalled was location (90%), followed by activity (77%), source (70%), aftermath (43%), and other details (26%). The results did not support Neisser's view that the vividness of flashbulb memories is produced by frequent rehearsal because self-reported amount of discussion was only weakly related to the amount of detail recalled. Moreover, if recall depends on reconstruction subsequent to the event, it is difficult to see why the age at encoding has such a strong effect on retention. Winograd and Killinger concluded that, because older children were capable of a deeper level of understanding, their encoding of the event was more elaborated and they formed a richer memory representation.

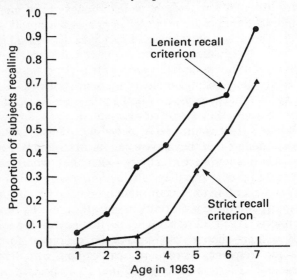

FIG. 5.5   The proportion of subjects who could recall President Kennedy's assassination as a function of age at the time of the event (from Winograd & Killinger, 1983).

In addition to the controversy about whether flashbulb memories derive special qualities at the stage of encoding or from subsequent reconstructions, there is some doubt whether these memories should be regarded as "special" at all. Rubin and Kozin (1984) argued that so-called flashbulb memories are not essentially different in character from other vivid memories. They found that subjects rated some events of personal importance, such as graduating from high school, or an early romantic experience, as having flashbulb clarity, and the vividness of these memories was also related to rated values for surprise, emotionality, and consequentiality. Their findings failed to reveal any features that would clearly distinguish flashbulb memories from other vivid autobiographical memories.

CHILDHOOD MEMORY

There is a great deal of rather conflicting folklore on the subject of childhood memory. On the one hand, it is said that people remember very little of the experiences of their early years. On the other hand, some childhood memories appear to be retained with great vividness. Most people would agree that, if they attempt to recall their personal history, they can retrieve a fairly continuous record for the years after the age of six or seven, but, for the period before this age, memories are sparse and fragmentary, consisting of isolated vignettes of particular events. Freud (1901) described this phenomenon as "childhood amnesia".

Childhood Amnesia

The term "childhood amnesia" is used as a label for deficient recall, and does not necessarily imply that memory is completely lost. Initially, claims of childhood amnesia rested on clinical reports, anecdotes, and intuitions, but more recently there have been attempts to give a more precise definition and to provide an empirical demonstration. Wetzler and Sweeney (1986) pointed out that what needs to be demonstrated is deficient recall for the early childhood years, which is independent of age at retrieval (current age) and of the length of the retention interval. That is, adults of all ages should exhibit a similar degree of childhood amnesia, and the loss of memory in the childhood years should be greater than would be predicted by the decay function whereby forgetting increases with the passage of time. This approach concentrates on a quantitative criterion for childhood amnesia rather than on qualitative aspects of childhood memories. Figure 5.6 shows a hypothetical distribution of memories across a 20-year life span. Wetzler and Sweeney examined the data from several studies of autobiographical memory, and found distributions approximating closely to this hypothetical one, with accelerated forgetting (i.e. disproportionate loss of memories) for ages below five.

Another way to probe this "dark age" is to ask people to produce their earliest memory. Dudycha and Dudycha (1941) noted that the average age for earliest memories was around 42 months and Halliday (personal communication) obtained a similar result with a mean of 39 months. Sheingold and Tenney (1982) focused on a specific episode that took place at a known age: the birth of a sibling. They interviewed four-year-old children whose

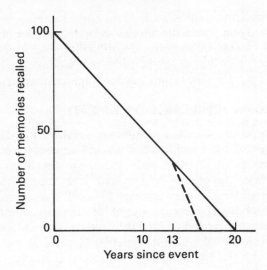

FIG. 5.6   The hypothetical distribution of memories across the lifetime of a 20-year-old subject. Solid line represents a linear function of normal forgetting; broken line represents the accelerated forgetting due to childhood amnesia (from Wetzler & Sweeney, 1986). Copyright (1986) by the American Psychological Association. Reprinted by permission of the author.

sibling had been born within the last year, and eight-year-olds and twelve-year-olds whose siblings had been born when they were four. At interview, they were asked specific questions, shown in Fig. 5.7. The children's mothers were also questioned to provide confirmation of their answers. The four-year-olds answered a mean of 13 questions out of 20 and, on average, 9 of their answers were confirmed by their mothers. The scores for amount recalled showed only minimal differences between children of different ages. The 12-year-old children remembered the event of 8 years ago as well as the younger children for whom it was more recent. For this highly salient event, there was almost no forgetting. Sheingold and Tenney also examined college students' memory for the birth of siblings and found a sharp discontinuity in memory between the ages of three and five. Students who were younger than three when their sibling was born recalled almost nothing about the circumstances, whereas those who were four at the time recalled an impressive amount of information. This discontinuity is reflected in Fig. 5.8. Different studies therefore place the boundaries of childhood amnesia at different ages, ranging from three (Sheingold & Tenney) to between six and eight (Freud).

A range of explanations for the phenomenon of childhood amnesia are on offer (White & Pillemer, 1979). According to the Freudian explanation,

1. Who told you that your mother was leaving to go to the hospital?
2. What were you doing when you were told that she was leaving?
3. What time of day was it when she left to go to the hospital?
4. Who went with her? Did you go?
5. Who took care of you right after your mother left to go to the hospital?
6. What did you do right after your mother left?
7. How did you find out that the baby was a boy or girl?
8. Who took care of you while your mother was in the hospital?
9. What things did you do with that person while your mother was in the hospital?
10. Did you visit your mother while she was in the hospital?
11. Did you talk to your mother on the telephone while she was in the hospital?
12. How long did she stay in the hospital?
13. Who picked your mother and the baby up?
14. What day of the week did they come home?
15. What time of day was it?
16. What did you do when your mother and the baby arrived at home?
17. What was the baby wearing when you first saw it?
18. What presents did the baby get?
19. Did you get any presents at that time?
20. How did you find out that your mother was going to have a baby?

FIG. 5.7   Questions about the birth of siblings used by Sheingold and Tenney (1982). From *Memory observed: Remembering in natural contexts*, by Ulric Neisser. Copyright © 1982 W.H. Freeman and Company. Reprinted with permission.

early memories are present but, with the rejection of infant sexuality, memories are repressed and cannot be recalled to consciousness. The deficit is thus a retrieval failure. Freud identified those early memories which can be recalled as "screen" memories, fabricated to block out emotionally painful realities. Other theories attribute the dearth of early memories to inadequate encoding, neurological immaturity, or developmental changes in cognitive mechanisms. It has been argued that very young children lack the linguistic ability to encode their experiences verbally, and lack the schemas within which they can represent and organise event memories (Schachtel, 1947). They may fail to use encoding strategies which elaborate and enrich the memory representation with semantic associations (Winograd & Killinger, 1983), or they may encode memories in ways that are inappropriate for the retrieval processes used at a later age. According to this explanation, developmental changes in coding and organisation produce a mismatch between the original coding and the subsequent retrieval cues. An example of this kind occurs when you try to

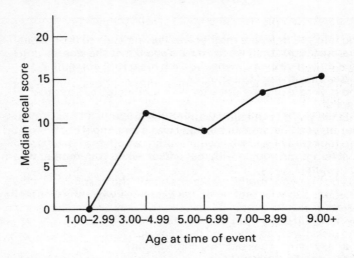

FIG. 5.8   Amount recalled about birth of a sibling as a function of age at the time of the event (from Sheingold & Tenney, 1982). From *Memory observed: Remembering in natural contexts*, by Ulric Neisser. Copyright © 1982 W.H. Freeman and Company. Reprinted with permission.

remind a child of a particular event, such as a family trip to visit a relative. Your descriptions of the journey, the destination, and the relative fail to evoke any memory in him, but it turns out eventually that he remembers the event in terms of the ice cream he was given at lunch. This type of example raises the possibility that we are underestimating the number of events which can be remembered from early childhood because we do not find the right triggers to elicit them.

Children's Scripts

Recent research on children's memory for events has centred on questions about the acquisition of scripts and the function of scripts in supporting memory. Early memories might be forgotten, it is suggested, if young children lack scripts. Following Schank and Abelson (1977), Nelson and Gruendel (1986) identified five features that define a script:

1. Scripts are organised sequentially.
2. They are organised around a central goal.
3. They are generalised and include slots for variable elements.
4. They are similar across individuals who share the same experience.
5. They are consistent across repeated experiences.

Figure 5.9 shows examples of some of the scripts supplied by three-year-old children in response to questions and prompts. Scripts for other events like getting dressed and going shopping were also elicited. These examples show that young children's event knowledge conforms to the defining features of scripts. Their scripts show temporal sequencing of actions, central goals, are consistent, and are expressed in a general form. Older children produced longer scripts with more detail and elaboration. Younger children's scripts were similar in form, but more skeletal. This finding supports Winograd and Killinger's conclusion that developmental differences in amount recalled stem from differences in the degree of elaboration at encoding.

Hudson (1986) examined children's organisation of memory for events within the framework of schema-plus-tag, or context-plus-index models, whereby specific autobiographical events are organised in long-term memory in terms of their relationship to general event representations. Routine, repeated events which conform to the same pattern are absorbed into a general event representation and are not remembered as distinct occasions. Novel, unique, or deviant occasions are retained as specific memories, although linked to the relevant general event representation. Autobiographical memories can therefore include a blend of specific knowledge about what happened on a particular occasion, and general knowledge which has been abstracted from past experience of similar occasions. Hudson pointed out that this form of representation is essentially a developmental one, as the general event representations are progressively built up out of accumulating specific event representations. She sought evidence for qualitative changes in children's memory for events that might reflect this development. She expected to find age differences in the relative proportions of general event knowledge, and specific event knowledge.

In her first study, she examined three- and five-year-olds' memory for specific episodes of routine events that had occurred the previous day (e.g. "What happened when you had dinner at home yesterday?"). She also studied their general knowledge about this class of event (e.g. "What happens when you have dinner at home?") All the children produced more information in answer to the general dinner script question than in answer to the specific episode question. There were no age differences in the relative proportions of general event knowledge and specific event knowledge in their answers. They had relatively little recall for the last occurrence of a routine event, but when asked to recall a novel event, such as a trip to the zoo or circus, their replies showed rich and detailed memory for these unique events.

In a second study, Hudson asked five- and seven-year-olds about events that had been experienced a varying number of times. There was evidence that increasing familiarity with an experience produced increasing

Making Cookies

Well, you bake them and eat them. (3;1)

My mommy puts chocolate chips inside the cookies. Then ya put 'em in the oven ... Then we take them out, put them on the table and eat them. (4;5)

Add three cups of butter ... add three lumps of butter ... two cups of sugar, one cup of flour. Mix it up ... knead it. Get it in a pan, put it in the oven. Bake it ... set it up to 30. Take it out and it'll be cookies. (6;9)

First, you need a bowl, a bowl, and you need about two eggs and chocolate chips and an egg-beater! And then you gotta crack the egg open and put it in a bowl and ya gotta get the chips and mix it together. And put it in a stove for about 5 or 10 minutes, and then you have cookies. Then ya eat them! (8;8)

Birthday Party

You cook a cake and eat it. (3;1)

Well, you get a cake and some ice cream and then some birthday (?) and then you get some clowns and then you get some paper hats, the animal hats and then and then you sing "Happy Birthday to you," and then then then they give you some presents and then you play with them and then that's the end and they go home and they do what they wanta. (4;9)

First, uhm ... you're getting ready for the kids to come, like puttin' balloons up and putting out party plates and making cake. And then all the people come you've asked. Give you presents and then you have lunch or whatever you have. Then ... uhm ... then you open your presents. Or you can open your presents anytime. Uhm ... you could ... after you open the presents, then it's probably time to go home. if you're like at Foote Park or something, then it's time to go home and you have to drive all the people home. Then you go home too. (6;7)

Well, first you open your mail box and get some mail. And then you see that there's an invitation for you. Read the invitation. Then you ask your parents if you can go. Then you ... uhm ... go to the birthday party and after you get there you usually wait for everyone else to come. Then usually they always want to open one of the presents. Sometimes then they have three games, then they have the birthday cake then sometimes they open up the other presents or they could open them up all at once. After that they like to play some more games and then maybe your parents come to pick you up. And then you go home. (8;10)

FIG. 5.9 Examples of scripts for making cookies and for birthday parties from children aged 3–8 years (Nelson and Greendel, 1986).

136

schematisation, with more general information and fewer particular details being reported. A further study examined children's memory for an untypical episode. New York children who made fairly frequent trips to museums were questioned about a particular trip to the Jewish Museum which was unusual. One year later, memory for this specific occasion was well retained, but it had not been incorporated into the general museum script, and this general museum script had not been modified by the novel experience.

Hudson also found that recall of specific memories of particular occasions depended on the cues that were used. Those children who could not remember the Jewish Museum visit after one year when they were asked "What happened when you went to the Jewish Museum?" succeeded in recalling the occasion when asked about the archaeological activities that were shown in the museum. These children had filed the episode under an "archaeology" tag. This finding confirms the view that what seems like a loss of early memories may be due to a mismatch between the index or tag in the filing system and the retrieval cue. As children's experience increases, and their knowledge of the world accumulates, the indices they use to tag specific episodes are likely to approximate more closely to probable retrieval cues, thus reducing the chance of mismatches.

Taken together, these studies showed that the relationship between general event representations and specific event memories that characterises adult memory is apparent in children as young as three years old. Structurally and functionally, autobiographical memory in young children is equivalent to autobiographical memory in adults. Routine events are absorbed into the general script; unique events are stored separately. There was no evidence of age-related changes in this basic structure between the ages of three and seven, but there was evidence that changes in autobiographical memory occurred as a function of increasing experience rather than age, and affected content rather than structure.

In spite of this impressive evidence that children's memories are highly organised, many of the early memories that people report do not seem to fit this pattern. In Cohen and Faulkner's (1988a) study 21% of the events recalled from the first decade of the life span were categorised as trivia. Whereas the other memories from this period were clearly linked to general event representations for school, family, holidays, pets, etc., these trivial memories were apparently unrelated to any script or general event knowledge. They were memories of isolated scenes that seemed relatively pointless and devoid of context, and were rated as low in emotionality, importance, and frequency of rehearsal. Examples such as "Sitting in the sandpit in the garden and looking at the sky through the leaves" or "Walking along a road towards a beach" have the quality of scenes recalled from dreams. It is not clear why these memories should have been preserved, or what significance, if any, they may once have had, since they seem to be detached from any organising framework.

It is probably simplistic to seek any single explanation for the dearth of memories from the early years of childhood. Generalised event representations are clearly present and are used to guide encoding and retrieval, but they are simple and skeletal in content, and specific episodes may be indexed with inappropriate tags so that they cannot be retrieved later. The existence of "trivia" memories also suggests the possibility that some specific memories are floaters that have drifted away from, or have never been firmly linked to the relevant general event representation. These memories would then be difficult to access and retrieve. Since the amount and nature of the input to the system appears to be a crucial factor in the development of memory organisation, it is tempting to speculate that there is some optimal mix of routine and novel experiences. If experience were too narrowly confined to an unvarying routine, scripts would be few and poorly elaborated; if experience were constantly changing, it would be difficult for the child to abstract general event knowledge and build general event representations.

Memory for personal experiences, as this chapter has illustrated, includes a wide-ranging variety of different types of memory. Researchers are forced to rely on relatively informal ways of gathering their data and cannot exclude or control the many factors that influence the encoding, retention, and retrieval of memories of personal experiences. In spite of these problems, theories and models developed in more formal cognitive studies are surprisingly successful at interpreting and making sense of the findings.

6 World Knowledge, Metaknowledge, and Expert Knowledge

TYPES OF KNOWLEDGE

There is more to everyday memory than mundane matters like remembering to put out the milk bottles. Everyday memory involves retrieving and using stored knowledge of many different kinds in the appropriate contexts. These different kinds of knowledge include knowledge acquired formally from education or training, as well as knowledge that is picked up incidentally. In the course of daily life a person may need to use knowledge of mathematics, of electrical wiring, of plant species, of cookery, of stock markets, and many more specialised topics. Everyday memory is not just concerned with the trivial and the commonplace.

This chapter examines memory for general knowledge about the world rather than specific knowledge about personal experiences; semantic knowledge rather than episodic knowledge. As we noted in Chapter 5, pp.114–115, this is not a sharp distinction, since the kind of semantic knowledge which consists of generalised event knowledge is built up by abstraction from personal experiences. However, the important difference between the two kinds of knowledge is that semantic knowledge consists of objective general facts and episodic knowledge consists of subjective specific facts. Within semantic knowledge, a number of further distinctions can be made which are important when we come to consider how knowledge is stored and organised in memory.

The knowledge stored in human memory forms a very large data base (Nickerson, 1977) but nobody knows, as yet, how large it is. In any case, the most interesting questions concern what information is stored in memory, and how it is organised and retrieved, rather than how much information is in store. Much of human knowledge is incomplete, inconsistent, vague, and uncertain. However much we know, we are constantly being confronted with demands for knowledge that we do not have, and, even when we do know it, we cannot always retrieve a given item of information when we want to. One of the most interesting and important questions, then, is how can we function with an information system that appears to have such serious shortcomings?

Before we can begin to address this question, we need to make some distinctions between different kinds of knowledge, because some of these distinctions affect the way that knowledge is organised, retrieved, and used.

General Knowledge and Expert Knowledge

General world knowledge is the kind of information that is shared by many educated adults in the same culture. It includes miscellaneous and relatively superficial information about history, geography, science, literature, current events, and so on. Expert knowledge, on the other hand, consists of a body of tightly integrated, domain-specific knowledge about some particular defined area such as nuclear physics, eighteenth-century chamber music, computer programming, or the habits of arctic terns. The difference between the two kinds of knowledge is mainly one of depth and interrelatedness. Although the distinction is not a sharp one, expert knowledge is more detailed, more cohesive and integrated, and less likely to be common to the majority of the population.

Explicit Knowledge and Implicit Knowledge

Nickerson emphasised the distinction between facts that have been learned explicitly, such as:

The sum of 2 and 4 is 6
Whales are mammals
The Aswan dam is in Egypt

and implicit, or tacit knowledge which consists of facts that are unlikely to have been learned explicitly, but which can be inferred from other knowledge, such as:

Julius Caesar had a mother
Giraffes have teeth
The Mississippi flows downhill

This distinction between explicit, pre-stored knowledge and implicit, inferential or computable knowledge was evident when map knowledge was analysed in Chapter 3, p.60. In any information system, whether it is a computer or a human memory, information may be pre-stored and represented explicitly, or it may computable by the application of inferential procedures to other information which is in store. There is a trade-off between pre-storage and computation. Pre-storage is very expensive in terms of storage space and, if large amounts of information are pre-stored, very efficient search and retrieval processes are required to locate and access particular items. For knowledge that is not very likely to be in frequent use (like the example about Julius Caesar's mother) it is obviously uneconomical to have it pre-stored. Having knowledge which is implicit, but not pre-stored, saves space, but implicit information takes more time to compute, and errors may occur if incorrect inferences are made.

Camp, Lachman, and Lachman (1980) demonstrated the psychological reality of this distinction between pre-stored and computable knowledge. They selected a set of questions likely to be retrieved by direct access. These were questions like:

What was the name of the flying horse in mythology?

Subjects either know or don't know that the answer is Pegasus. Many of the direct-access questions involved proper names because these are not computable—they cannot be inferred. Another set of questions were inferential questions such as:

What direction does the Statue of Liberty face?
What U.S. President was the first to see an airplane?

Subjects were unlikely to know the answers to these questions, but they could figure out the answer by inferential processes. Camp et al. found that reaction times to respond "true" to answers to direct-access questions averaged 1.97 seconds, whereas reaction times to respond "true" to answers to the inferential questions averaged 2.85 seconds. The additional retrieval time for inference questions reflects the reasoning processes necessary to retrieve the answer. The various types of inference that are used to access implicit knowledge are described in a later section on inferential knowledge.

Fuzzy Knowledge and Absolute Knowledge

Nickerson also distinguished between fuzzy relational knowledge and absolute knowledge such as quantitative facts. Relational knowledge includes facts such as:

Potatoes are bigger than peas
France is north of Spain
Alexander the Great lived before Napoleon

which represent relative differences in magnitude, location, and temporal order. He pointed out that people are more likely to know these kind of relationships than to know actual sizes, dates, weights, speeds, ages, monetary values, or whatever. This observation lends support to Nickerson's contention that much of our knowledge is approximate rather than exact. The model of the world that we have in our heads is vague and inexact. And, as he convincingly points out, this kind of approximate knowledge is all that is needed for most decisions and actions in everyday life. For most purposes, we do not need to know precise numerical values. We need to be able to make rough estimates and fairly crude relational judgements. Approximate or relational knowledge is also more economical in storage. Absolute quantitative facts would take up far more storage space and rarely be required. Much of our knowledge is also imprecise because it is probabilistic. Predictions about what the weather will be like tomorrow, when the plums will be ripe, the state of the bank balance next month, and the chances of catching a train, are couched in terms of probabilities. In these kinds of cases, precise knowledge would be more helpful, but is usually not available.

In human memory, reliance on fuzzy knowledge and implicit knowledge, and on inferential processes rather than on direct access to explicitly pre-stored information has the effect of making a limited amount of knowledge go a long way.

METAKNOWLEDGE

Insights about how general world knowledge is organised and retrieved from memory have come from the subjective self-reports that are generated when people are required to answer factual questions, and, at the same time, to report on their memory processes. Recent studies have used this method to probe people's ability to know about their own memories. The general term "metamemory" has been used, but Cavanaugh (1988) has pointed out that three kinds of knowing about memory can be distinguished:

1. *Systemic awareness* consists of knowing how memory works, what kinds of things are easy or difficult to remember, or what kinds of encoding and retrieval strategies produce the best results.
2. *Epistemic awareness* consists of knowing what we know, knowing what knowledge is in store, and being able to make judgements about its accuracy. This is metaknowledge.

3. *On-line awareness* consists of knowing about ongoing memory processes and being able to monitor the current functioning of memory, as in prospective memory tasks (Chapter 2, p.24). Cases of absent-mindedness occur as a result of failures of on-line awareness.

As Cavanaugh has noted, the three kinds of metamemory may be interrelated. In trying to recall a particular fact, epistemic awareness may be involved in knowing that the relevant information is in store; systemic awareness may guide the selection of search strategies and direct the search process; and on-line awareness might be involved in keeping track of the progress of the search. In the recall of general knowledge it is the epistemic kind of metamemory, or metaknowledge, which has received most attention.

Our ability to know what we know, and, even more importantly, to know what we don't know, is such a commonplace feature of everyone's mental processes that we tend to take it for granted, and fail to realise quite how surprising and how puzzling an achievment it is. Given the enormous range and quantity of information that an adult accumulates and stores over a lifetime, it is surprising that, when we are asked a question we can usually say at once and with reasonable confidence whether the answer is in memory or not. Paradoxically, we know whether the search for an answer will be successful before it has begun. An example of this ability comes from lexical decision tasks. People are able to decide that a letter string (such as *"brone"*) does not constitute a real word, and they make this decision so fast that it is hard to believe that they can be searching through the entire mental lexicon to find out whether *"brone"* is represented. The same ability to know what we know and what we do not know extends to facts as well as lexical items.

Knowledge on the Tip of the Tongue: the TOT State

Brown and McNeill's research (1966) into the tip-of-the-tongue phenomenon is a classic study of epistemic metamemory. When recall of knowledge is rapid and successful there is little or no conscious awareness of how that knowledge was retrieved. Direct access to information in the memory system is a fast and automatic process and is not accessible to introspection. Occasions when recall is slow, effortful, and indirect are much more illuminating to the researcher because people are able to report something about how they are searching and what fragments or items the search process turns up along the way.

Brown and McNeill focused on cases when a target is known but cannot be recalled. In these cases there is a temporary failure of the retrieval process, but recall is felt to be imminent. This phenomenon was called the

TOT state because the target item is felt to be on the tip of the tongue. The material used in their study consisted of rare words, and their findings are therefore relevant to the storage and retrieval of lexical knowledge rather than factual knowledge, but the basic method they developed has been adapted and used in other studies examining retrieval of general world knowledge. They assembled a large group of subjects and read out questions such as: "What is the word designating a small boat used in the river and harbour traffic of China and Japan?" and succeeded in inducing 233 TOT states. Of these 65% were classed as positive because, when the target word ("sampan") was supplied by the experimenter, it was recognised as the one that had been sought, indicating that the feeling of having the word on the tip of the tongue was a valid reflection of what was in the memory store. As in the studies of name blocks, described in Chapter 4, pp.102–106, people in the TOT state could often supply partial information about the target word, recalling the first letter, number of syllables, and location of primary stress. They also recalled candidate words which were not the target, but were similar in sound or meaning (e.g. "samurai" or "junk"), and they were able to judge the relative proximity of these candidates to the target.

Koriat and Lieblich (1974) have since pointed out that features such as number of syllables can sometimes be guessed accurately on the basis of knowing the class of the target word without having any idea of the specific target. For example, I might guess that the river boat had two syllables even if I had never heard of the word "sampan". This means that Brown and McNeill's data may contain an unknown proportion of guesses as well as genuine cases of retrieval of partial information. However, this does not significantly weaken their main conclusions that words are generically organised in memory into sets with similar meanings or with similar sounds. Recall of partial information, and of non-target candidates which resemble the target word, reflects this generic organisation. Top-down search processes first access a class of related words, and may stop short at this point without locating the specific target. It is worth emphasising, though, that these findings apply to indirect retrieval processes. They do not apply to rapid automatic direct access to a designated target, which does not necessarily follow the same route as TOT searches.

The TOT state should be distinguished from other states in which people feel confident that, given time, they will be able to remember some target piece of information. Suppose, for example, you are asked "What is the capital of Afghanistan?" You may feel recall is imminent because: (1) you know that you once knew it and have recalled it successfully on previous occasions; (2) you know that you have studied geography and learned lots of capital cities so you know you ought to know this one; (3) you know that you do know it and have a feeling of being almost, but not quite, able to retrieve it. Brown and McNeill described this feeling as like being on the brink of a sneeze.

The first two examples describe a rational inference you make about your own knowledge. The third, which resembles a physical sensation rather than a rational process, is the true TOT state. The feeling of knowing, described in the next section, could be the product of either rational inferences about one's own knowledge state, or TOT sensations.

The Feeling of Knowing: FOKs and the Knowledge Gradient

Lachman, Lachman, and Thronesberry (1981) developed Brown and McNeill's insights using a more experimental technique for investigating epistemic awareness and the retrieval of general world knowledge. Their experiment was divided into three phases. In Phase 1, subjects had to answer general-knowledge questions covering current events, history, sport, literature, etc. such as: "What was the former name of Muhammed Ali?" or "What is the capital of Cambodia?" They were told not to guess, but to give the correct answer or respond "Don't know" as quickly as possible.

In Phase 2, subjects were re-presented with all the questions to which they had responded "Don't know" and asked to make a "feeling of knowing" (FOK) judgement on a scale from 1=definitely do not know; 2=maybe do not know; 3=could recognise the answer if told; to 4=could recall the answer if given hints and more time. In Phase 3, after a short delay, the subjects were given four multiple-choice alternatives for each of the questions to which they had initially responded don't know, and had to select one of these alternatives and give a rating of confidence in the correctness of their choice. So, for example, the choices for the question about the capital of Cambodia were Angkor Wat, Phnom Penh, Vientiane, and Lo Minh. The confidence rating scale ran from 1= a wild guess; 2= an educated guess; 3= probably right, to 4= definitely right.

The results showed that high FOK ratings were positively related to the probability of picking the correct alternative and to the level of confidence. The response times in Phase 1 were also systematically related to the FOK ratings. Subjects took longer to say "don't know" when they thought they might possibly know the answer, so high FOK ratings of 3 or 4 were associated with long response times. When FOK was low, response times were fast. Confidence ratings in Phase 3 also reflected the correctness of the choice. Subjects were more confident when they picked the correct alternative and less confident when their choice was wrong. This experiment takes subjective self-ratings of FOK and of confidence, and validates them against objective measures of accuracy and response time. The results confirmed that there is not a simple two-state dichotomy such that people either know something or do not know it. Instead, there is a gradient of knowing which is reflected subjectively in the FOK and confidence ratings, and objectively in the speed and accuracy with which a target piece of information can be retrieved.

Similar findings emerged from a study by Gruneberg and Sykes (1978). They asked subjects to name the capitals of 25 countries and to give FOK ratings when they could not answer. FOKs were classed as positive (do know) or negative (don't know). They found that if they supplied first-letter cues for the missing names, the probability of correct recall was higher (0.38) if a positive FOK had been given, and lower (0.14) if the FOK had been negative. However, they also found that negative FOKs were associated with different probabilities of recall depending on whether the knowledge being queried was something known to most people in the group to which the subjects belonged. When the question related to information that is generally well known (e.g. a familiar capital city like Paris), a negative FOK was more likely to be wrong. The subject underestimated the probability that he could recall it. If the question related to some little-known information, a negative FOK was more likely to be accurate. The subjective FOKs of individuals were more accurate when they were consistent with an objective estimate of probability of recall based on group knowledge. These findings draw attention to the fact that, although it is generally fairly accurate, the FOK may sometimes be illusory. Krinsky and Krinsky (1988) found that when subjects failed to remember a state capital their FOK for the unrecalled capital city was distorted by a tendency to falsely recognise other large cities as the capital. For example, your estimate of your ability to recall the capital of West Germany will be inaccurate if you think Berlin is the capital. People cannot always judge what they will or will not be able to retrieve from memory. Gruneberg and Sykes also suggested that there may be individual differences in the accuracy of FOK ratings.

Individual Differences in Metaknowledge

Individual differences in epistemic awareness have been explored by Perlmutter (1978). She examined the effects of age and of level of education on several aspects of metamemory in a study that tested old and young adults of different levels of education. She reasoned that with increasing age an individual would accumulate an increasing amount of world knowledge. Age deficits in retrieval of facts could then arise if interference increased with the size of the knowledge base, or if strategies of retrieval were unable to handle the increased amount of information. Epistemic awareness might also decline in old age, since, as the knowledge base changes over time with the acquisition of new information and with forgetting old information, metaknowledge needs to be continuously updated. To express this idea in terms of the library analogy for knowledge storage is to suggest that the catalogue gets out of date in old age. Old people may then base judgements on what they previously knew rather than what they currently know.

Perlmutter also explored the possibility that age differences in systemic awareness might affect fact retrieval. Age differences in question answering would arise if old people are less able to select and implement optimal strategies of retrieval. Among the battery of tests, Perlmutter included a systemic awareness component consisting of 60 questions probing subjects' knowledge of how their own memories functioned. Examples are shown in Fig. 6.1. There was also a general-knowledge test of 24 factual questions and subjects were asked to give a confidence rating for their answers and, if they were unable to recall a fact, to predict their ability to recognise the correct answer. This was followed by a fact-recognition test, and again confidence ratings had to be supplied.

The results showed that the age groups did not differ in systemic awareness. They all thought it easiest to remember information that was related, organised, interesting, understandable, and concrete, and they reported using similar strategies. The old subjects remembered more facts in response to the general-knowledge questions, but there were no age differences in the accuracy with which old and young predicted whether they would be able to recognise the correct answer, and no age differences in confidence ratings. Overall, there were significant correlations between confidence and number of facts recalled and between prediction accuracy and fact recall. People who knew more facts were also better at knowing what they knew. This finding is a clear indication that the efficiency of epistemic awareness does not decline with the size of the knowledge base.

Although in Perlmutter's study FOK accuracy did not appear to decline in old age, Camp (1988) reported that elderly people believed that their ability to remember facts had declined, but that their ability to "figure out" answers by making inferences had improved. However, when they were tested and compared with young people, the results showed exactly the opposite. The elderly were better at fact recall but poorer at inferential retrieval. These results suggest that elderly people are not necessarily accurate in their assessment of their own memories.

It is not clear, therefore, whether metamemory ability declines in old age, but there is evidence that, in children, it improves with age. Flavell and Wellman (1977) found that nine-year-old children were better able to predict whether they would recognise correct answers than five-year-old children. Other aspects of metamemory also show developmental trends. Kreutzer, Leonard, and Flavell (1975) asked children from four to ten years questions like:

When you can not remember something do you find it upsetting?
Do you have more difficulty remembering things when you are tired?
Do you have more difficulty remembering things when you are
    pressured?
Do you have more difficulty remembering things when you are
    anxious?
Are you more likely to forget things when your mind is preoccupied?
Over the years have you become more aware of your memory?
Over the years have you noticed any changes in your memory?
Do you use memory aids more often than you previously did?
Over the years has your memory improved?
Over the years has your memory become worse?
Do you think your memory will change as you get older?
Do you think your memory will get better when you get older?
Do you think your memory will get worse when you get older?
Do you think your memory will always stay about as it is now?
Do you think you will forget things more easily when you get older?
Do you think you will remember more details as you get older?
Do you consciously try to memorize things more than you used to?
Do you remember some kinds of things better than others?
Do you find it easier to remember organized things than unorganized
    things?
Is it easier to remember visual things than verbal things?
Do you find it easier to remember bizarre things than usual things?
Do you find it easier to remember things you are most interested in?
Do you find it easier to remember concrete things than abstract things?
Do you find it easier to remember things that are related to each other
    than things that are not related to each other?
Are there some kinds of things that are really hard to remember?
Are you especially likely to forget unpleasant things?
Do you have more difficulty remembering details than generalities?
Do you find it more difficult to remember things you are not interested
    in?
Do you find it more difficult to remember unfamiliar than familiar
    things?
Do you find it more difficult to remember things you do not really
    understand?

FIG. 6.1   Items from a metamemory questionnaire (from Perlmutter, 1978). Copyright
(1978) by the American Psychological Association. Reprinted by permission of the author.

If you wanted to phone your friend and someone told you the phone
number, would it make any difference if you phoned right away, or if
you got a drink of water first?

Suppose your friend has a dog and you ask him how old his dog is. He
tells you he got his dog as a puppy one Christmas but can't remember

which Christmas. What could he do to help him remember which Christmas he got his dog?

Awareness of appropriate strategies for remembering phone numbers or retrieving dates of events increased with age. The pattern of age effects in old and young suggests that metamemory efficiency improves with experience but is unaffected by the size of the knowledge base.

Decisions About Ignorance: Knowing That You Don't Know

How do people know that they don't know something? Glucksberg and McCloskey (1981) explored their intuition that there are two basic types of "don't know" decision. One type is a slow, low-confidence decision. If, for example, someone is asked "Is Kiev in the Ukraine?" he or she may ponder for several seconds and eventually reply "Don't Know" hesitantly. In contrast, a question like "What is Jimmy Carter's favourite colour?" might elicit a fast, high-confidence "Don't Know".

Glucksberg and McCloskey considered that the two different kinds of response might reflect two different knowledge states. When a person has some knowledge that is relevant to the question (e.g. that Kiev is in the U.S.S.R.; that Ukraine is in the U.S.S.R.) this relevant knowledge is accessed and evaluated to find out whether an answer to the question is implicit and can be inferred from it. The slow don't know response is produced only after it is clear that the relevant knowledge will not yield an inference which answers the question. When a person has no knowledge relevant to the question (e.g. knows nothing at all about Jimmy Carter's taste in colour) a rapid response can be made. Because the initial search for relevant facts draws a blank, the process stops short. Subsequent stages of evaluation or attempted inferencing do not occur, so the response is faster.

To test these intuitions Glucksberg and McCloskey ran several experiments. In one of these, the subjects learned a set of statements such as:

John has a pencil
John doesn't have a shovel
Bill has a bowl
Bill has a magazine

They were then presented with test sentences to which they had to respond True (e.g. *John has a pencil*); False (e.g. *John has a shovel*); or Don't know (e.g. *John has a magazine*). As predicted, reaction times to respond Don't know were fastest. For both the True and the False judgements subjects had some information in store (about John and a pencil or about John and a shovel) and had to evaluate whether the relationship in the stored statement matched the relationship in the test sentence. For the Don't know judgement there was no information about John and a magazine that needed to be considered.

In another experiment they compared reaction times to respond to different questions about real-world knowledge. There were three types of question:

1. Known questions, e.g. "Was John F. Kennedy a Democrat?" It was expected that most subjects would know the answer to these questions.
2. Don't know–relevant questions, e.g. "Does Ann Landers have a degree in journalism?" It was expected that most subjects would not know the answer but would know the relevant fact that Ann Landers writes a syndicated advice column.
3. Don't know–no relevant questions, e.g. "Does Bert Parks have a degree in journalism?" In this case subjects would not have any knowledge relevant to the question.

Responses to the Don't know–no relevant questions were, on average, 300 milliseconds faster than responses to the Don't know–relevant questions. These results confirm Glucksberg and McCloskey's model for the two different kinds of Don't know response, but this may be oversimplified as an account of how people make decisions about ignorance in everyday life. In the test situation, Don't know was a perfectly acceptable response to make. In everyday life, Don't know is a last-resort response which is usually unhelpful. If the information is sought for some practical purpose, in order to make a decision or implement a course of action, it is more useful to make a plausible guess than give up and admit ignorance. Suppose, for example, that you urgently need a shovel to clear snow from your garage door so that you can get the car out. You don't have shovel, but does your neighbour, John, have a shovel? Even if you have no directly relevant knowledge about John and shovels, you may have other knowledge which makes it plausible to guess that he probably has one (he has a lot of tools, does building jobs, etc.). Plausible inferences or probabilistic judgements are more useful than admissions of ignorance, and may therefore be made instead of the slow Don't know response elicited in formal tests. Glucksberg and McCloskey have fudged the difficult problem of how we decide when an inference based on relevant knowledge is plausible enough, or probable enough, to constitute an answer to the question, and when it is too uncertain so that it is better to decide we don't know.

Knowledge Sources

Another aspect of metaknowledge involves knowing where your knowledge came from. This may seem to be somewhat irrelevant, but it is important when making judgements about the accuracy or authenticity of knowledge.

Much of the information that comes our way in everyday life is incorrect and we are constantly confronted with the need to decide whether to accept it and modify our existing knowledge structures accordingly, or to reject it outright, or to seek some further confirmation. If you state some fact which other people find novel or surprising, they will often ask you "How do you know?" If you can remember that you acquired the information from a reputable source, such as a work of reference, an acknowleged expert, or a person recognised to be knowledgeable, your statement is likely to be accepted. Similarly, you almost certainly apply the same kind of "source test" yourself when you encounter some new information before you accept it as true. McIntyre and Craik tested memory for the source of information. Their subjects were given general-knowledge questions, but when they responded Don't Know, answers were supplied by one or other of two experimenters. One week later the subjects were tested for recall of the facts and were also asked to state the source of the information, i.e. which experimenter had supplied the information. Young subjects recalled 60% of the sources correctly, although elderly subjects made more errors. In naturally occurring situations people may remember the general context in which they acquired some information even if they cannot state the source precisely. They may remember that the information was acquired from a television programme, during a course of study, or from somebody they met at a party. Knowing where knowledge came from provides a useful indication of its authenticity .

INFERENTIAL KNOWLEDGE

Although explicit knowledge can be accessed directly, implicit, or tacit, knowledge has to be retrieved by means of inferential processes or computation. Much of our everyday knowledge about the world is implicit and different kinds of inferences are used to access it. Graesser and Clark (1985) have described the way that some of these different kinds of inferences can be classified in "inference taxonomies".

Types of Inference

The first dimension of this taxonomy, pointed out by Collins (1979), distinguishes between *inferences based on knowledge and inferences based on metaknowledge*. Inferences based on knowledge include deductive reasoning (e.g. Socrates is mortal because he is a man and all men are mortal) and inductive reasoning (e.g. Jane has a short skirt, and Anne has a short skirt, so short skirts must be fashionable). Inferences based on metaknowledge are inferences based on what you know about your knowledge (e.g. "It can't be true because I would have known it if it were true" or "Everybody knows that and I know what most other people know so I must know it too"). The kind of negative inference based on "lack of knowledge" is also an example of an inference based on meta-knowledge.

A second dimension in the taxonomy of inferences distinguishes between *functional inferences* and *set inferences*. Functional inferences include inferences about causes, consequences, and goals (e.g. "It must have rained overnight because the road is full of puddles"). The most common kind of set inferences are deductions whereby we infer that a member of a subset must have the properties of the superordinate set. Subsets derive properties from their superordinates by a process known as "inheritance". We infer, for example, that a robin lays eggs because robins are a subset of the superordinate set of birds, and the superordinate concept bird has the property *lays eggs*. So robins inherit the property of being able to lay eggs. Inductive generalisations are also inferences that operate on sets. When enough examples of a property have been noted in different subsets, it may be inferred that the property belongs to the superordinate set. If you find that Renaults are reliable and Citroens are reliable, you may infer that French cars are reliable. Another kind of set inference is an analogical inference whereby we infer that the properties of one set also belong to other similar sets. So, if oranges are good for you, you may infer that grapefruit, which are similar, are also good for you.

A third dimension in the taxonomy of inferences contrasts *spatial, tempora, and semantic inferences*. Spatial inferences about distance, location, and orientation were discussed in Chapter 3, p.61, and temporal inferences about the dates of events in Chapter 5, p.128. Some semantic inferences are based on knowledge about word meanings. So, for example from the statement that "John is a husband " it can be inferred that John is human, male, adult, and married. Another kind of semantic inference is based on knowledge represented in schemas, scripts, or generalised event knowledge structures. So, when we hear that John ate in a restaurant, we can infer that he paid for his meal and supply default values for the menu. The specific event inherits components from the script by inferential processes. Other kinds of semantic inference that occur in the comprehension and interpretation of discourse are discussed in Chapter 7, p.205.

A fourth dimension is the difference between *positive* and *negative inferences*. Because we seldom store negative information explicitly, most negative facts have to be inferred.

Some of the more formal kinds of inference, used in formal logic or in mathematical and statistical reasoning, are not so relevant to everyday memory for various reasons. The kind of fuzzy knowledge that is typical in real-world situations is often not precise enough for the application of formal logical procedures. People have to be formally taught how to make these inferences and they are more applicable to solving formal artificial problems than naturally occurring situations. However, although people do not use some kinds of formal reasoning very readily or accurately (Braine, 1978), they do use what he calls natural logic, and processes of estimation and probabilistic reasoning to make rough-and-ready judgements about quantities and frequencies. The next section describes some of the more informal kinds of inferences that are made in everyday situations and which serve to extend the range and scope of the explicit knowledge we have stored in memory.

Negative Inferences

Negative information is not usually stored in memory. Although some negative facts which are especially important may be stored explicitly (e.g. *Fatty food is not good for you; the pub is not open until 7 p.m. on Sunday*), it would be uneconomical to devote a large amount of storage space to memory representations of what is not the case. Deciding that something is not true usually requires an inference. Collins, Warnock, Aiello, and Miller (1975) analysed the process and modelled negative inferencing in a simulation program called SCHOLAR which operated on a geography database, using this as an example of general world knowledge. They distinguished between closed and open sets of knowledge. Closed sets of knowledge are relatively rare, but if you know all the counties of England and Wales, or all the different species of gulls, then these are closed sets, and you can answer "No" to questions like "Is a tern a kind of gull?" or "Is Loamshire an English county?" by searching exhaustively through the relevant knowlege set. However, most sets of knowledge are open, either because the boundaries are ill-defined or changing, or because a person's knowledge is incomplete. So, for example, if you do not know all the counties it would not be possible to give a negative answer with certainty. Or, if you were asked a question like "Is X a famous actor?" it would be difficult to answer negatively since the class of famous actors is ill-defined and constantly changing.

However, people have a number of tricks or strategies to enable them to make negative inferences even if they cannot be certain to be correct. One of these is the *I would have known it if it were so* strategy, which Collins et al. call a lack of knowledge inference. I may decide that X is not a famous actor on the grounds that I don't know it and I would have known it if he were. To apply this strategy effectively, the following stages are required:

1. I do not have this information in store. This decision requires accurate epistemic awareness of what I do and do not know.
2. My knowledge in this domain is complete or includes all the important facts. This stage requires knowledge of the domain boundaries and of the relative importance of items of information.

3. This fact is important, so I would have encountered it and remembered it if it were part of the knowledge domain.

Other strategies for generating negative inferences rely on recognising that a putative fact cannot be true because it is directly contradicted by some other item of well-established knowledge, or because it is implausible in the light of other known facts. You can answer "No" to questions like "Is a sparrow a wren?" or "Is a cat a dog?" because the two things are mutually exclusive. You can answer "No" to "Is a cat a bird?" because a cat is a mammal and birds and mammals are mutually exclusive. You can answer "No" to questions like "Is Germany an island?" because islands have a defining property and Germany does not have this property, and you can answer "No" to "Is Paris in England?" because you know that Paris is in France and a city cannot be in two different locations.

Causal Inferences and Estimation Inferences

Knowledge about causal factors enables people to figure out answers to specific questions when they don't already have the required information. They can extend their existing knowledge by making functional inferences which are probably true. In an example cited by Collins et al., a student was asked "Where in North America do you think rice might be grown?" and answered "Louisiana". When the teacher probed the reasons for this reply, it emerged that the student had used his knowledge that growing rice requires plenty of water, flat land, and a suitable climate, together with his knowledge of which states fulfilled these conditions, to generate the conclusion. Knowledge about causes allows people to infer the probable consequences and vice versa. If someone has food poisoning I can infer that he ate infected food; if he drinks a large quantity of alcohol I can infer that his driving will be impaired.

Mathematical inferences are commonly used in rough estimations of speed, distance, time, size, and weight. Camp (1988) reported that when an elderly man was asked "How far is it from Paris to New York?" he replied " Well, Lindberg flew there in about 36 hours with an average speed of about 100 mph, so I'll say that it's about 3600 miles." Or, in an example cited by Collins et al. the question "How many piano tuners are there in New York City?" elicited the answer "Well, there are three or four in New Haven which has about 300,000 people. That's about one per 100,000. New York City has seven million people so that would make 70. I'll say about 50 or 60." In arriving at this estimate, the respondent is assuming a roughly linear relationship between population size and number of piano tuners, and then correcting downwards to adjust for a deviation from linearity.

Analogical Inferences

In everyday life we use analogical reasoning to extend the knowledge we have derived from past experiences so as to apply it to new experiences and handle novel situations. In the piano-tuner example, the respondent used New Haven as an analogy for New York City. In everyday life we often work out how to cope with a current problem by recognising that it is similar to some other situation we have encountered before. Suppose, for example, that you are making strawberry jam and it fails to set. You remember that you had a similar problem previously when making raspberry jam and the solution was to add lemon juice. Recognising that making strawberry jam is analogous to making raspberry jam enables you to apply the same solution to the current problem. In this example the analogy is an obvious one because the two cases are very similar, but sometimes analogies are not so readily apparent.

Gick and Holyoak (1980) studied the ability of subjects to perceive a not very obvious analogy, and use it to solve a problem. They first read a story about a general who wanted to capture a fortress located in the centre of a country with many roads radiating outward from the fortress. All the roads have been mined so that, although small groups of men can pass along them safely, a larger force would detonate the mines so that a full-scale attack is impossible. The solution is to divide the army into small groups and have them converge simultaneously on the fortress along different roads. Subjects were later given Duncker's (1945) radiation problem in which a patient has a malignant stomach tumour. It is impossible to operate, but the patient will die unless the tumour is destroyed. This can be done with rays only if they reach the tumour at sufficiently high intensity, but at this intensity they would destroy the healthy tissue surrounding the tumour. The solution is to focus low-intensity rays from different directions, so that they converge simultaneously on the tumour site. On the surface, the two problems are totally dissimilar but at a more abstract level they are analogous.

These examples highlight the fact that recognising analogies depends on the level of abstraction at which the two scenarios are represented in memory. If they are represented in too much detail the surface dissimilarities obscure the analogy. When they are expressed at a more abstract level, as a generalised event representation (the need to bring a high level of force to bear on an area plus some factor which only allows direct access to low levels of force), the analogy between the two problems is obvious and it is readily apparent that the simultaneous convergence solution, which solved the military problem, can also be applied to the tumour problem.

However, most of Gick and Holyoak's subjects were unable to perceive and make use of the analogy spontaneously, unless they were given a strong hint that it would be useful. In one experiment, some of the subjects were given the military story, and also a second analogue story about a fire at an oil rig. The firefighters needed to spray a large quantity of foam onto the fire, but did not have a hose large enough to deliver a sufficient quantity. The solution was to direct foam onto the fire from smaller hoses, spraying from different directions. Subjects who were given both of the analogue stories were more likely to perceive that the analogical solution could be applied to the tumour problem than subjects who only heard one of the analogue stories.

It is possible that in everyday life people also need to build up repeated similar experiences before they can abstract analogical inferences success-fully. A current situation can only be perceived as analogous to similar previous experiences if people can recognise that it matches some pre-viously encountered situation in relevant respects. Because two situations are never exactly identical, analogies rest on fuzzy matches. Knowing what degree and kind of similarity constitutes a useful analogy is an important aspect of everyday competence.

All these examples show that human knowledge, though limited, is extremely elastic. What we don't know we can infer, guess, estimate, or predict. We can produce a plausible, if uncertain, answer. It is relatively rarely that we are completely at a loss.

MAINTENANCE OF KNOWLEDGE: EVIDENCE FOR A PERMASTORE?

How permanent is knowledge once acquired? In his 1976 talk Neisser suggested that one of the important questions that memory research should address concerns what people retain of the knowledge they acquired during the years of their formal schooling. Educators have studied child-ren's memory for what they learn at school over relatively short retention intervals of months rather than years, but when we come to assess the value of education in the longer term we want to know how much people remember in the years after they have left school. What, if any, of the information we acquire with so much effort in our schooldays constitutes permanent knowledge? Because these issues have to be studied over long time spans, they are outside the scope of traditional laboratory methods, and have been neglected until recently, when the more adventurous approach of everyday memory research has encouraged some psych-ologists to tackle them.

Harry Bahrick has conducted a series of studies of long-term retention of Spanish learned at school. Surmounting formidable methodological prob-lems, his study (Bahrick, 1984b) spanned retention intervals of up to 50 years and attempted to identify the conditions of original learning which determine the longevity of the knowledge acquired. The subjects were 773 individuals who had learned Spanish in high school. The time elapsed between studying the language and being tested varied from 0 to 50 years. A control group of 40 subjects who had never received any instruction in Spanish was also included in the study to establish a baseline for performance that could be achieved by guessing, or by incidentally acquired knowledge. The subjects who had learned Spanish supplied information about the level of their original training (how many courses they had taken), the grades they had attained, and how much they had used the language during the retention interval. The tests included reading comprehension, and recall and recognition tests for vocabulary, grammar, and idioms. The results showed that retention was predictable from the level of original training. People who had learned more remembered more. When the recall test scores were expressed as a percentage of the original grades about 40% of the original performance was maintained after 50 years, and on recognition tests about 60% was maintained.

Interim use of the language was negligible, so that no effects of rehearsal were evident. The most interesting finding can be seen in Fig. 6.2. Knowledge declined exponentially for about 3–6 years, but after this period retention stabilised, and there was little further loss for a period of up to 30 years before a final slight decline. Much of the original knowledge therefore remains accessible after 50 years. According to Bahrick, this knowledge has entered the permastore. On the basis of the discontinuous character of the retention function, he argued that there had been a discrete transition of knowledge into the permastore and that a minimum level of original training was necessary for this transition to take place. When the original training was insufficient, the knowledge would not be entered into the permastore and would only be retained for a shorter period.

Commenting on these results, Neisser (1984) suggested that there was no need to assume the existence of a knowledge permastore. Whereas Bahrick's explanation assumes that language learning involves acquiring responses that are *reproduced* when retrieval takes place, Neisser argued that knowledge is *reconstructed*, rather than being reproduced. In his view, the enduring component of language knowledge does not consist of specific responses, but of generalised schemas, for example a structured system of knowledge of the Spanish language which enables people to reconstruct correct responses. Acquisition of these knowledge schemas depends on the level of original training, as Bahrick's data confirmed. According to this interpretation, the information that is lost in the early years of the retention interval consists of isolated bits and pieces not closely related to the general schema. Neisser claims that retention of systematic schematised knowledge is enduring because it is protected from interference by its

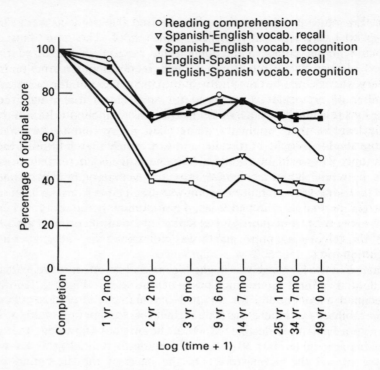

FIG. 6.2   Retention functions for Spanish vocabulary and reading comprehension (from Bahrick, 1984b). Copyright (1984) by the American Psychological Association. Reprinted by permission of the author.

unique and specialised nature. Schema-based knowledge is not forgotten because other knowledge is not sufficiently similar to cause interference. On this interpretation, the discontinuity in Bahrick's retention curves does not reflect two different stores, a vulnerable store with a five-year span and a permastore, but two different kinds of knowledge: isolated items and integrated schemas.

Neisser's account is not wholly convincing. Although it is plausible to suppose that language learning involves acquiring a schema for the grammar of the language which might enable people to reconstruct the grammar, it is not so clear that knowledge of its morphological and orthographic structure would enable them to "reconstruct" vocabulary. It might be expected, then, that knowledge of grammar would show a long-term retention plateau, but knowledge of vocabulary would be less well retained. However, in Bahrick's data, the retention function is similar in shape for both grammar and vocabulary.

In a follow-up to an earlier study, Bahrick and Phelps (1987) re-tested subjects who had learned 50 English–Spanish word pairs in laboratory conditions 8 years earlier. They found that 2 variables predicted the likelihood of permastore retention. After 8 years, memory for Spanish vocabulary was affected by the spacing of the original learning sessions and the number of presentations required for acquisition. The number of presentations reflects the ease of initial learning. Overall, about 10% of the originally learned words could still be recalled. Of words that had been learned easily 14% could be recalled, but of words learned with more difficulty only 2% could be recalled. Memory was also better when the intervals between the original study sessions were longer. These data indicate that long-term retention of knowledge (or, in Bahrick's phrase, entry to the permastore) depends on the conditions of acquisition. On Neisser's view, schema acquisition would be dependent on the amount and depth of the original learning, and the type of knowledge rather than on factors like spacing.

Bahrick, Wellman, and Hall (Note 1) designed an experiment to test Neisser's ideas. They measured speed of learning and retention for English–Spanish word pairs, and for pairs consisting of an English word and a Spanish nonword. They compared the performance of students who studied Spanish with students who studied other languages and had no knowledge of Spanish. The students of Spanish were assumed to have acquired general schemas of the language. It was expected that they would perform better with the English-Spanish word pairs, and, if having general schemas of a language allows people to guess or reconstruct vocabulary, as Neisser claims, they should also have done better with the nonwords, since these nonwords were constructed to conform to the characteristics of real Spanish words. The results showed that, although the students of Spanish did slightly better on the real Spanish words, they had no advantage on the nonwords. Bahrick et al. therefore concluded that people cannot use schemas to reconstruct vocabulary which they have forgotten.

More studies of long-term retention of different kinds of knowledge are required to show which interpretation is correct. However, Bahrick's finding that knowledge acquired at school can persist for 50 years without re-activation in the interim is of great theoretical and practical importance.

Naveh-Benjamin (Note 8) has studied retention of knowledge acquired in university courses of philosophy, psychology, and anthropology, comparing a zero retention interval with retention intervals of one and two years. He was particularly interested in how the knowledge structures changed over time. In order to examine this, he first asked the university teachers who had taught the courses to arrange different elements of knowledge into conceptual hierarchies with general concepts at the highest level, and specific concepts at the lowest level. When the subjects were tested, they were shown a conceptual hierarchy with some empty nodes and had to select items from a set of alternatives and place the correct item at the correct node. This test revealed a loss of information from 70% at the zero retention interval, to 46% after two years. The loss of information was greatest at the lowest level of the conceptual hierarchy, whereas the higher-level concepts were better retained. The test also showed that the relationships between higher-order concepts and low-level specific examples were especially vulnerable to the effects of the passage of time. Knowledge became fragmented as people tended to forget the links between concepts.

Knowledge Updating

Whether or not some of our knowledge is immutably lodged in a perma-store, other knowledge sometimes has to be revised. Some of the facts we thought to be true turn out to be false, or to need modification. New knowledge supersedes old knowledge which is outdated, irrelevant, or contradicted. As in any information storage system, the information that is stored in memory needs to be corrected and updated.

Some researchers who have studied the process of knowledge updating have noted a *knew-it-all-along effect* (Fischoff, 1977; Wood, 1978). When people have been given new facts that contradict their previous knowledge they appear to be unable to remember what they originally believed, and claim to have known it (i.e. the new fact) all along. Apparently, the new knowledge is immediately assimilated with the previous knowedge, and any inconsistencies are eliminated so as to produce an updated version. An update-and-erase mechanism of this kind may be an efficient kind of information storage, but it represents a limitation of metamemory. The "knew-it-all-along" effect appears to indicate that, although people may know what they know, they are not very accurate at knowing what they used to know.

Hasher, Attig, and Alba (1981) examined the fate of discredited infor-mation. In their first experiment, subjects were divided into three groups, a No-feedback group, a Discredited feedback group and an Undiscredited feedback group. In Phase 1, all the subjects rated a set of plausible statements about current affairs, the arts, sports, etc., on a seven-point true–false scale. In Phase 2 all the subjects reviewed the statements, which were divided into two sets. No-feedback subjects received no further information about any of the statements. Both groups of Feedback sub-jects (discredited and undiscredited) were initially told that one set of statements was true and one set was false. The Discredited feedback group then received discrediting information. They were told that there had been a mix-up, and the experimenter had made a mistake and the statements identified as true were actually false and vice versa. The Undiscredited Feedback subjects did not receive this discrediting information. In Phase 3 all the subjects were asked to re-rate all the statements. They were all told to try to remember their original ratings, and the subjects in the Discredited feedback condition were also told to ignore what the experimenter had said about the truth/falsity of the statements.

The results showed that the No-feedback group did not change their original ratings. Subjects in the Undiscredited feedback group changed their ratings to conform with the experimenters' feedback, increasing their ratings for statements called true, and decreasing ratings for items called false. Subjects in the Discredited feedback group corrected their ratings in line with the disconfirmed feedback. These subjects did not simply discard the discredited feedback and return to their original judgement: They updated their knowledge in line with the feedback-plus-correction, thereby demonstrating the knew-it-all-along effect.

An example helps to make this complicated design clearer. Suppose subject A is in the Discredited feedback group, subject B is in the Undiscredited feedback group. In Phase 1 they both rate the statement:

The story of Aladdin originated in China

and give it 3 on a scale running from 1 to 7 (false to true). In Phase 2 both are told the statement is true. Then A, but not B, is told there has been a mistake and it was actually false: The story originated in Persia. When both are asked to repeat their original ratings, B shifts from 3 to 6 in line with the undiscredited feedback, but A shifts from 3 to 1 in line with the discrediting feedback. A "knew all along" that it was false, while B "knew all along" that it was true.

In a second experiment, Hasher et al. succeeded in inducing subjects to ignore the disconfirmed information. It was more effectively discredited when they were told it had been deliberately misleading, not just a mistake. This time the re-ratings did not differ from the original ratings, showing that the subjects had returned to their original knowledge state. This finding suggests that old knowledge is not necessarily completely erased when it is contradicted, but can be recovered. The results also showed that it was easier to shift a belief from false to true than from true to false. People are more reluctant to change their views in response to falsifying evidence. A similar bias has been noted in studies of problem solving (e.g. Wason, 1960) in which subjects generate a hypothesis in an attempt to solve a problem, and resist evidence that the hypothesis is false.

In everyday life, knowledge updating is likely to be much more complex than in Hasher et al.'s experiment. There are three different processes that make knowledge updating necessary. One of these is contradiction, as in the experiment. You may believe that the highest mountain in Britain is

Snowdon until someone tells you this is not true. If the new information is sufficiently authoritative, you will probably discard the original belief. Another process that necessitates knowledge updating is change. Little Willy changes from a small boy into a young man, or the neighbours trade in their Metro for a Volvo, or the new bypass is now the quickest route to the city. In these cases, the old knowledge is not so much wrong as obsolete. Another process that enforces knowledge revision is the accumulation of counter-examples. A belief that cream and butter are good for you may need revising in the face of growing evidence that high-cholesterol foods are damaging to health.

In some of these examples, knowledge updating is a gradual process with old knowledge being eroded over time, and gradually giving way to a new belief. While this process is going on a person may dither between two contradictory beliefs, or may be in a state of suspended disbelief, or may simply be confused. When knowledge updating occurs as a result of change, the old knowledge is not necessarily forgotten or discarded, but may be maintained alongside the new knowledge. Naturally occurring knowledge updating is much more complicated and variable than the kind of knowledge updating that has so far been studied in laboratory experiments.

EXPERT KNOWLEDGE

How does an expert differ from a novice? When someone ceases to be a novice and becomes an expert in some particular knowledge domain, changes which are both qualitative and quantitative have taken place in the knowledge structures stored in memory. This is broadly true whether we are talking about formal knowledge domains like chess or computer programming, or less formal ones like birdwatching or cookery. In spite of the fact that knowledge structures and reasoning strategies vary from one domain to another, some of the qualities that characterise an "expert", and some of the changes that are associated with expertise, are similar in different domains.

Differences in Amount of Knowledge

It is, of course, almost tautologous to state that experts know more than novices about their area of expertise. They are also able to acquire and retain new information better than novices, and this fact is not quite so obvious. It might be supposed that, as the amount of knowledge in store increases, search processes would be more complex and it would become more difficult to locate and retrieve particular items of information to order. However, this is not what happens. So, how does an expert manage to handle a greatly expanded amount of knowledge without being overwhelmed by it?

McCloskey and Bigler (1980) argued that knowledge is divided up into subsets. Although an expert knowledge base is larger than a novice one, the expert can focus on the relevant subset and ignore other subsets so that he or she does not need to search through more information, and does not take longer to retrieve a target item. To support this argument, they carried out an experiment in which subjects learned facts about persons. All the facts were of the form:

The (occupation) likes (animal or place name)

For example:

The banker likes rabbits
The lawyer likes Italy

For each person, the subject learned from one to six facts which were either all from the same category (e.g. all about animals), or from different categories. In the test phase they were presented with statements (such as *The banker likes rabbits, and asked to verify these as true or false.* Response times were measured. The key finding was that subjects could verify a true statement about a person just as fast when they had learned six facts about that person as when they had only learned one fact about that person, as long as the critical fact belonged to a different category from the other five facts. That is, verifying that the banker liked rabbits was not impeded by knowing that he also liked Italy, Minneapolis, Brighton, Thailand, and Orkney. However, verification was slower if the additional facts belonged to the same category. It did take longer to decide that the banker liked rabbits if the subject also knew that the banker liked wolves, emus, hamsters, snakes, and pigeons.

These results appear to show that (at least when operating with clearly defined categories) people can focus on relevant subsets of information. McCloskey and Bigler suggested that one difference between experts and novices might be that experts are better than novices at organising stored knowledge into subsets. Knowledge is not always handed out already neatly packaged into well-defined subsets like bankers and rabbits, and the learner has to impose his or her own organisation on new information. The idea that experts retrieve facts by focusing search on relevant subsets also presupposes that they are efficient at identifying which is the relevant subset, and this may not be so easy in a non-trivial knowledge domain. However, there is growing evidence linking the superiority of experts over novices when memory is tested to the ability to organise knowledge into subsets, groups, or chunks. As is well known, the capacity of short-term memory is extended when items can be grouped together and treated as chunks (Miller, 1956).

Organisation in Memory

Playing Chess

Chase and Simon (1973) carried out a classic study of the differences between expert and novice chess players. Three subjects with different levels of expertise, a beginner, a class A player, and a Master, were allowed five seconds to study a chess board with a game in progress, and were then asked to reconstruct the board positions from memory. If the reconstruction was not complete and accurate then the original board was re-presented and viewed again, and the procedure was repeated until a perfect reconstruction was achieved. The Master needed fewer attempts to achieve a perfect reconstruction than the class A player or the novice. On average, the Master placed 16 pieces correctly at the first attempt to reconstruct a middle game; the class A player placed 8 pieces correctly; and the beginner only 4. However, when the subjects were asked to reconstruct chess boards in which the pieces were placed at random, there were no differences between them. This result showed that the Master did not just have superior memory ability. Expertise does not "improve your memory" in general; experts only have better memories for meaningful, properly structured information in their particular knowledge domain.

Chase and Simon believed that chess experts perceive board positions in terms of relations between groups of pieces, so, whereas novices have to memorise the position of each individual piece, the expert only has to remember the group. They tested this "perceptual chunking hypothesis" in a further study. Subjects again had to reconstruct board positions, but this time, instead of relying on memory, they were allowed to look back at the original board as often as they needed to. Monitoring the number of "looks" revealed the size and composition of the perceptual chunks. The expert player memorised larger chunks with each glance at the board, and each chunk represented a meaningful cluster of related pieces. The expert organised information into chunks in accordance with the relational patterns resulting from the attacking and defensive moves that occur in the game.

Reitman (1976) obtained a similar result when she compared expert and novice Go players. Other researchers have since confirmed that expert knowledge is more highly organised than novice knowledge, using different techniques to identify the chunks and studying different knowledge domains.

Computer Programming

Adelson (1981) used a technique similar to Chase and Simon's to compare expert and novice computer programmers, and also demonstrated that they used different types of organisation. The subjects saw 16 lines of code taken

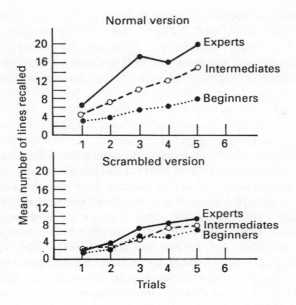

FIG. 6.3   Lines of code recalled by experts, intermediate programmers, and beginners (from McKeithen et al., 1981).

from three different programs scrambled together. They had 20 seconds' viewing, followed by 8 minutes for free recall. As the view–recall sequence was repeated, differences in the organisation of recall began to emerge. Experts began to sort out the mixture and group together lines of code that came from the same programs. Novices grouped together lines that looked alike. The experts were using their knowledge to form meaningful higher-level chunks of information and were able to recall more.

In a further study, Adelson (1984) showed that the representations formed by programmers can be characterised as either concrete represent-ations, which instantiate procedural information about how the program operates, or as more abstract representations instantiating declarative knowledge about the higher-level principles of the program. Experts were more likely to form the abstract type of representation spontaneously, although they could shift to the concrete form if required to do so. McKeithen, Reitman, Rueter, and Hirtle (1981) also tested expert and novice programmers' ability to recall a 31-line computer program presented either in normal or in scrambled order. Figure 6.3 shows that for normal programs, recall increased with level of skill, but when the pro-grams were scrambled there was no difference. When novices and experts were asked to recall key words from programs, novices appeared to use shallower processing, grouping items by first letters, or by natural-language associations (e.g. "long" "and" "short" "bits" "of" "string"), whereas experts grouped keywords according to their function in programming. The experts also showed much less variability than the novices. Experts tended to use similar groupings, whereas the novices differed from each other.

Electronics

Egan and Schwartz (1979) compared the ability of skilled technicians and novices to reproduce symbolic drawings of electronic circuits. First, they asked an independent expert to indicate how the elements in the display should be grouped according to function. In the test, they found that, for the skilled technicians, the order in which elements were reconstructed, and the pauses in the process of re-drawing, both corresponded to the functional groupings, but this was not true of the novices. Egan and Schwartz emphasised that the experts also imposed functional groupings on their recall even when the original circuits they had been shown were scrambled. They pointed out that this finding indicates that the organisation demonstrated by experts is conceptual chunking rather than perceptual chunking as Chase and Simon originally suggested. The experts are not perceiving patterns in the material but are creating them by reorganisation in memory.

Baseball

Similar findings also emerge from more mundane knowledge domains. Spilich, Vesonder, Chiesi, and Voss (1979) compared individuals who had a lot of knowledge about baseball with others who had little knowledge of the game. Subjects listened to an account of a baseball match lasting five minutes. Afterwards high- and low-knowledge individuals differed in the kind of information they recalled as well as the kind of errors they made. Free-recall protocols of high-knowledge subjects showed that they recalled more of the actions which produced significant changes in the outcome of the game; they recalled more goal-related actions and these were integrated into sequences. Low-knowledge subjects recalled less information and made more errors in which they confused the players or confused different actions. For people who know little or nothing about baseball, memorising the commentary was like learning nonsense material. Because they did not understand how actions were related to goals, they were unable to differentiate important events that affected the outcome from irrelevant or unimportant events.

Waiters and Bartenders

Expertise influences the kind of strategies that are employed by waiters and bartenders to memorise orders. Ericsson and Polson (cited in Chase & Ericsson, 1982) studied the memory organisation of a skilled waiter who could retain 17 menu orders in memory without writing anything down. In an experimental test of his ability, he could remember up to 8 orders, each consisting of a main course (8 alternatives with directions about how they should be cooked), a starch (3 alternatives), and a salad with dressing (5 alternatives). The waiter mentally rearranged the orders into categorical groupings (for example, one Blue cheese, two Oil and vinegar, one Thousand island) and used a first-letter mnemonic to encode this as BOOT.

Beach (1988) compared the mnemonics used by expert and novice bartenders. Novice bartenders relied on verbal rehearsal of mutiple orders, but the experts provided themselves with external cues by setting up the appropriate types of glasses for each drink along the bar as they heard each order. This strategy was more effective.

These studies demonstrate, across a range of different knowledge domains, that experts organise information differently from novices. They are more likely to organise information into groups instead of treating it on an item-by-item basis. The groupings they use are in accordance with the functions, rules, or frequently occurring patterns of the knowledge domain, and this organisation into groups, chunks, or subsets of knowledge enables the expert to restrict search to relevant parts of the knowledge base when retrieving information. The superior memory of the expert is also due to the accumulated knowledge of the rules, patterns, and constraints that govern information in the knowledge domain. This allows the expert to infer missing information, or reconstruct missing elements from partially remembered information.

Attitudes and Interests

The transformation of a novice into an expert is not, however, just a matter of accumulating more and better structured knowledge. The development of expertise brings about other changes which also affect memory for material in the knowledge domain. There are changes in emotional and motivational factors.

Football

Morris, Gruneberg, Sykes, and Merrick (1981) carried out a study designed to show how knowledge of football (soccer) affects ability to remember scores. They measured level of expertise by administering a soccer-knowledge questionnaire. There was a strong correlation between performance on the questionnaire and memory for new scores. It was not clear how the high-knowledge subjects were able to achieve superior recall since there is no obvious way to chunk or group a list of teams and their scores. The scores do not conform to learned patterns and even the most knowledgeable subjects were not able to predict them.

Morris, Tweedy, and Gruneberg (1985) explored this problem in a further series of experiments. Subjects were first given a questionnaire to measure soccer expertise. Then, general memory ability was tested by a free-recall test for a list of common words. Finally, free recall was tested for a set of real football scores and a set of simulated scores. Simulated scores were prepared by recombining teams and scores in a plausible way. An important feature of the design was that subjects knew which were the real scores, and which were simulated.

The results showed that soccer knowledge correlated at 0.82 with memory for the real scores, but only at 0.36 with the simulated scores. Free recall of common words correlated at 0.67 with memory for the simulated scores and not at all with memory for the real scores. Morris et al. concluded that for the high-knowledge individuals the real scores had real implications, and therefore aroused greater interest and activated processes of elaborative encoding. For example, the soccer expert would consider how the scores affected the teams' standing and future prospects. Simulated scores, although similar on the surface, failed to activate deeper-level encoding and were treated like the word lists.

In a second experiment, subjects were asked to rate their degree of support (positive or negative), their amount of knowledge about each team, the importance of each match outcome, and the predicted result. Memory for the actual scores was then tested and correlated with each of these ratings. Both degree of support and amount of knowledge were related to recall, but judged importance and accuracy of prediction were not related. This lack of relation between judged importance and recall caused Morris et al. to revise their view that elaborative encoding of the implications of the scores produced better retention. Instead, they argued that the emotional response aroused by support for particular teams seemed to be the crucial factor. High-knowledge individuals were more emotionally involved and therefore remembered the scores better.

International Relations

Tyler and Voss (1982) studied a very different knowledge domain and also found evidence of a relationship between level of expertise, attitudes toward the facts, and recall of information. They assessed subjects' knowledge of the U.S.S.R. and its relations with other countries by means of a questionnaire. They also assessed the extent to which the subjects were pro- or anti-Soviet in their attitudes. The subjects were subsequently tested for recall and recognition of short texts, ostensibly taken from Pravda, commenting on other countries. Some of the texts were congruent with expectations and prior knowledge about the U.S.S.R.'s international relations, and other texts were incongruent and violated these expectations. The results were complicated. Higher knowledge was related to a more pro-Soviet attitude. For the congruent texts, a positive attitude was associated with better memory, but knowledge was not a significant predictor. For incongruent texts, memory was determined by knowledge but not attitude. Tyler and Voss claimed that subjects with a high level of knowledge probably engaged in additional processing in an attempt to interpret the incongruent texts which did not fit their expectations.

In both the football study and the U.S.S.R. study, expert knowledge was associated with a change in emotion, attitude, or interest which appeared to have some effect on memory for information in the knowledge domain. It is perhaps less plausible, though, to suppose that expertise in electronics or computer programming would produce emotional changes that enhance recall of circuits or strings of code. It is more likely that different factors (including both organisational strategies and attitudes) affect different kinds of knowledge.

Mental Representations of Expert Knowledge

Different models of representation have yielded different accounts of the way knowledge structures change as novices become experts. This section outlines the accounts provided by models of categorical organisation, by schema theory, and by production systems.

Categorical Organisation

Experts may structure their knowledge differently from novices, forming different categories; using different attributes to distinguish between categories; and representing relationships between categories differently.

Rosch et al. (1976) proposed that categories are organised in conceptual hierarchies as shown in the example in Fig. 6.4. Within a given hierarchy they distinguish a "basic level". The basic level is the one at which the concepts are most clearly defined and best differentiated from other related categories. The basic level is also the one that is cognitively most accessible, the level at which we most often think and communicate with each other. In the furniture hierarchy, the concept of chair is basic and the superordinate and subordinate levels are less accessible. However, Rosch et al. found some evidence that the basic level shifts with expertise, moving

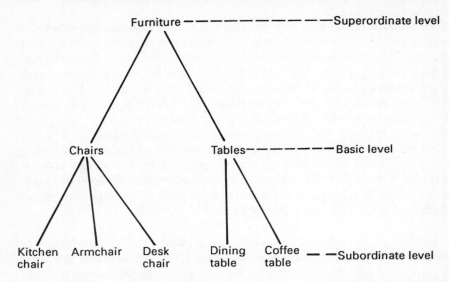

FIG. 6.4   A conceptual hierarchy for the category "furniture", showing the basic level of representation.

downward in the hierarchy. In their study, they encountered a subject who was an aeroplane mechanic, and who distinguished between many different types of plane, so that, whereas an ordinary person would identify an object as "a plane", he identified it as "a twin-engined Cessna". Similarly, for an expert on antique furniture, a chair is not just a chair, but a late Chippendale mahogany dining chair. For experts, the preferred, or basic level of categorisation seems to be lower down the hierarchy, more specific and more highly differentiated. Such a shift also necessarily entails an increase in the number of categories, since the expert makes finer-grain distinctions.

Murphy and Wright (1984) set out to test some of these intuitions and observations in a systematic study comparing the knowledge structures of experts and novices. They studied four groups of people with differing levels of expertise in clinical psychology: *Experts* were fully trained with years of experience; *experienced counsellors* had less formal training but considerable experience; *beginning counsellors* had done voluntary work and taken undergraduate courses; and *novices* were students just starting an introductory psychology course.

All the subjects were asked to consider three types of emotionally disordered child, the aggressive, the depressive, and the disorganised. They were asked to list as many as possible of the characteristics typical of each disorder. The results are shown in Fig. 6.5. As expected, the number

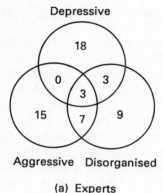

(a) Experts

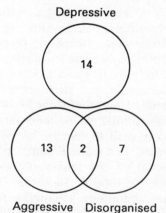

(b) Experienced counsellors

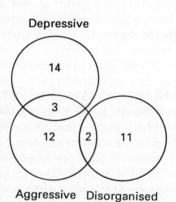

(c) Beginning counsellors

(d) Novices

FIG. 6.5   Venn diagrams representing the frequency of occurrence of consensual features in each diagnostic category as a function of level of expertise. Numbers in each area indicate the number of features agreed upon by 25% or more of the subjects in that group (from Murphy & Wright, 1984). Copyright (1984) by the American Psychological Association. Reprinted by permission of the author.

of features listed increased with expertise, and the experts listed twice as many as the novices. Inter-subject agreement was also much greater among the experts. However, contrary to expectations, the experts' concepts had greater overlap with each other, as can be clearly seen in the figure. For the experts, the three types of disorder were actually less well differentiated because they listed more characteristics as belonging to more than one category of disorder.

Murphy and Wright confirmed this finding in a further test. The subjects were given a list of characteristics (e.g. has low self-esteem; isolates self from others) and asked to rate how well each characteristic described each type of child. These ratings again showed that the novices had simple, well-defined, distinctive concepts. They tended to think that particular characteristics were displayed by one type of child and not by the other types. The experts' concepts were less clear cut and well defined. They recognised that different types of child might exhibit the same characteristics, so that, for example, low self-esteem might be characteristic of both depressive and aggressive types. Although this finding seems counter-intuitive, it does make a good deal of sense. The novice has probably learned a concept like "the depressive child" from textbook descriptions of prototypical cases. The expert has encountered a much greater range and variety of cases and recognises that, in the real world, categories are not so sharply differentiated. Although in some knowledge domains, expertise may bring about increasing precision of categorisation, in other domains concepts may become less distinctive with increasing knowledge.

A study by Chi and Koeske (1983) has attempted to plot qualitative differences in the structure of knowledge across different levels of expertise. They studied the knowledge base of a 4-year-old boy who had a consuming interest in dinosaurs. Numerous books on dinosaurs were regularly read to him by his parents and he had a collection of model dinosaurs. In a name-production task, they asked the child to produce the names of all the dinosaurs he knew and he eventually produced the remarkable total of 46 names. These were divided, on the basis of his mother's intuitions, and on the frequency with which they were mentioned in the books, into 2 lists, one of 20 well-known dinosaurs and one of 20 less well-known dinosaurs. In order to plot the child's knowledge structures, a guessing game was played. Either the experimenter listed two or three attributes (e.g. appearance, habits) and the child had to guess the name of the dinosaur with those attributes, or the roles were reversed.

The child's knowledge networks, illustrated in Figs. 6.6 (the well-known set) and 6.7 (the less well-known set) show the links between different dinosaurs (evidenced by the sequence of responses in the name-production task), and the links between dinosaurs and attributes (evidenced by responses in the guessing game). As the figures show, dinosaurs in the well-known set have more links between them, and the sub-groups (shown by the dotted lines) of armoured dinosaurs (A) and plant-eaters (P) are more cohesive with more internal linkages. In the less well-known set the patterns of interlinkage are different. Fewer attributes are known and the sub-groups are less cohesive. These differences in the structure of

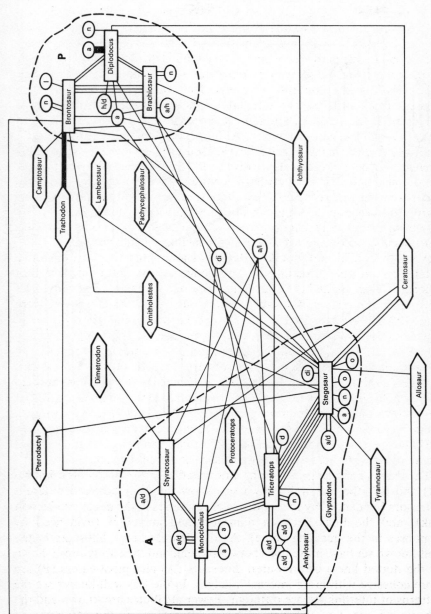

FIG. 6.6 Network representation for the target dinosaurs in the better-known list (A – armoured; P – giant plant-eaters; a – appearance; d – defence mechanism; di – diet; h – habitat; l – locomotion; n – nickname; o – other) (from Chi & Koeske, 1983).

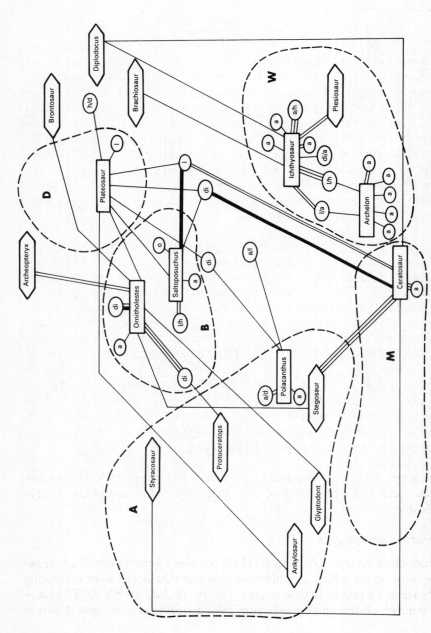

FIG. 6.7 Network representation for the target dinosaurs in the lesser-known list (A – armoured; B – bird- or egg-eaters; D – duckbills; M – giant meat-eaters; W – water dwellers; a – appearance; d – defence mechanism; di – diet; h – habitat; l – locomotion; n – nickname; o – other) (from Chi & Koeske, 1983).

well-known and less well-known knowledge were correlated with memory performance. The well-known dinosaurs were better recalled in a memory test, and, when the child was re-tested one year later, they were better retained.

Schema Theory

Schema theory accounts for developing expertise in terms of the acquisition of schemas. The expert has schemas which are well-developed, accurate representations of the generalised knowledge in the domain. Schemas supply frameworks that impose organisation and grouping on new information, and new knowledge can be economically stored by assimilation to this pre-existing framework. At retrieval, missing information can be derived from the schema by inheritance or by default (see pp.71–72).

The novice starts off with only the most rudimentary schemas for the relevant knowledge domain. According to Rumelhart and Norman (1978), three processes are at work in producing the developed schemas of the expert:

1. *Accretion*: New information is added to existing schemas so that the database is expanded without changing its basic principles. So, for example, basic chess-playing schemas for attack and defence might "grow" to accommodate new patterns as these become familiar.

2. *Tuning*: Comparatively minor alterations may be made to existing schemas, gradually modifying, for example, the slots and values to conform to newly acquired knowledge. The restaurant schema (or script) may be tuned in this way to include paying at a check-out as well as paying the waiter at the table.

3. *Restructuring*: Restructuring occurs when new knowledge is discrepant with existing schemas so that major changes are required. New schemas are created either by copying old ones and modifying them, or by deriving new generalisations from recurring patterns and building new schemas to instantiate these general principles.

As a result of these processes, the expert has more schemas than the novice, and has schemas that are more powerful and more widely applicable.

Production systems

Production systems (Anderson, 1983) provide a general model of knowledge acquisition which specifies the changes that occur with increasing expertise more precisely than schema theory. In Anderson's ACT* (adaptive control of thought) production systems architecture, two different kinds of knowledge are stored in long-term memory. Declarative memory stores factual knowledge, including temporal, spatial, and semantic information. Procedural knowledge consisting of knowing what to do, how to act, is stored in production memory and consists of production rules.

Productions are processing elements each consisting of a *condition* + *action* rule. Each rule takes the form of an IF clause followed by a THEN clause. The IF clause specifies a state of affairs, the THEN clause specifies the action. When the pattern of a current state of affairs matches the pattern described in the IF condition, the production is activated and the action is elicited, as in:

IF the sink is full of dirty dishes
THEN do the washing up

In recent formulations Anderson has elaborated the nature of this pattern-matching process. A set of related productions constitute a production system, and goal-related productions are organised in hierarchies with higher-level goals and subgoals.

Production systems provide a general-purpose cognitive system which can give an account of many different kinds of skill and knowledge. The chess player acquires a set of productions whereby patterns of pieces on the board form the conditions for making particular moves. The doctor acquires productions relating symptoms to treatments. All experts have a repertoire of rules for recognising situations and taking appropriate actions.

According to the production systems account, becoming an expert involves a number of processes. First the novice acquires declarative knowledge by learning relevant facts. This stage is followed by gradual proceduralisation of the declarative knowledge which is transformed from propositions into production rules. The novice medical student learns facts about the circulation of blood and the consequences of bleeding. At a later stage he or she acquires the production:

IF bleeding needs to be controlled
THEN apply pressure above the site of the wound

In Anderson's model, learning involves other processes in addition to proceduralisation. New productions are added and old ones are modified. *Strengthening* occurs when productions are used frequently so that they are activated more readily. Correspondingly, productions which are seldom used lose strength and become harder to elicit. *Composition* takes place when sequences of productions, which reliably occur together and relate to the same goal, are integrated into a single higher-level production. The conditions of several separate productions are amalgamated into a single complex condition which triggers the whole sequence of actions.

Generalisation is a process whereby the condition of a production is represented more generally so that the action has a wider range of applicability, and can extend to similar but novel situations. For example, the novice driver may learn:

IF the road surface is icy
THEN reduce speed

On the other hand, the more experienced driver generalises the condition to include other kinds of dangerous road surface such as loose grit or oil slicks.

Productions systems are versatile and flexible and this model can account for some of the observed differences in performance between novices and experts. Proceduralisation and strengthening make responses faster, and composition accounts for the higher-order chunking in memory which characterises expert performance. It does not account for the effects of emotional and attitudinal factors observed by Morris et al., or for the blurring of conceptual boundaries noted by Murphy and Wright. The great advantage of this model, however, is the way it links knowledge to behaviour and helps us to understand how expertise influences what people do as well as what they know.

7 Memory for Conversation, Prose, and Stories

Much of the information that we store in memory is not acquired first hand through our own experience. It is acquired at second hand through reading or through listening to other people talk about their experiences. This chapter explores what is known about memory for information acquired in this way. Memory for spoken information and memory for written information are treated separately because they differ in important ways. Intake of written information is self-paced. The reader can pause, back-track, or take a coffee-break. The listener must keep pace with the rate of speech, which is determined by the speaker. However, in both cases, the input is sequential and both tasks place heavy demands on the working memory system, which must hold segments of the input temporarily until they can be related to what comes later. The meaning of the first part of a sentence often cannot be grasped until the rest of the sentence has been analysed. The meaning of part of a conversation or part of a story may be obscure until the rest has been processed. With any form of linguistic input, working memory has to function as a temporary holding store where new information can be related to previously acquired information and where parts of a message can be integrated with other parts.

The first section of this chapter, which deals with memory for spoken information, emphasises the role of pragmatic factors such as intentions and attitudes. The second part of the chapter deals with written information and is more concerned with how this is structured in memory. Listening to speech usually takes place in a social context and is therefore strongly influenced by social and pragmatic factors like the intentions and personalities of the speaker and the hearer, the context of the utterance, and the social conventions that govern the exchange. These factors are of less importance when information is written. Reading is a more private and solitary occupation and a lot of written material is decontextualised. That is, the writer of the message may not know when, where, or by whom it will be read. Hence written material must be much more formally structured, and must conform to accepted rules and formats, if it is to be intelligible to a range of potential readers. In conversation the structure of the message is much less important because comprehension can be assisted by intonation, gesture, facial expression, repetition, and recapitulation.

MEMORY FOR CONVERSATION

Problems in Studying Conversation

Cognitive psychologists have devoted a great deal of work to memory for written texts, but relatively little to memory for conversations. Conversation occupies a central role in the everyday life of most people, but is one of the most difficult areas of human behaviour to analyse and measure. From the linguist's point of view, naturally occurring conversation is a disaster area. It is always surprising to read a transcript of a conversation. What seemed to be perfectly sensible when you were listening to it is exposed as incoherent, disjointed, ungrammatical rambling when you see it written down. When people are speaking to each other they violate linguistic rules; their utterances are full of gaps and are often not completed; and much of the information which is exchanged is never spoken at all. Indeed, a great deal of conversation is not designed as an exchange of information at all, but is simply a form of social interaction. People use conversation as a means of relating to each other, and what they actually say is often unimportant. This kind of conversation has very little content. It probably leaves little trace in memory, and is of more interest to social psychologists than to cognitive psychologists.

When conversation does function as an exchange of information, memory for that information can, in principle, be tested. This requires an objective record of the conversation, but tape recordings omit many important aspects of conversation, such as context, gestures, and facial expressions. These may be captured by video recordings, but natural conversation is easily distorted when people know they are being filmed. Apart from these methodological problems, there are special difficulties in studying conversation. Factors such as emotion, motivation, context and setting, and personal relationships, both past and present, which cognitive psychologists often try to exclude from studies of memory, are an integral and essential part of conversation. These factors exert powerful effects in naturally occurring conversation, but are impossible to control or to specify precisely. Because of the great variety of different types of conversation it is difficult to formulate general conclusions about memory for conversation, but some common threads do emerge from the studies that are described in the following sections.

Memory for conversation obviously rests on preceding processes of speech perception and language understanding. Detailed consideration of these processes lies outside the scope of this book, but some aspects that are of particular importance in understanding conversation are described next.

Pragmatics in Conversation

Pragmatics is the term used to describe the functional aspects of conversation. Conversation can have many different functions besides the exchange of information. For example, it may be designed to entertain, to advise, to annoy, to complain, and so on. The pragmatic aspect of the meaning of an utterance derives from the speaker's intentions and purposes. The intended meaning of an utterance may be quite different from its literal meaning. So, for example, the utterance "I'm tired" may be used to convey that it is no good asking the speaker to mow the lawn; that the speaker would like some sympathy and attention from the hearer; or that the speaker is justified in being unco-operative. Indeed, people sometimes say the exact opposite of what they intend the hearer to understand. If someone says "You've been a great help" when she has received no help at all, the utterance is intended to convey a reproach, and she is using sarcasm instead of a literal statement to underline the reproach.

Conversational Implicature

Complex implications like these run through everyday conversation. They cannot be derived by linguistic or by logical analysis, so how do we understand these implied meanings? The philosopher Grice (1967) claimed that conversation is normally governed by a *co-operative principle* consisting of a set of maxims or conventions observed by the speaker and the hearer. These are:

1. *Quality*: A speaker should normally say what is true, and a hearer normally assumes that what he is being told is true.
2. *Quantity*: The speaker should say as much as is necessary and neither more nor less.
3. *Relation*: The speaker's utterances should be relevant to the topic. The hearer works on the assumption that what is said is in some way relevant, and will try to figure out the relevance if it is not immediately obvious.

4. *Manner*: The utterances should be clear and orderly. The speaker normally aims to be understood and should not be obscure or ambiguous.

In practice, these conventions are often violated, either deliberately or involuntarily. Speakers may sometimes lie, mislead, joke, be sarcastic, verbose, ambiguous, irrelevant, or unintelligible. Nevertheless, hearers make the default assumptions that what is said is true, is in some way relevant, and that they ought to be able to understand it, and only abandon these assumptions when there is some evidence that the co-operative principle is not being observed.

Speech Acts

The pragmatic aspect of the meaning of utterances has been analysed in terms of speech acts (Searle, 1969). Not all utterances are simple statements of fact. In some cases, the speaker is performing an act by saying something. The speaker who is promising, requesting, or blessing is performing a speech act. Speech acts like commanding, rebuking, or threatening are designed to produce some desired effect on the hearer. The function of such utterances is to convey the intentions of the speaker, or, in some cases, to bring about changes in the behaviour or state of mind of the hearer. Other kinds of speech act are expressives, such as apologising, commiserating, deploring, which convey the speaker's state of mind. Speech acts are sometimes indirect. Instead of directly requesting "Please pass me the sauce" the speaker may use an indirect speech act, saying "Can I pass you the sauce?" Applying Gricean maxims, the hearer can figure out that this is a request rather than an offer. He knows he already has the sauce, and he knows that the speaker knows he already has the sauce. By assuming that the utterance must be relevant in some way, he is able to infer the indirect intended meaning. In one of Grice's own examples, a stranded motorist says "I'm out of petrol." A passer-by responds "There is a garage round the corner." The motorist needs to apply the maxim of relation to recover the conversational implicature that the garage sells petrol and is probably open.

The Given-New Contract

Clark and Haviland (1977) expressed some of the same ideas in their claim that speakers and hearers operate with a given–new contract. An utterance usually contains both given information (old information which is known to both the speaker and the hearer) and new information (information which is known only to the speaker). There is a co-operative principle whereby the speaker indicates the given information, making clear who or what is being talked about so that the hearer can identify the topic, and then supplies some new information about it which is true and is not already known to the hearer, as in "Have you heard about Harry? He's gone to Majorca." Violations of the given–new contract (like just saying "He's gone to Majorca", without indicating the given information) are apt to elicit responses like "What are you talking about?" from the hearer.

Bridging Inferences

Sometimes the hearer must refer back to a previous utterance in order to identify the given information. The utterance "Jane left early" refers back to a previous statement "The film was boring." The hearer has to infer that Jane left the cinema to escape further boredom. This type of inference which links new information back to a given topic is called a *bridging inference*. The listener who makes a bridging inference is acting on the Gricean co-operative principle and observing the maxims of relation and manner in assuming that the information about Jane must make sense and must relate to something. There are other principles that govern conversational exchanges, such as the *order-of-mention contract*, whereby events are normally mentioned in the order in which they occurred (as in "They got married and had a baby"; "He borrowed a fiver and I never saw him again") unless otherwise indicated. The point to note about all these examples is that in conversational exchanges the actual words used convey only a part of the meaning. Conventions of interpretation supply additional elements over and above the literal meaning.

Memory for Wording and Memory for Meaning

When people remember conversations, what do they remember? Empirical studies of memory for sentences, models of psycholinguistic processing, and models of memory such as schema theory all claim that memory for the surface form (the actual words and syntactic form) is lost very rapidly, and what is stored in memory is a more abstract representation of the meaning. The classic experimental demonstration of this phenomenon was carried out by Sachs (1967). In her experiment subjects listened to tape-recorded passages. One of the sentences they heard was: "He sent a letter about it to Galileo, the great Italian scientist". A test sentence was presented after a delay of approximately 0, 25 or 50 seconds. The subject had to decide if the test sentence was identical with the original or if it had been changed. There were four kinds of test sentence:

He sent a letter about it to Galileo, the great Italian scientist.
He sent Galileo, the great Italian scientist, a letter about it.
A letter about it was sent by him to Galileo, the great Italian scientist.

Galileo, the great Italian scientist, sent him a letter about it.

Version 1 is identical to the original. Versions 2 and 3 both preserve the meaning of the original although the wording has been changed. In version 4 both the wording and the meaning are changed. Subjects could detect changes of wording (2 and 3) at the zero delay but after 50 seconds these judgements were at chance level. Memory for the original wording had been lost, but changes of meaning, as in version 4, could still be detected with about 80% accuracy. This evidence suggests that verbatim wording (the surface form) is briefly stored in short-term memory, but only the semantic interpretation is retained in long-term memory.

According to this view, people remember the gist of a conversation, but, after a few seconds, they normally have little or no verbatim memory of what they have heard. Of course, it is recognised that people can remember speech word for word if they set out to memorise it and are given enough time and repetitions. People memorise poems and speeches in this way, but it is not considered the normal mode for remembering naturally occurring conversations. However, everyday experience does suggest that verbatim memory might be more common than Sachs's findings indicate. We are all familiar with verbatim raconteurs who report exchanges like " I said to her —, so she said to me—" in direct speech. Of course, this kind of recall may be only a quite inaccurate reconstruction, but most people feel confident that they can sometimes quote the exact words someone has said. Several studies of memory for conversation have addressed the question of whether any verbatim memory persists, and under what conditions.

John Dean's Memory

Neisser (1982a) analysed John Dean's memory for the conversations he had with President Nixon. Testifying to the Watergate Committee in June 1973, Dean described dozens of conversations with the President and with members of his Administration. Unknown to Dean, all the conversations that took place in Nixon's Oval Office were tape-recorded and transcripts were made available. Dean's recollection of these naturally occurring conversations could therefore be checked against the transcripts. Neisser analysed the recall of two conversations, one of which took place nine months before the hearing and one three months before. The first conversation is shown in Fig. 7.1(a). The President (P) and Robert Haldeman (H), the chief of staff, are discussing the fact that only five men and two minor White House officials (Hunt and Liddy) have been indicted for the Watergate break-in, so their efforts to conceal the involvment of higher officials seem to have been successful. Fig. 7.1(b) shows Dean's recall of this conversation.

P: Hi, how are you? You had quite a day today, didn't you? You got Watergate on the way, didn't you?
D: We tried.
H: How did it all end up?
D: Ah, I think we can say well, at this point. The press is playing it just as we expected.
H: Whitewash?
D: No, not yet – the story right now –
P: It is a big story.
H: Five indicted plus the WH former guy and all that.
D: Plus two White House fellows.
H: That is good; that takes the edge off whitewash, really. That was the thing Mitchell kept saying, that to people in the country Liddy and Hunt were big men. Maybe that is good.
P: How did MacGregor handle himself?
D: I think very well. He had a good statement, which said that the Grand Jury had met and that it was now time to realize that some apologies may be due.
H: Fat chance.
D: Get the damn (inaudible).
H: We can't do that.
P: Just remember, all the trouble we're taking, we'll have a chance to get back one day. How are you doing on your other investigation? (*Presidential Transcripts*, p. 32)

P: Yes (expletive deleted). Goldwater put it in context when he said (expletive deleted) everybody bugs everybody else. You know that.
D: That was priceless.
P: It happens to be totally true. We were bugged in '68 on the plane and even in '62 running for Governor – (expletive deleted) thing you ever saw.
D: It is a shame that evidence to the fact that that happened in '68 was never around. I understand that only the former director [*J. Edgar Hoover, former head of the FBI*] had that information.
H: No, that is not true.
D: There was evidence of it?
H: There are others who have information (*Ibid.*, p. 34).

D: Three months ago I would have had trouble predicting there would be a day when this would be forgotten, but I think I can say that 54 days from now [*i.e., on election day in November*] nothing is going to come crashing down to our surprise.
P: That what?
D: Nothing is going to come crashing down to our surprise (*Ibid.*, p. 36).

P: Oh well, this is a can of worms as you know, a lot of this stuff that went on. And the people who worked this way are awfully embarrassed. But the way you have handled all this seems to me has been very skillful, putting your fingers in the leaks that have sprung here and sprung there. The Grand Jury is dismissed now?
D: That is correct ... (*Ibid.*).

FIG. 7.1(a)   John Dean's conversation on 15th September, 1972 (from Neisser, 1982a).From Memory observed: Remembering in Natural Contexts, by Ulrich Neisser. Copyright © 1982 W.H. Freeman and Company. Reprinted with permission.

On September 15 the Justice Department announced the handing down of the seven indictments by the Federal Grand Jury investigating the Watergate. Late that afternoon I received a call requesting me to come to the President's Oval Office. When I arrived at the Oval Office I found Haldeman and the President. The President asked me to sit down. Both men appeared to be in very good spirits and my reception was very warm and cordial. The President then told me that Bob – referring to Haldeman – had kept him posted on my handling of the Watergate case. The President told me I had done a good job and he appreciated how difficult a task it had been and the President was pleased that the case had stopped with Liddy. I responded that I could not take credit because others had done much more difficult things than I had done. As the President discussed the present status of the situation I told him that all I had been able to do was to contain the case and assist in keeping it out of the White House. I also told him there was a long way to go before this matter would end and that I certainly could make no assurances that the day would not come when this matter would start to unravel (*Hearings*, p. 957).

FIG. 7.1(b)   John Dean's recall of the conversation nine months later (from Neisser, 1982a). From Memory Observed: Remembering in Natural Contexts, by Ulrich Neisser. Copyright © 1982 W.H. Freeman and Company. Reprinted with permission.

Neisser points out that, even considered as gist, hardly any of the recalled version is accurate. Nixon did not say the things he is reported to have said (e.g. asking Dean to sit down; that H had kept him informed of Dean's handling of the case; that he was pleased the case stopped with Liddy). Dean himself did not say that he could not take credit or that the matter might unravel later. Nevertheless, Neisser argues that Dean's account is correct at a much more general thematic level. They did discuss the cover-up and Nixon was clearly aware of it. Some of Dean's distortions, such as "The President asked me to sit down", can be seen as script-based intrusions, derived from an arriving-at-a-meeting script. Others are changes bringing the conversation into line with what (with hindsight) should have been said. For example, Dean would like to have warned the President that the cover-up might fall apart, since it eventually did. He would like the President to have appreciated what a difficult task he had. Under further interrogation, Dean repeated his statement in a way suggesting that he was recalling his earlier recall, rather than recalling the original conversation.

Dean's recall of the second conversation was more accurate. In this conversation, he made a more or less prepared speech warning the President of the precariousness of their position. Neisser points out a number of factors that might account for the superior recall of this conversation. The original conversation took place only three months previously, so the time elapsed was shorter. Dean himself did most of the talking and had prepared what he wanted to say. There were only two participants instead of three. And, finally, the conversation conformed more closely to the way he wanted to present himself. It was apparent that Dean had often conflated or transposed different conversations. Many of the conversations were fairly similar in content, and were therefore remembered like repisodic events (see Chapter 5, p.118). Two findings emerge most strongly from this study. Firstly, recall is strongly influenced by motives, personality, and wishful thinking. Secondly, we need to distinguish several different levels of memory for conversation. Memory that is inaccurate at the lower levels of verbatim recall, and even at the level of gist recall, may still be correct at a much more general level of thematic recall.

Bekerian and Dennett (1988) analysed the memory of a defendant for the summing-up speech made by the judge at the trial at which he was found guilty and sentenced. Six months later he recalled 49% of the main points but only 30% of the less important details. There was a marked bias toward recall of the points put forward by the prosecution which the defendant considered unfair and prejudiced. Like the John Dean study, this demonstrates the effects of attitudes on recall of what has been said.

Memory for Lectures and Seminars

In contrast with the study of John Dean's memory, other research has revealed that people do remember some kinds of utterance verbatim. Keenan, MacWhinney, and Mayhew (1977) examined memory for utterances made in the course of a linguistics seminar and discussion. They were interested in memory for pragmatic information, as well as memory for meaning and for surface structure. They distinguished between utterances with high or low interactional content. Those with high interactional content (HIC) have a pragmatic role and a personal significance. They carry information about the speaker's attitude, beliefs, or relations with the listeners. Utterances with low interactional content (LIC) are impersonal and factual. Examples are:

I think you've made a fundamental error in this study. (HIC)
I think there are two fundamental tasks in this study. (LIC)

The authors predicted that HIC utterances would be more memorable than LIC ones, and that people would be more likely to remember the exact wording of HIC utterances than LIC ones. This latter prediction was based on their intuition that the exact words are of critical importance in the interpretation of HIC exchanges, since choice of words determines whether such an utterance is polite or insulting, joking or serious.

Thirty hours after the seminar took place, participants were given a recognition test with multiple choices including the original utterance reproduced verbatim (the target) and two foils, a true paraphrase of the original statement and a new statement. As predicted, subjects recognised more HIC target utterances (56%) than LIC ones (19%). The difference betweeen recognition responses made to targets, and recognition responses made to true paraphrases, was taken as a measure of verbatim memory since a true paraphrase can only be recognised as different from the original sentence if memory for the exact wording is preserved. For HIC sentences, recognition of targets exceeded recognition of true paraphrases by 38%. For LIC sentences recognition of the verbatim target was only 1% more frequent than recognition of the paraphrase. In order to confirm that these differences were caused by the interactional role of the sentences, Keenan et al. carried out a control experiment. The HIC and LIC sentences from the original experiment were arranged in a list, and presented to new subjects who had not attended the original discussion. When the sentences were taken out of context in this way, they lost their interactional content, and this time the recognition test showed no difference between the sentences previously classified as HIC or LIC. Keenan et al. concluded that it is only when sentences have a pragmatic role and a personal significance for the hearer that they are remembered verbatim.

A similar result was obtained by Kintsch and Bates (1977) in two experiments on recognition memory for statements from a lecture. Figure 7.2 shows examples of statements made in two lectures, one on intelligence

Sentence Category	Experiment 1	Experiment 2
	Topic Statement	
Old	The doctrine of natural biological evolution formed the rationale for Galton's study of the eminent families of Britain.	The closed energy model is still critical for the psychoanalytic approach to therapy.
Paraphrase	Galton compared the eminent families of Britain with the natural biological variations that figure so preeminently in the doctrine of evolution.	The psychoanalytic approach to therapy still depends critically on the concept of a closed energy system.
New	The inheritance of human intellect implied for Galton the practicability of supplanting inefficient human stock by better strains.	The concept of a limited energy system explains a great deal about neurotic development.

Sentence Category	Experiment 1	Experiment 2
Paraphrase	None.	The development of neurosis can be explained in large measure by the concept of a limited energy system.
Detail Statement		
Old	Galton was the brilliant younger cousin of Darwin.	Around 1887, Freud was working with Joseph Breuer, studying the method of free association.
Paraphrase	Darwin was the older cousin of the extremely intelligent Galton.	Freud learned the method of free association from Joseph Breuer around 1887.
New	The phrenologists had tried to do the same thing before but failed.	In 1885, Freud spent time with Jean Charcot studying hypnosis as a clinical method.
Paraphrase	None.	Freud studied hypnosis as a clinical method under Jean Charcot in 1885.
Extraneous Statement		
Old	Isadora Duncan suggested to George Bernard Shaw that they should combine her beauty and his intelligence; Shaw however objected that the child might turn out with his looks and her brains.	Oh, speaking of anxiety, that reminds me. Marcia and I will not be able to answer questions between now and next Tuesday.
Paraphrase	Isadora Duncan told Bernard Shaw that she wanted a child from him in order to combine her beauty and his intelligence: Shaw, however, was afraid the child might get her brains and his looks.	Oh, speaking of anxiety, I forgot to mention that Marcia and I won't be answering questions until the exams are in on Tuesday.
New	The Spartans purposefully bred their strongest warriors with their most beautiful maidens, but in the end they became just as decadent as the Athenians, who had more fun all along.	In case I didn't mention it, Marcia and I will try to have the papers back to you a week from Tuesday.
Paraphrase	None.	Oh, if I didn't tell you before, Marcia and I plan to give you back the papers a week from Tuesday.

FIG. 7.2 Statements extracted from lectures on intelligence testing (Experiment 1) and on psychoanalysis (Experiment 2) (from Kintsch & Bates, 1977). Copyright (1977) by the American Psychological Association. Reprinted by permission of the author.

testing, and one on psychoanalysis. These were divided into topic statements which made general points; detail statements which supplied illustrative details; and extraneous statements which were jokes or announcements irrelevant to the main theme. These extraneous statements are similar to the HIC sentences in the Keenan et al. study in that they have interactional significance. In Experiment 1, a recognition test was given two days after the lecture. Kintsch and Bates found that extraneous statements were remembered better than topic or detail statements which did not differ. Verbatim memory, as shown by the ability to distinguish between old statements and their paraphrases, persisted for all three types of statement, but, in line with the results of Keenan et al., subjects were more likely to remember the exact wording of extraneous statements. A second experiment, with a five-day delay before the recognition test, produced substantially the same results, although verbatim memory was further reduced at this longer retention interval.

According to the predictions from schema theory, topic statements should be remembered best because they are more important, more relevant, and at a higher level of generality. Kintsch and Bates suggested a number of reasons why this did not turn out to be the case. The extraneous statements benefit from distinctiveness, standing out from the rest of the material. Both detail and extraneous statements are also more concrete than topic statements, and, as can be seen from the example of an extraneous statement in the lecture on psychoanalysis, they may be richer in pragmatic information. The studies by Kintsch and Bates and by Keenan et al. converge in identifying pragmatic utterances as more likely to be remembered verbatim than factual ones.

Peper and Mayer (1978) studied the effects of note-taking on memory for lectures. In their study, one group of students took notes; the other group listened without taking notes. Those who did not take notes were better at remembering technical symbols and specific ideas, but the note-taking group were better at remembering the important general ideas, and their recall was more likely to include intrusions of relevant material acquired elsewhere. The act of note-taking therefore appeared to help the listeners organise the material, to select out the higher-level information, and to integrate it with what they already knew. Those who listened passively were more likely to remember details verbatim, but had not grasped the main ideas so well. Kintsch and Bates did not report whether their students took notes during the lectures or not. Perhaps failure to recall the topic statements was due to not taking notes.

An important point about memory for spoken information emerged from a study by Neisser (1988). He held a series of weekly seminars and later tested students' ability to remember statements made in the seminars. Free recall was tested first and cues were supplied if necessary, but students were able to respond "Don't know" when they could not recall an item. The statements recalled were mostly at a general level, and specific information was less likely to be recalled. Although much of the material could not be remembered, subjects made very few errors. A recognition test was given after the recall test, and produced a very different pattern of results. When the subjects had to select an old target statement from two foils they made errors. Neisser showed that recognition memory was distorted by attitude. Those students who, at a separate confidential interview, disclosed that they had a positive attitude toward Neisser as a teacher, selected foils in which he made helpful encouraging statements. Those who had negative attitudes attributed to him foil statements which were unhelpful and critical. This study underlines the fact that the recognition paradigm is an unnatural way to test memory for utterances and is liable to induce errors and distortions. If Kintsch and Bates had tested recall instead of recognition, they might well have found superior memory for topic statements. If people are encouraged to report what they can remember and admit what they have forgotten, then memory may be sparse, but it is more likely to be accurate. Researchers tend to use recognition paradigms simply because these are much easier to score, but the memory that is elicited in recognition tests is more easily contaminated by attitudes and by beliefs about what is plausible or probable.

Memory for Requests

Keenan et al. showed that pragmatic utterances were more likely to be remembered verbatim than purely factual statements which had no pragmatic function. However, Kemper and Thissen (1981) obtained results showing that some kinds of pragmatic utterances are more likely to be remembered word-for-word than others. They focused on requests. The examples below show how these could vary in syntactic form (imperative, declarative, or interrogative); in the presence or absence of "please"; the use of modal or auxiliary verbs like will, can, or should; the use of linguistic hedges; and the indirect statement of wishes or needs. These factors combine to produce requests of varying degrees of politeness or directness.

Rake the leaves.
Please rake the leaves.
Would you rake the leaves.
Why don't you rake the leaves.
I think you should rake the leaves.
I would like you to rake the leaves.
I think the leaves need to be raked.

Kemper and Thissen showed subjects cartoons. Each cartoon depicted a speaker–hearer pair of different status (e.g. a waiter–diner pair or a boss–secretary pair). In the caption one member of the pair was making a request either for money or for the other person to do something. When memory for the captions was tested the results showed that the verbatim form of the request was most likely to be remembered if the wording violated normal social conventions, so that a low-status speaker used an impolite form to a high-status hearer (e.g. the waiter saying "Sit there" to the diner) or a high-status speaker used a super-polite indirect form to a low-status hearer (e.g. the boss saying something like "I think it would be a good idea to type these letters"). These results indicate that pragmatic utterances which are surprising and distinctive are most likely to be remembered verbatim.

Memory for Courtroom Testimony

A study of memory for courtroom testimony by Harris (1978) showed that memory is influenced by pragmatic implications. In an earlier experiment (Harris & Monaco, 1976) sentences like:

The housewife spoke to the manager about the increased meat prices.
The paratrooper leaped out of the door.

were sometimes remembered as:

The housewife complained to the manager about the increased meat prices.
The paratrooper jumped out of the plane.

In these examples, the original version has been elaborated by inferential processes to unpack the pragmatic implications. When memory is tested, people often cannot remember what was explicitly stated and what was only implied. The same tendency was apparent in Harris's 1978 experiment simulating courtroom testimony. Subjects were told to pretend they were members of a jury, and listened to a five-minute account of a burglary. In a later recognition test, they claimed that statements were definitely true, and had been explicitly asserted, when in fact they had only been implied in the original testimony. These constructive errors occurred even when subjects were warned to avoid them. Explicit and implicit information appears to be integrated into a global memory representation of the meaning and cannot be distinguished. This phenomenon is further evidence of a bias toward remembering meaning and forgetting what has actually been said.

Memory for Conversations in Soap Operas

Bates, Masling, and Kintsch (1978) tested recognition memory for utterances occurring as part of the conversation in TV soap opera episodes. This study was particularly concerned with memory for reference. In a recognition test, subjects had to select the sentence they had originally heard from a set of alternatives. One set of sentences was used to test memory for names and pronouns. When the original target sentence contained a pronoun, the true paraphrase test sentence substituted the name of the person referrred to (or vice versa), and the false paraphrase test sentence substituted the name of some other person in the drama, as shown in the following:

I wanted to get that Pendleton work done while he was out of the office. [original target sentence]

I wanted to get that Pendleton work done while Robert was out of the office. [true paraphrase]

I wanted to get that Pendleton work done while Willis was out of the office. [false paraphrase]

Another set of sentences was used to test memory for explicit and implicit references. When the original target sentence contained an elliptical clause, the true paraphrase substituted a full clause which correctly and explicitly instantiated it (or vice versa). The false paraphrase substituted a full clause which incorrectly instantiated it:

We're doing everything we can to make sure she does, Ada. [original target]

We're doing everything we can to make sure she keeps the baby, Ada. [true paraphrase]

We're doing everything we can to make sure she regains consciousness, Ada. [false paraphrase]

In a third set of sentences, characters originally referred to by their proper names were referred to by their roles or occupations in the paraphrases.

Subjects viewed a videotaped episode lasting 20 minutes and were tested immediately afterwards. The percentage of false paraphrases that were rejected was used as an index of memory for meaning. The percentage of targets selected minus the percentage of true paraphrases selected was used as an index of memory for verbatim surface form. The results showed that memory for meaning was near perfect. Subjects also showed a significant amount of retention of the surface form of the utterances, but this varied for different types of item. Explicit forms of reference were more likely to be remembered exactly than the elliptical or implicit forms. Use of a proper name was more likely to be remembered than use of a pronoun, and a role was remembered better than a name. Bates et al. concluded from these results that, in natural conversation, surface form is remembered if and when it has some functional significance. The choice of a particular form of reference in conversation is not arbitrary, but has the function of distinguishing or drawing attention to the referent.

Memory for Voices

The surface form of an utterance does not consist only of its lexical and syntactic form, but also includes the voice characteristics of the speaker. Everyday experience leads us to believe that our ability to remember voices is reliable. It is not unusual to pick up the phone and immediately recognise the voice of a friend who has not been heard from for many years. Although this voice is totally unexpected and there are no contextual cues to aid identification, we are still able to identify the speaker. On other occasions, we may be unable to put a name to the voice, but yet be confident that it is a familiar voice and not the voice of a stranger. Clifford (1983) contrasted these situations with the circumstances in which a witness, or a victim, has heard an unfamiliar voice during the commission of a crime and is asked to identify it later. Identification of once-heard voices is not nearly as good as identification of familiar voices. Bricker and Pruzansky (1966) found that people were 98% correct in identifying the familiar voices of people they worked with, but this contrasts with the findings from experiments using strange voices. In an early experiment by McGehee (1937), 740 listeners heard a passage of prose being read aloud. Recognition tests were given after intervals ranging from 1 day to 5 months. In the recognition test, 5 different readers read the original passage and listeners had to identify which voice they had heard before. Recognition accuracy was 80% for a delay of up to 1 week; 69% after 2 weeks; 51% after 3 weeks; and 35% after 3 months.

Clifford's review indicates that the accuracy of voice recognition is slightly reduced if the speech sample is small, and is seriously damaged by distortions such as whispering. In an experiment designed to study the effects of delay, target voices uttered the sentence: "I will meet you outside the National Westminster Bank at 6 o'clock tonight." In the recognition test, there were 2 target voices and 22 distractors. Trainee nurses served as subjects. Recognition accuracy declined from 55% at 10 minutes delay to 37% at 2 weeks delay.

Clifford points out that naturally occurring situations are unlike the experimental situation in that the listener is not forewarned that he or she will be required to recognise the voice. Forewarning appears to make a substantial difference to performance. In a naturalistic study, Clifford tested the ability of shopkeepers and bank clerks to recognise the voice of a male stooge who entered the bank or shop, introduced himself, explained that he had lost his cheque book and card, and asked what steps he should take. The researcher later asked the shop assistant/bank clerk to participate in a voice-identification test. In this situation, when testing was not anticipated, identification was at chance level after four hours delay.

Memory for voices is clearly not as good as our intuitions may suggest. Strange voices are unlikely to be recognised after a delay unless the listener has made a deliberate effort to commit the voice to memory, and even when the listener has tried to remember the voice, recognition is poor after two or three days. However, the fact that in some circumstances people can remember a speaker's voice for hours or days is a further indication that memory for the surface form of utterances is not necessarily lost as rapidly as in the experiment by Sachs.

Memory Capacity for Spoken Information

How much information do listeners remember? How can information be structured or "put across" so that it is remembered better? What factors influence the amount of information that is recalled?

Intention to Remember

In everyday life we usually take part in conversations without any expectation that we will be required to remember what has been said, but intuitively we would guess that memory would be better if we made an effort to memorise the conversation. It is surprising, therefore, that in a study by Kausler and Hakami (1983) the intention to remember did not produce any significant improvement. Young and elderly subjects received a series of 12 topics for discussion. The experimenter asked 3 questions on each topic. Subjects had to answer yes or no and explain their reasons. Those in the incidental condition did not know that memory would be tested, but those in the intentional condition were expecting a memory test. Half the topics were about personal matters such as being embarrassed or feeling irritable, and half were impersonal topics such as the United States space programme. When asked to list the topics which had been discussed, the young subjects recalled 67% and the elderly 55%, but there was no difference between the intentional and incidental conditions, nor between personal and impersonal topics. After only a short interval, people are apparently not very good at remembering what they have been talking about. However, the experimental situation, with many topics arbitrarily selected and rapidly switching, is quite unlike natural conversation in which topics arise out of the context and associative links lead from one to the next.

Weather Forecasts and Traffic Reports

Wagenaar (1978) has investigated how much people remember from radio broadcasts, using weather forecasts and traffic reports. Examples are shown in Fig. 7.3.

The weather report contains 32 idea units. The construction is complex. Information about time and place is interleaved, and there are no main

---

A weather forecast
Forecast for tonight and tomorrow: In the evening in the southern part of the country a good deal of cloud, within the southeastern region some temporary rain, otherwise some cloudless periods but tomorrow, in the afternoon, some local showers, especially in the north and west regions. Wind moderate to strong, along the coast occasionally high to stormy earlier from the southwest, later veering to the northwest. Minimum temperature about 10°C, on the Wadden Shallows a few degrees higher. Maximum temperature from 16°C in the northwest to 22°C in the southeast regions.

A traffic report
On the following roads traffic jams are reported. A2 Den Bosch in the direction of Utrecht, between Outemborg and Vianen a jam of 6km. A27 Gorkum in the direction of Vianen, between Lexmond and Vianen, a jam of 3km. A29 Hellegatsplein in the direction of Rotterdam, at the entrance of Heinenoord tunnel a jam of 2 km ...

FIG. 7.3   Material used to test memory for radio broadcasts (from Wagenaar, 1978).

verbs. The traffic report (in full) contains 70 idea units and needs a detailed knowledge of geography to understand it. Memory was tested by cued recall, using cues like "clouds" or "location of jams". Memory for the weather report showed a ceiling of about 8 idea units. The longer traffic report had a ceiling of 17 ideas. In general, the percentage of a message that was recalled declined with message length. Not surprisingly, drivers recalled the traffic report better than non-drivers.

A second experiment tested ability to remember pre-selected information. Before hearing the message, subjects were told they should try to remember those parts of the weather forecast relating to a particular region, or those parts of the traffic report relating to a particular route. The results showed that the subjects had difficulty in extracting and selectively storing the relevant parts of the weather forecast. Wagenaar pointed out that the complex structure made it difficult to select a part without first analysing the whole. Because of its simpler structure, selecting relevant information from the traffic report proved easier, and there was a 20% improvement in the amount recalled. The study highlights the importance of message structure and of prior knowledge in determining how much is remembered.

In another study of memory for weather forecasts, Wagenaar and Visser (1979) compared a radio message (speech only) and three different kinds of television broadcast. The TV forecasts had different visual components: a talking head, a map with symbols appearing on it as the items were mentioned, and a map with a man pointing to the symbols. They found that the amount recalled was the same for the radio message and for the map with symbols. Both the talking head and the pointing man acted as distractors and actually impaired recall. The amount of information retained from weather forecasts is quite sharply limited and gimmicky visual aids are no help.

Doctor–Patient Dialogues

When patients come away from consultations with their doctors they remember alarmingly little of the advice and information they have received. Ley (1978) has summarised the findings of various studies of memory for medical information and has shown that there are ways of presenting information which significantly improve the chances that it will be remembered. Estimates of how much people remember of what the doctor has told them range from 46% to 63%. Elderly people remember less than the young, and those with medical knowledge remember more than those who are medically naive.

The patient's anxiety also affects how much is remembered. There appears to be a Yerkes–Dodson relationship between anxiety and forgetting. Forgetting is greatest when anxiety is very low or very high, and intermediate levels of anxiety produce better recall. The amount of information given is linearly related to the amount recalled, with the percentage that is remembered declining as the total amount presented is increased. Although the perceived importance of the information does affect recall, patients do not seem to be very good at spontaneously picking out the most important elements of the conversation to remember. Memory for diagnostic information is best and memory for advice and instructions is poorest, although, in practical terms, this is the most important. This result appears to be largely due to a primacy effect. The first items of information are the best retained, and many doctors present their diagnosis first. Ley's research showed that recall of advice and instructions could be improved from 50% to 87% if this information were presented first, and its importance stressed. Accordingly, Ley generated six suggestions for doctors:

1. Give instructions and advice first.
2. Stress the importance of instructions and advice.
3. Use short words and short sentences.
4. Use explicit categories, stating, for example, this is what treatment you will need; these are the tests that will be done; this is what is wrong; this is what will happen to you; this is what you must do to help yourself. The doctor should announce each category in this way, and then supply the information.

5. Repeat information.
6. Be specific. For example, say "you must lose 7 lbs" rather than "you must lose some weight".

Four general practitioners adopted these suggestions and found a 10–20% increase in the amount of information retained.

Limits of Capacity

These studies reveal some of the constraints on memory for conversation. Speech is a rapidly fading continuous signal. The listener must perceive, interpret, and encode the message during the brief period it is available in working memory and before it has decayed or been displaced by the new material which is continuing to come in. Since conversations, lectures, and broadcasts almost always contain more information than people can remember or want to know, the listener must select what is important and discard what is redundant, irrelevant, or uninteresting. When the listener is equipped with prior schemas (e.g. the patient has medical knowledge, or the driver is familar with the routes), and when the new messages are well organised with the important elements clearly highlighted, this process of selective encoding can be achieved. When the message is poorly organised, the listener is forced to spend too long on interpretation and selection, and cannot keep pace with the input. In a lecture you can easily fall behind the speaker while trying to take notes and organise them under headings. In conversation, the listener has the additional task of generating contributions. You can easily miss what is being said while thinking of what you want to say yourself. On the other hand, interactive conversation has the advantage that you can ask the speaker to repeat the message or to speak more slowly. In dialogues, the speaker normally adjusts the style, amount, and rate of information to suit the listener.

Remembering Through Conversation

There is one aspect of memory for conversation that is not often considered. Conversation is not just something to be remembered, but can also be used as a means of remembering. In everyday life remembering is not necessarily a solo performance. If we cannot remember something we commonly appeal to family, friends, or colleagues for assistance. Shared experiences are recalled collaboratively with different individuals supplying missing elements and cueing each other. Middleton and Edwardes (Note 7) have studied remembering as a joint collaborative effort. They recorded occasions when parents and their young children looked through the family photograph album together. Together they identified the scene and people depicted, elaborated the details of the scene, placed it in context of time and place of occurrence, interpreted what was happening, and used inferential reconstruction to assign causes and consequences to the event. Children and parents compared reactions and contributed additional remembered information. Even when conversations are not designed, like these were, as collaborative acts of remembering, many everyday conversations include explicit reminders, cues which reinstate shared memories, and appeals for help in remembering.

MEMORY FOR PROSE AND STORIES

We need to remember many different kinds of written information including poems and stories, factual texts such as newspaper articles or technical reports, letters, prayers, legal agreements, or instructions for operating the video recorder or the washing machine.

The content of these different kinds of material spans the whole range of human experience and imagination and serves many different functions. Written information may be designed to entertain, to inform, to instruct, to convey emotions and states of mind, to preserve traditions and rituals. Most of the pragmatic functions of speech can also be served by writing. The speech acts described in the previous section should really be called *language acts* since they can be performed either in speech or in writing. Psychologists have rather lost sight of this pragmatic aspect of written language because research has concentrated on laboratory experiments, and has only explored a restricted range of written material. Memory for written information in everyday contexts has been neglected. Outside the laboratory we use writing much more pragmatically. Consider the following examples:

IOU £30
4 pints, please
Gone to lunch, back at 2 p.m.
No Smoking
I am happy to accept your invitation ...
I write to offer my sincere sympathy ...

We use writing to promise, to request, to inform, to warn, to agree, to sympathise, just as, at other times, we use speech.

Another important difference between laboratory research on memory for prose and stories and everyday-life situations is that, in most experimental studies, subjects know that they will be tested so that learning is intentional. In everyday life we often read texts without deliberately trying to memorise what we read. Most of the information acquired from written material is acquired incidentally. Even when we read a newspaper article with interest, and with the intention of improving our knowledge of the topic, we do not always memorise as if preparing to be tested. Laboratory experiments usually test memory for short texts or stories of only a few hundred words after a single reading or a short study period, and testing usually takes place after only a short interval. For these reasons, experiments on memory for prose and stories are not very similar to naturally occurring memory for written information and may not be representative.

Techniques for Effective Study of Texts

We know relatively little about how people set about trying to learn a large body of material from written texts in naturally occurring situations. Yet people in many jobs need to commit to mind the contents of technical reports, memoranda, newspaper or journal articles, technical or academic books, the details of a legal case, or a part in a play. Students need to cram large amounts of material in order to be able to regurgitate it in examinations. Robinson (1946) outlined a set of recommendations known as the SQ3R method, and a similar study technique (Rowntree, 1970) is known as PQRST.

The SQ3R method lists the prescribed stages of study as survey, question, read, recall, review. In the PQRST method the stages are preview, question, read, state, test. In the preview, or survey stage, the reader is advised to look quickly through the headings, and identify the main topics and ideas that are covered. This operation is designed to supply an organising framework, which is why headings are sometimes called advance organisers. At the question stage, the reader formulates questions about the information which is to be extracted from the material and sets goals in the form of answers to be sought. The third step is to read through the text in order to find the answers to the questions. This goal-directed reading is an active and purposeful search. The next step (recall or state) consists of writing down or saying a brief answer to each of the questions, and in the final stage (review or test) the student reviews the knowledge that has been acquired.

Wilson and Moffatt (1984) reported the results of a study in which the PQRST technique was used to try to improve the performance of a student suffering from a verbal memory disorder following a head injury. Studying with this technique took three times as long as without it, but produced superior recall and recognition of the material. Common sense suggests that the success of this method must depend crucially on the student's ability to extract the main ideas at the preview stage and to formulate the most relevant questions. The most appropriate organising framework is not always readily apparent unless the reader already has prior knowledge of the topic.

There is obviously a close relationship between how we understand what we read, how we encode it, and how we remember it. The main focus of this chapter is on what is remembered, but the processes which create the memory representation have to be taken into account as well. Theoretical interpretations of memory for texts and stories are controversial and several different models are currently being debated.

The Role of Event Schemas

Recent studies of memory for texts and stories have emphasised the role of schemas. It is important, however, to distinguish between two different kinds of schema, which can be characterised as *event schemas* and *story schemas*. Event schemas consist of knowledge about the subject matter of the story. The event schemas activated in remembering a Trollope novel, for example, might include knowledge of Victorian social life and political history, foxhunting, country houses, and ecclesiastical preferment. Story schemas, however, consist of abstract, content-free knowledge about the structure of a typical story: They are described in a later section. This section is concerned with the role of event schemas.

Some of the earliest studies of memory for stories were carried out by Bartlett (1932). He introduced the idea that schemas, or mental frameworks built up from prior knowledge and experience, are influential in shaping and moulding the memory of a story. In one of his experiments he asked people to read through a story about Indians in British Columbia, called *The War of Ghosts*. The last part of the story was as follows:

So the canoes went back to Egulac, and the young man went ashore to his house, and made a fire. And he told everybody and said: "Behold I accompanied the ghosts, and we went to fight. Many of our fellows were killed, and many of those who attacked us were killed. They said I was hit, and I did not feel sick."
He told it all, and then he became quiet. When the sun rose he fell down. Something black came out of his mouth. His face became contorted. The people jumped up and cried. He was dead.

The following is a subject's reproduction of the story, produced immediately afterwards:

In the evening he returned to his hut, and told his friends that he had been in a battle. A great many had been slain, and he had been wounded by an arrow: he had not felt any pain, he said. They told him that he must have been fighting in a battle of ghosts. Then he remembered that it had been queer and he became very excited.
In the morning, however, he became ill, and his friends gathered round. He fell down and his face became very pale. Then he writhed

> and shrieked and his friends were filled with terror. At last he became calm. Something hard and black came out of his mouth and he lay contorted and dead.

Bartlett identified three schema-induced processes: sharpening, levelling out, and rationalisation. Examples of the changes resulting from these processes can be found in this reproduction. Sharpening can be seen in the details that are added by elaborative inferences (the young man being wounded *by an arrow*; the idea that his audience was composed of *his friends*; the fact that they *gathered round* and *were filled with terror*). Rationalisation is evident in the substitution of *had not felt any pain* for *did not feel sick* as being more consistent with an arrow wound. Some details (*the canoes, making a fire*) have been levelled out or omitted. According to Bartlett, the story has been revised in memory to fit with the cultural expectations and experience of the reader.

The contribution of prior knowledge to story recall has been strikingly demonstrated in several different experimental paradigms. The results are particularly dramatic when people are asked to remember a story for which they have no pre-existing event schema.

Remembering without a Schema

Bransford and Johnson (1973) in a classic series of experiments showed that people remember very little of a text if they do not have an appropriate schema. They constructed two texts which are reproduced in the following paragraphs. The first text describes a situation so bizarre that without some clues the readers could not figure out what was going on.

> If the balloons popped the sound would not be able to carry, since everything would be too far away from the correct floor. A closed window would also prevent the sound from carrying since most buildings tend to be well insulated. Since the whole operation depends on a steady flow of electricity, a break in the middle of the wire would also cause problems. Of course, the fellow could shout, but the human voice is not loud enough to carry that far. An additional problem is that a string could break on the instrument. Then there would be no accompaniment to the message. It is clear that the best situation would involve less distance. Then there would be fewer potential problems. With face to face contact, the least number of things could go wrong.

One group of subjects who were given no context and no title with this text remembered an average of only 3.6 ideas out of 14. Another group were shown a picture illustrating the text which made it clear that a guitar player standing in the street is trying to serenade a lady in the top floor of a high-rise building, and has used balloons to hoist a loudspeaker up to her level. Those who saw this picture before they read the text remembered 8 ideas. Using a "serenade" schema they were able to make sense of the text and encode a meaningful representation. Showing the picture after the text had been read failed to improve performance.

The second text describes a commonplace situation, but in such an abstract and obscure way that it was again difficult to know what it was about.

> The procedure is actually quite simple. First you arrange things into different groups. Of course, one pile may be sufficient depending on how much there is to do. If you have to go somewhere else due to lack of facilities that is the next step: otherwise you are pretty well set. It is important not to overdo things. That is, it is better to do too few things at once than too many. In the short run this may not seem important, but complications can arise. A mistake can prove expensive as well. At first the whole procedure will seem complicated. Soon, however, it will become just another facet of life. It is difficult to foresee any end to the necessity for this task in the immediate future, but one can never tell. After the procedure is completed, one arranges the materials into different groups again. Then they can be put into their appropriate places. Eventually they will all be used once more, and the whole cycle will have to be repeated. However, that is part of life.

One group of subjects read this text with the title *Washing Clothes* supplied before they read it; one group had the title supplied after reading the text; a third group had no title at all. With no title subjects recalled only 2.8 ideas out of 18. With the title supplied before, the score increased to 5.8 ideas, but the title-after group recalled only 2.7. These results clearly indicate that when new information cannot be related to an appropriate schema very little is remembered. Of course, the situation is a very artificial one. In everyday life there are normally plenty of contextual cues to tell us what schemas are appropriate for what we read. Written material comes with titles, headings, and illustrations, and the situation in which it is encountered also gives clues as to its content. Bransford and Johnson's material violates both the co-operative principles by being deliberately obscure and the given–new contract by not making clear what is being referred to.

In theory, the use of schemas could facilitate several different stages of memory. At the encoding stage, the active schema guides the selection of relevant information, influences the interpretation, and integrates the new information with pre-existing knowledge. At the retrieval stage, schemas may facilitate recall by supplying an organisation or plan to direct search, and a framework which enables forgotten material to be reconstructed. The finding that schemas are only effective if they are activated before reading texts suggest that the role of a schema is to facilitate the encoding stage, and not to facilitate retrieval, but the results of other experiments suggest that the primary role of schemas is to aid recall.

Changing Schemas

Anderson and Pichert (1978) constructed an ingenious text which described how two boys played truant from school and spent the day at the home of one of them because the house was always empty on Thursdays. The text described the house as an older house set in attractive grounds well back from the road. Various possessions of the family such as a ten-speed bike, a colour TV, and a rare coin collection were mentioned, as well as features of the house such as its leaking roof and its damp basement. Altogether the text contained 72 ideas which were rated by a separate set of subjects for importance to either a home-buyer (e.g. leaking roof; attractive grounds) or a burglar (coin collection; nobody home on Thursdays).

Half the experimental subjects were told to read the text from the point of view of a home-buyer, and half were told to read it from the point of view of a prospective burglar. After a 12-minute filled delay subjects were asked to recall the text in as much detail as possible. Following a further 5-minute delay, a second attempt at recall was made. This time, half the subjects were given a changed perspective: Home-buyers were switched to the burglar perspective and vice versa. The rest of the subjects retained their original perspective and simply recalled the material again trying to retrieve more information.

The point of this design is that, if schemas operate only at the encoding stage, supplying a new, different schema at the retrieval stage should not assist recall. In fact, however, subjects who shifted to a different schema recalled 7% more ideas at the second attempt than at the first. Those who did not change perspective actually recalled slightly less. In a follow-up experiment, Anderson and Pichert showed that the change of schemas influenced which ideas were remembered as well as the amount recalled. Recall of ideas that were important according to the new schema increased by 10%, and recall of ideas that were important to the previous schema, but not the current one, declined by 21%. Anderson and Pichert also recorded subjects' introspections about how they had studied and recalled the information. Most said they had selectively attended to the schema-relevant facts while they were encoding. However, the results demonstrated that they must also have encoded some schema-irrelevant facts since they were able to retrieve these later. The subjects reported that, at retrieval, they used the new schema to search memory and recover additional information. Why, then, did Bransford and Johnson's subjects fail to benefit when they were given the "Serenade" schema or the "Washing clothes" schema after reading the text at the time of recall? The answer must be that the Bransford and Johnson texts were too incomprehensible to encode at all. If information has not been encoded in the first place, then a schema supplied at the time of recall cannot guide retrieval. Everyday experience suggests that the role of schemas is flexible and dynamic, and affects encoding, storage, and retrieval. If I read a newspaper article about government plans for changes in taxation, I encode the information within my pre-existing schema for the tax system. When I want to discuss it later with a friend, I use this schema to search for and retrieve the new information. But information which is originally encoded within one schema can sometimes be completely re-interpreted in the light of new information and transferred to a new schema. Films and novels often have surprise twists built into the plot which require reorganisation of this kind. The apparently innocent nice guy turns out to be the villain. In these examples, changing schemas seems to involve recoding the information that is in store, rather than just using a different search plan to retrieve it.

Inferential Processes in Memory for Texts

Garnham (1985) distinguishes three kinds of inference that are made in comprehending texts:

1. *Logical inferences*, which follow from the meaning of words. For example, the statement that a robin is a bird logically entails that it is an animal.
2. *Bridging inferences*, that relate new information to previous information, are made in understanding text as well as in understanding conversation.
3. *Elaborative inferences* extend and enrich new information with previously acquired schema-based knowledge about the world.

Bridging Inferences

The function of a bridging inference is to identify what is being referred to. Sometimes the bridge that has to be built is between one part of the text and another part and consists in *resolving an anaphor*. An anaphor is a word or phrase which has the same referent as an expression in another part of the text. The commonest example is when a proper name or noun phrase ("Mr. Biggs" or "the baker") is used initially and a pronoun ("he") is used later. Understanding that "he" and "Mr. Biggs" refer to the same person is called resolving the anaphor. Resolving the anaphors is a necessary part of achieving *local coherence* within the text. Anaphors are often easily resolved by simple linguistic rules or conventions. Given the gender of the pronoun there may be only one possible referent. Where there is more than one possibility, the antecedent which immediately precedes the anaphoric expression is assumed to be its referent. In some cases, though, anaphors are more difficult to resolve and depend on prior knowledge of the topic, as in the example:

Ann polished the wardrobe with a soft cloth and oiled its hinges.

The reader depends on knowledge of wardrobes and cloths to identify the referent of *its*. Here is another example from the instructions for assembling a gas fire:

For tapered inset fires place the four loose radiants in the gaps between the fixed radiants and the rear board turning them until they locate in their lower position.

It is (fairly) clear that *them* refers to the loose radiants since presumably the fixed radiants could not be turned.

Elaborative Inferences

Sometimes what is written is not intelligible on its own and inferences are required to elucidate the meaning. In today's fourth leader in *The Times* I read: *Since Mikhail Gorbachov stole some of the ideas of the banned Polish union Solidarity, Warsaw has been in confusion*. To make much sense of this I need to know something about Solidarity's ideas, what Gorbachov has been up to, and how Warsaw would be likely to react. Prior knowledge is required to infer and make explicit what has only been stated vaguely or elliptically.

We also use prior knowledge to infer causes, consequences, and instruments as in the following examples:

The house burned to the ground (it was on fire)
The fragile glass was dropped on the stone floor (it broke)
She cut a slice of bread (with a knife)

It is not clear whether these kinds of inference are constructed on-line as the material is being read, or whether they are constructed later in order to answer questions or reproduce the information. The fact that people are often unable to distinguish between information that has been explicitly stated and information which has been inferred (as with the pragmatic implications discussed on p.192) suggests that inferences are built into the memory representations as they are encoded. However, the finding that inferred items can be effective cues for eliciting recall is more difficult to interpret. In a study of instrumental inferences McKoon and Ratcliff

(1981) showed that "ladle" was an effective cue for retrieving a sentence about stirring the soup, although it had been inferred, not explicitly stated. People may have inferred that the soup was stirred with a ladle when they first read the sentence, or they may have only made the inference when the cue was supplied. It is possible that we make some inferences at the time of encoding if they are obvious ones, or if they are necessary to make sense of the material. Other inferences, which are not so obvious or not so necessary, may only be made as a result of later probing.

Whether inference making is immediate or deferred, it is abundantly clear that what people remember when they have read a text goes beyond the words they saw on the page. The memory representation of the new information is integrated with prior knowledge of the topic and schemas supply missing information, probable values, and plausible interpretations.

Some Problems with Event Schemas

What Do We Remember?

When we remember written information, what is it that we remember? In the discussion of memory for conversation it was noted that, although people remember the meaning of what has been said better than they remember the wording, they do retain the surface form of some utterances. Clark and Clark (1977) stated that memory for texts and stories is not so much memory for meaning as memory for the products of comprehension. This view fits well with some of the introspective evidence. When I try to recall a novel which I read a few months ago, I remember none of the exact words. My memory of the characters and events is detailed, but consists largely of products of comprehension such as the visual images that I constructed from the author's descriptions, and the emotions that were produced by the story.

But introspection also suggests that in some cases memory for the surface form of written information persists as well. When I try to remember the contents of a letter from a friend I remember some of the phrases exactly. I also remember the colour of the writing paper, the handwriting, and the pattern and position of words on the page. These introspections are inconsistent with a schema-theory interpretation of memory for texts, whereby we remember generalised ideas and not exact words or details.

Schema theory also has difficulty in accounting for experimental results that show that exact wording is sometimes retained. For example, Yekovich and Thorndike (1981) found that some sentences from narrative stories could be distinguished from true paraphrases after a delay of one hour; and Hayes-Roth and Thorndike (1979) found that a verbatim cue (i.e. one of the original words) facilitated recall of a sentence better than a synonym cue. Alba and Hasher (1983) have argued that the retention of lexical and syntactic information, and schematically unimportant details, as shown in these and other experiments, is not compatible with a schema theory account of memory for text. However, there are several different versions of schema theory.

The Schema-Plus-Tag Model

The schema-plus-tag version developed by Graesser and Nakamura (1982) and described in Chapter 5, pp.112–114, can account for the fact that schema-irrelevant information is often retained better than schema relevant information. According to this model, the memory trace of a text consists of a pointer to the relevant generic schema. This schema is copied into the specific memory trace which interrelates both the prior knowledge and the new knowledge, including what was explicitly stated and what was only implied, plus a set of tags, one for each item of atypical or irrelevant information. They tested this model in an experiment in which subjects read a restaurant script which contained both typical and atypical actions:

> That evening Jack wanted to go out to dinner so he called a friend who recommended several good restaurants. Jack took a shower, went out to his car, picked up his girlfriend and gave his girlfriend a book. He stopped the car in front of the restaurant and had the valet park the car. They walked into the restaurant and sat for a few minutes in the waiting area until the hostess escorted them to their table. They sat down at the table, the waitress introduced herself, and they ordered cocktails. Jack talked to his girlfriend and asked how her job was doing, and they decided what to eat. Jack cleaned his glasses, paid the bill and bought some mints. Then they left the restaurant and drove home.

The schema-irrelevant, or atypical, actions in this script were judged to be:

Jack gave his girlfriend a book
He asked his girlfriend how her job was doing
He cleaned his glasses
He bought some mints

The other actions were judged to be typical in a restaurant script. (It is strikingly evident from this material that what is judged to be typical of a visit to a restaurant is highly culture-specific.) The results showed that recognition was better for atypical actions than for typical ones at all retention intervals. Recall was initially better for atypical actions, but after

3–4 days typical actions were recalled best. According to the model, typical actions are difficult to recognise since people do not know whether the actions are familiar because they were read in the test passage, or whether they are familiar because they are part of previously acquired schematic knowledge. Atypical actions which are specifically tagged are therefore easier to recognise. At short delays, atypical actions are also easy to recall, but, as the retention interval increases and memory for the passage decays, retrieval depends increasingly on schema-guided search, so schema-relevant actions are more likely to be recalled. This modified version of schema theory can therefore account for the fact that memory for schema-irrelevant facts which are odd or unexpected is sometimes superior to memory for facts that are more routine and predictable.

Word-perfect Memory

In memory for prose and stories, the general rule appears to be that the meaning, the gist, the most important and most relevant facts are preserved and a few specific details may also be retained for a relatively short period of time. The exception to this pattern is material which has been deliberately "learned by heart". In this case, verbatim memory can persist for a lifetime, although it may take numerous repetitions to acquire. Rubin's (1977) study of very long-term verbatim memory revealed that this type of memory is quite different from memory for the gist of texts.

During the course of their education, most people learn by heart some material such as prayers and psalms, poems, and speeches from Shakespearean plays. Rubin tested American college students' memory for the Preamble to the Constitution, the 23rd Psalm, and Hamlet's soliloquy. The students reported having memorised these items some time in the past, but had not recalled them during the past 3–4 years. When memory was tested, it was apparent that very long-term verbatim memory displays regular and distinctive characteristics. There were very few constructive errors. Recall was either perfect or it failed completely. For the Preamble and for Hamlet's speech, most people recalled about 20 words from the beginning and then came to a full stop. Recall of the psalm showed a less marked primacy effect, and was influenced by the rhythmic structure. Recall is clearly organised in terms of surface structure, since breakdowns occur at syntactic boundaries. The surface units are remembered as associative chains, and, if one link in the chain is missing, the rest is usually lost. However, where the material has a clear rhythmic structure, this can serve to reinstate items beyond the gap. This phenomenon, which appeared in Rubin's data, is also clearly seen when somebody is repeating a poem and fills a missing line with dummy syllables and then recovers the words on the next line as in:

Up the airy mountain,
Down the rushy glen,
Di dum,di dum,di dum
Di dum, di little men.

This very long-term verbatim memory acquired by arduous rote learning is clearly quite different from the kind of memory for texts and stories that is acquired from a single reading.

Hunter (1979) has analysed the memory feats of story-tellers and singers in non-literate societies. Theirs are not word-perfect verbatim recitals but reconstructions according to formulaic rules. The story-teller introduces new ingredients to suit the current audience while adhering to a traditional structure. The use of strong rhythms and group chanting aids retrieval.

Mental Models

Johnson-Laird (1981) argues that stories are represented as mental models (described in Chapter 3, p.64). According to this view, the reader (or listener) constructs a mental model of the events recounted in the story. To construct a mental model of a story is to imagine what was happening. A mental model is a global representation integrating information from different parts of the story. It is constructed on-line as the story unfolds, and represents the scene, characters, and events, incorporating spatial, temporal, and causal relations. Construction of the model depends on two factors: coherence and plausibility. Coherence is a function of the pattern of co-reference, which is the way that successive sentences are linked together in a chain of anaphoric references with, for example, a pronoun in one sentence referring back to a name or noun phrase in the preceding sentence. Plausibility is the product of temporal, spatial, and causal relations which may be stated, or inferred by the reader. The distinction between these factors is illustrated in the following examples, taken from Johnson-Laird (1981, p.368):

Version A.
Jenny was holding on tightly to the string of her beautiful new balloon. She had just won it and was hurrying home to show her sister. Suddenly, the wind caught it and carried it into a tree. The balloon hit a branch and burst. Jenny cried and cried.

Version B.
She had just won it and was hurrying home to show her sister. Suddenly, the wind caught it and carried it into a tree. Jenny was holding on tightly to the string of her beautiful new balloon. Jenny cried and cried. The balloon hit a branch and burst.

Version C.
Jenny had just won a beautiful new balloon and was hurrying home to show her sister. Suddenly, the wind caught it and carried it into a tree. Jenny was holding on tightly to the string of her balloon. She cried and cried. It hit a branch and burst.

Version A is coherent and plausible. The referents of *she* (Jenny) and *it* (the balloon) are perfectly clear. The temporal sequence of events, their causes and effects, are plausible in that they are consistent with prior knowledge. In Version B, the sentences are jumbled. The referential continuity is broken, it is hard to resolve the anaphors, and the sequence of events seems implausible (she is still holding the string after the balloon has been carried away). In Version C, the referential continuity is restored by changing around the proper names or noun phrases and the pronouns, but the sequence is still implausible.

Johnson-Laird reported experimental results which showed that stories in well-structured versions (like A) are remembered much better than those in jumbled versions like B. Stories like version C are remembered slightly better than B, but still worse than A. There are also many other studies that demonstrate that when stories are presented in a disordered sequence, they are re-ordered in memory and recalled in a more coherent sequence. Mandler (1978) presented the Beach story, shown in Figs. 7.4a and b in two different versions, a canonical one and an interleaved one. Subjects who received the interleaved version tended to separate the sandcastle episode and the dog episode in their recall, and produced a version closer to the canonical one. Mandler interpreted these findings in terms of story schemas (see the next section), but they can also be taken as evidence for a mental model.

The mental model account has the advantage of relating verbal information to the real world. It also fits well with the introspective evidence that

---

Canonical Version
One day at the beach, a girl named Tammy was building a sand castle, while her friend Susan played with a frisbee. Suddenly, a big wave rolled right out of the ocean and splashed over the edge of Tammy's castle. Tammy thought her sand castle would be washed away and she wanted to save it. Quickly she took more sand and made the walls thicker. Then she made a ditch in front of the castle. The next wave filled the ditch but it didn't reach the castle. Soon the tide went out and Tammy's castle was safe from the waves. Meanwhile, a big black dog grabbed Susan's frisbee and started to chew on it. Susan was afraid of the dog but she wanted to get her frisbee back. She got a sandwich out of her lunchbox and held it out for the dog. The dog dropped the frisbee and ran off with the sandwich. Susan didn't get any lunch that day but she was happy that she had saved her frisbee.

FIG. 7.4a   Canonical version of the beach story (from Mandler, 1978).

Interleaved version
One day at the beach, a girl named Tammy was building a sand castle, while her friend Susan played with a frisbee. Suddenly a big wave rolled right out of the ocean and splashed over the edge of Tammy's castle. Meanwhile, a big black dog grabbed Susan's frisbee and started to chew on it. Tammy thought her sand castle would be washed away and she wanted to save it. Susan was afraid of the dog but she wanted to get her frisbee back. Quickly Tammy took more sand and made the walls thicker. Then she made a ditch in front of the castle. Susan got a sandwich out of her lunchbox and held it out for the dog. The next wave filled the ditch but it didn't reach the castle. The dog dropped the frisbee and ran off with the sandwich. Soon the tide went out and Tammy's castle was safe from the waves. Susan didn't get any lunch that day but she was happy that she had saved her frisbee.

FIG. 7.4b   Interleaved version of the beach story (from Mandler, 1978).

memory for stories includes visual images instantiating spatial relations. However, it does not account for the fact that some of the verbatim surface form of a story is sometimes retained.

Story Schemas and Story Grammar

A story schema consists of knowledge about the way stories are typically structured, which is derived from repeated experiences of hearing and reading stories. A limitation of story schemas is that they apply only to stories which follow a fairly traditional pattern, and not to other kinds of texts like newspaper articles, essays, or novels with a more innovative structure. Story schemas are content-free, that is, they are independent of the particular topic of the story. Unlike the mental model, which depends heavily on concrete knowledge of the real world, story schemas are highly abstract. They incorporate knowledge of story structure that reflects the existence of a story grammar. A story grammar is a system of rules that define the units of which a story is composed, and the relationships between these units. These are re-write rules, which can be used to re-write the story into its component units, and to re-write each component into subcomponents. One version of these rules is shown here. Other, slightly different versions, have also been put forward, e.g. Mandler, 1984.

Story—setting + theme + plot + resolution
Setting—characters + location + time
Theme—goal
Plot—episode(s)
Episode—event + reaction

Resolution—event or state
Goal—desired state

These re-write rules generate a hierarchical tree structure with subordinate nodes branching out from the superordinate node (*story*). To illustrate this structure, take the story of Jenny and the balloon. This can be decomposed into the numbered statements:

1. Jenny was holding tightly to the string of her beautiful new balloon
2. She was hurrying home to show it to her sister
3. A gust of wind caught it and carried it into a tree
4. It hit a branch
5. and burst
6. Jenny cried and cried

Figure 7.5 shows how the re-write rules generate a hierarchical tree structure for this story. A more complex story would be represented at more levels.

Story-grammar models generate several empirical predictions about memory for stories. The most important ones are that stories which conform to the canonical structure and the canonical rules will be remembered better; disordered stories will be re-ordered in memory; elements of the story which are higher in the hierarchy will be remembered better than

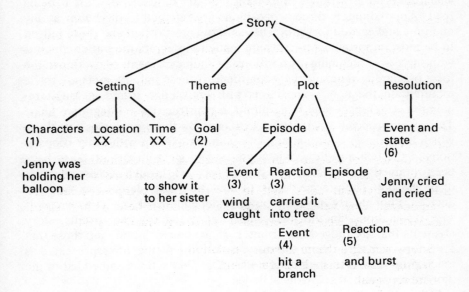

FIG. 7.5   A hierarchical tree structure for the story of Jenny and her balloon.

elements at the lower or terminal nodes; and missing components will tend to appear as intrusions in recall. Jean Mandler (1984) reviews experimental results which confirm these predictions and suggest that story schemas have psychological reality.

Hierarchical Models

The main objection to story grammars is, as we have already noted, that they only fit a restricted type of story. A more general hierarchical model, which applies to descriptive texts as well as stories, has been proposed by Kintsch and Van Dijk (1978) and Van Dijk and Kintsch (1983). The hierarchy in their model reflects the importance or generality of different propositions in the text. Instead of a text being fitted to a pre-existing, content-free framework based on knowledge of story structure, this kind of hierarchy is generated on-line by the semantic content of the particular text which is being read.

According to this model, sentences are analysed into propositions. The reader establishes local coherence by analysing the co-reference and relationships between adjacent sentences, and also establishes global coherence by extracting a set of *macropropositions*. These macropropositions constitute the summary, or gist, of the text and form the top level of the hierarchy. Macropropositions are the product of integrative processes which take place within a short-term memory buffer as the text is being read. Approximately three propositions are retained in the buffer at any one time and carried forward. These are the most recent and those judged to be most important. Attempts are made to integrate the buffer contents with successive incoming propositions by finding elements of overlap in the form of shared arguments between them. If these fail, attempts are made to integrate the new propositions with knowledge stored in long-term memory. Inferences may be required to construct these integrative links. The macropropositions that are extracted by these processes are those which have the greatest amount of argument overlap with other propositions in the text and those which are judged most important. They have been retained in the buffer and carried forward through successive cycles of processing. The precise details of how the reader determines "importance" are not clearly specified, but may depend on the reader's own goals and expectations. In the hierarchical representation that results, story elements that are judged important, such as the resolution, and those that are interwoven throughout the story, such as the theme, are represented as macropropositions at high-level nodes. Detailed actions embedded in the plot are represented at low-level nodes.

Many studies have shown that people are more likely to remember the high-level propositions than the low-level ones (e.g. Meyer, 1975).

Yekovich and Thorndike (1981) undertook an investigation of this so-called *levels effect*. They designed their study to show whether the levels effect originates from preferential encoding of important propositions or from retrieval strategy. On the Kintsch and Van Dijk model, important propositions are remembered better because, at the encoding stage, they are continually being reinstated in the buffer and carried forward to a fresh cycle of processing. Alternatively, the privileged recall of high-level propositions might arise at the retrieval stage if the hierarchical representation functions as a top-down retrieval plan. If search starts at the top of the tree, retrieval probability would decrease as it progressed downward through the levels.

In their experiment, Yekovich and Thorndike presented four stories that were similar in general structure, but different in content. The stories mapped onto hierarchies which had from 5 to 16 levels. Testing was either immediate or after a delay of one hour. A free-recall test was followed by a recognition test, in which subjects had to identify test statements as old (i.e. original), true paraphrase, or false. The results showed a clear levels effect in recall, but not in recognition. Figure 7.6(a) shows how the proportion of propositions recalled decreased from Level 1 (the top of the hierarchy) to Level 5+ (the bottom levels). But Fig. 7.6 (b) shows that there is no clear relationship between levels and recognition. The finding that the levels effect is confined to recall shows that the hierarchy influences retrieval, not encoding. Differential encoding would be reflected in recognition as well as in recall. Top-down search was also demonstrated by

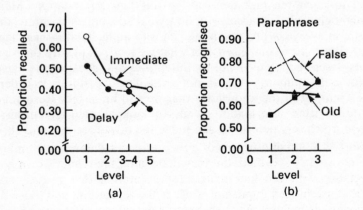

FIG. 7.6   (a) Recall proportions for story propositions as a function of level in the organisational hierarchy. (b) Proportion of correct responses to the different item types on the recognition test as a function of level in the organisational hierarchy (from Yekovich & Thorndike, 1981).

the finding that the probability of recalling a subordinate proposition, given that its superordinate had been recalled, was higher (0.63) than the probability of recalling a subordinate proposition given that its superordinate had not been recalled (0.24).

In the data from the recognition test, shown in Fig. 7.6(b), the proportion of correct rejections of true paraphrases reflects the persistence of verbatim memory. This proportion was larger for propositions at the lowest levels of the hierarchy. Thus, although macropropositions are remembered in terms of their meaning, lower-level specific details are more likely to be remembered verbatim. Overall, the results of this study are consistent with texts and stories being represented in a hierarchical organisation in memory, which is used to guide search when the material is recalled.

Which account of memory for texts and stories is most convincing, mental models or hierarchical representations? Mental models have the intuitively appealing feature of treating memory for stories and memory for real-world events as essentially the same. However, the temporal, spatial, and causal relationships represented in mental models are not necessarily hierarchical, so mental models have difficulty in accounting for the emergence of the levels effect in recall. In considering alternative models it should be emphasised that the type of representation may well vary with the aims and intentions of the reader. Most of the empirical findings come from experiments in which readers expect to be tested. One possibility is that hierarchical organisation is a mnemonic strategy developed to meet the task demands in this kind of situation. Mental models might give a better account of how we read a novel for interest and for pleasure in everyday life, when the aim is to understand rather than to remember. We want to make sense of what we read, to picture the scenes and events described, to evaluate the intentions and goals of the characters, to guess the outcome. We do not normally read stories in order to memorise them, or in the knowledge that we will be tested. Research on memory for written information needs to look at naturally occurring examples more closely before we can judge the power, scope, and appropriateness of different models.

8 Overview: Conclusions and Speculations

In reviewing research on memory in the real world this book has included such a wide range of different memory functions and such a diverse collection of findings and observations that it is a difficult task to formulate any general conclusions. No unitary theory emerges. Nevertheless, having surveyed most of the functions that an everyday memory system needs to perform, we are in a better position to identify the general characteristics that such a system needs to have. And, if we cannot construct an architecture of everyday memory, at least we can identify some of the concepts and theories that prove most useful in the interpretation of memory in the real world.

MEMORY IN THE REAL WORLD: ENCODING

Memory as an Overloaded System

Characteristics of the memory system can be seen as having evolved to meet the demands imposed on the system by the environment and by our way of life. Researchers tend to restrict consideration of everyday memory to here and now, that is, to urban Western society in the present day. It is instructive, however, to take a longer and broader view. In the kind of simple rural communities that were the norm a few centuries ago, and which still persist in remoter parts of the world, the demands on memory were relatively slight. People rarely encountered an unfamilar face. They carried out the same activities in daily and seasonal routines all their lives.

They rarely travelled beyond the immediate well-known terrain. The same songs and stories were regularly repeated. Contrast this sort of life and the minimal demands it makes on the memory system with a twentieth-century urban lifestyle. We are continuously confronted with strange faces; we meet new people; we travel to new places and have to navigate in unfamiliar terrain; we have to learn new skills and perform new activities; we are bombarded with written and spoken verbal information for almost every waking moment. The result is that in modern urban society the memory system is grossly overloaded.

Memory Must Be Selective

We can support the overloaded memory system to some extent by the use of external aids. As life gets busier and more complicated we rely more and more on information technology. We store information in data banks, in personal computers, in filofaxes, but memory is still overloaded. To cope with this overload the system must be selective. Selective attention and selective perception act to limit the inflow of information, but, even so, we still perceive far more than we could hope, or wish, to remember. In many laboratory experiments selectivity emerges as errors, but in the real world selectivity is both a virtue and a necessity. In everyday life, an ideally efficient memory system would make maximum use of external aids and devote its resources selectively to high-priority items, filtering out irrelevant or less important information.

MEMORY IN THE REAL WORLD: REPRESENTATION

Memory Must Be Dynamic

Besides being enormously complex and rich in information, today's environment is also constantly changing. We move houses, change jobs, and travel around. The skills we learn need frequent updating. The media inform us daily of new events. We need a dynamic memory system to cope with changing circumstances and a changing physical environment. We need to be able to update the knowledge we have stored and to transform the models of the world we construct in our heads. We have to revise the concepts we have acquired, or throw them out and acquire new ones. Fixed memory structures are liable to become obsolete or to be inappropriate for the current situation. We noted in Chapter 2 that the kind of mental models needed for planning or problem solving are dynamic models which are assembled as required. And Schank developed the idea of MOPs (p.115) as part of a dynamic system which could draw on high-level general components and low-level specific components to construct appropriate memory representations on demand. Fixed memory structures are uneconomical to store because the same high-level elements need to be reduplicated in many different representations. Dynamic memories are readily revised, updated, and modified, whereas fixed memories would rapidly become redundant in a changing world.

Memory Must Link Past, Present, and Future

In the real world, memory acts as a bridge between the past, the present, and the future. It stores retrospective information, monitors current input and output, and constructs and stores future plans. This integration of past, present, and future in a unified personal history is achieved by interactive processes. New memories are stored within pre-existing knowledge structures; old memories are modified by new ones; prospective plans are built out of elements abstracted from past experience. This intricate interaction of past, present, and future allows us to maintain a coherent identity and to develop flexibly and adaptively in knowledge and experience.

Memory Must Be Able to Construct Hypothetical Representations

A distinguishing feature of the human mind is its capacity for "displacement" in thought. It is because we are able to think about things that are displaced in time and in space, and things that are not the case, that we are able to plan, to predict the outcome of actions and events, to prepare for eventualities. Our ability to construct detailed and accurate hypothetical representations of possible states of affairs is crucial for survival. To meet this requirement we have to have a constructive memory system. In the real world, a memory system which could only copy the information it received would be hopelessly maladaptive. It would also be incapable of invention, imagination, and creative art.

Memory Must Store Both General and Specific Information

From a functional point of view it is easy to see the value of a memory system which abstracts and stores generalisations from experiences. Generalisation allows us to apply the knowledge acquired from one experience to a new experience that is similar but not exactly the same. The ability to store general memories allows us to know what to do in a new restaurant or a different shop, to drive an unfamiliar car, or switch to a different job. However, everyday memory also needs to store some information specifically, because, in some situations, general information is of little use. We need to remember specific names and specific faces. We need to remember precise information about routes and places and about where objects are located. It is probably true to say that specific information of this kind does not need to be stored for such a long duration as general information. It is not so important to remember names and faces from the remote past as those you have encountered more recently, and whereas general information about restaurants is always useful, there is not much point in remembering the menu and prices in a specific restaurant you dined in ten years ago. Studies of autobiographical memory in Chapter 5 showed that repeated experiences tend to be collapsed into a generalised representation and specific events are only stored if they are especially salient or unusual. Findings reviewed in Chapter 7 showed that memory for verbal information exhibits a similar mechanism, retaining a general representation of the gist of what has been read or heard, together with a relatively short-lived specific representation of the verbatim form. The usefulness of general information extends over an indefinite period, but a lot of specific information can be discarded as life moves on.

Memory Must Store Information Implicitly

A generalising mechanism is essentially a selective one which reduces the amount of information held in store. Another aspect of the memory system that results in economical storage is the way large amounts of information are only stored implicitly or inferentially as described in Chapter 6. Explicit pre-stored knowledge is only the tip of the knowledge iceberg, nine-tenths of which is submerged and consists of implicit information. The two forms of information storage are associated with different forms of retrieval, direct access and indirect search. Explicit information can be accessed directly, but implicit information can only accessed indirectly by inferential processing.

MEMORY IN THE REAL WORLD: RETRIEVAL

The Importance of Memory Processes

Recent work has concentrated more on the nature of memory representations, so that the importance of memory processes has been underplayed. Most of the characteristics of the memory system that have been outlined so far are ones which have the effect of easing the burden on storage and placing greater demands on retrieval processes. Memories which are dynamic need to be assembled. Processes of transformation may be needed to rotate, align, expand, or contract the internal analogues we construct of the real world. Processes of selection, abstraction, and generalisation are needed to protect the system from overload. Hypothetical representations have to be constructed and implicit information has to be recovered by inferential processes. Complex matching processes are required to integrate new information with representations of past experience, and in order to perceive analogies between current problems and previously encountered ones.

Retrieval Strategies

As memories proliferate, retrieval must necessarily become more difficult. Studies of retrieval in everyday life have revealed some of the main strategies used. The retrieval mechanism makes use of the way memory representations are organised in terms of categories, time periods, and levels of generality/specificity. When people search for remote memories, as described in Chapters 4 and 5, they use complicated search strategies such as partitioning the search context and searching relevant categories or relevant time periods, searching downwards from the higher levels of general schemas, or upwards from idiosyncratic markers placed on specific items at the lower levels. The striking difference that generally emerges between performance on tasks requiring recognition and tasks requiring recall suggests that retrieval is the most vulnerable aspect of everyday memory.

Serendipitous Recall

In experiments, errors of retrieval are considered to occur when retrieval fails and the target item cannot be recalled, or when retrieval is inaccurate and a non-target item is recalled instead. In everyday life, however, a high proportion of memory retrieval is spontaneous and involuntary. Memories often come to mind without any deliberate attempt at recall. These involuntary memories are not incorrect substitutes for a target which is being sought: They are spontaneous and serendipitous. External perceptual or verbal cues or internal cues from current thoughts trigger such memories involuntarily. A memory system that retrieves information involuntarily, as well as in response to deliberate recall attempts, is particularly suited to the demands of the real world. In many situations we cannot deliberately seek target information because we do not know what the target is. Involuntary memories, triggered by cues in the current situation, can be of analogous past experiences which contain useful hints, warnings, or reminders. For example, when buying a new washing machine, I involuntarily recalled a previous experience of buying domestic equipment which reminded me to check the small print to see if the guarantee included labour costs as well as parts. A retrieval system which only provides information when you already know what it is you want to know is much less versatile.

THE EFFICIENCY OF THE MEMORY SYSTEM

Research has tended to emphasise the errors that occur in everyday memory functions. The picture that emerges is of an error-prone system. This emphasis is partly an artefact of research methodology. In experiments it is usually more informative to set task difficulty at a level where people make errors so that the nature of the errors and the conditions which provoke them can be identified. Diary studies such as those recording TOTs and slips of action have also concentrated on failures rather than on successes. People do make plenty of naturally occurring errors in ordinary life situations, but, arguably, the methodology has produced a somewhat distorted view of memory efficiency. In daily life, memory successes are the norm and memory failures are the exception. People also exhibit remarkable feats of remembering faces and voices from the remote past, and foreign-language vocabulary and childhood experiences over a lifetime. As well as such examples of retention over very long periods, people can retain very large amounts of information over shorter periods, as when they prepare for examinations, and sometimes, as in the case of expert knowledge, they acquire a large amount of information and retain it for an indefinitely long time. Considering how grossly it is overloaded, memory in the real world proves remarkably efficient and resilient.

REFERENCE NOTES

1. Bahrick, H. P., Wellman, C. L., & Hall. L. K. (1987). *The effect of language schema on learning and retention of vocabulary.* Paper presented at the Second Conference on Practical Aspects of Memory, Swansea, Wales.[1]

2. Harris, J. E. & Sunderland, A. (1981). *Effects of age and instructions on an everyday memory questionnaire.* Paper presented at the British Psychological Society, Plymouth.[2]

3. Koriat, A. & Ben-Zur, H. (1987). *Remembering that I did it: Processes and deficits in output monitoring.* Paper presented at the Second Conference on Practical Aspects of Memory, Swansea, Wales.[1]

4. Loftus, E. F., Smith, K. D., Johnson, D. A., & Fiedler, J. (1987). *Remembering when: Errors in the dating of autobiographical memories.* Paper presented at the Second Conference on Practical Aspects of Memory, Swansea, Wales.[1]

5. McIntyre, J. S. & Craik, F. I. M. (1987). *Adult age differences for item and source information.* Paper presented at the meeting of the Experimental Psychological Society, Oxford (July).

6. Meacham, J. A. & Leiman, B. (1975). *Remembering to perform future actions.* Paper presented at the meeting of the American Psychological Association, Chicago (September).

7. Middleton, D. & Edwardes, D. (1986). *Conversational remembering in families.* Paper presented at the Second European Conference on Developmental Psychology, "European Perspectives", Rome.

8. Naveh-Benjamin, M. (1987). *Telling the same story twice.* Paper presented at the Second Conference on Practical Aspects of Memory, Swansea, Wales.[1]

9. Sehulster, J. R. (1987). *Broader perspectives on everyday memory.* Paper presented at the Second Conference on Practical Aspects of Memory, Swansea, Wales.[1]

10. Sinnott, J. D. (1984). *Prospective/intentional and incidental everyday memory: Effects of age and the passage of time.* Paper presented at the meeting of the American Psychological Association, Toronto.

11. West, R. L. (1984). *An analysis of prospective everyday memory.* Paper presented at the meeting of the American Psychological Association, Toronto.

[1] Now published in: Gruneburg, M. M., Morris, P. E., Sykes, R. N. (Eds.) (1988). *Practical aspects of memory: Current research and issues.* (*Vols. 1 & 2*) Chichester: John Wiley & Sons Ltd.

[2] Now published in: *The Canadian Journal of Psychology*, 1987, *41*, 175–192.

References

Alba, J.W. & Hasher, L. (1983). Is memory schematic? *Psychological Bulletin, 93,* 203–31.

Adelson, B. (1981). Problem solving and the development of abstract categories in programming languages. *Memory and Cognition, 9,* 422–33.

Adelson, B. (1984). When novices surpass experts: The difficulty of a task may increase with expertise. *Journal of Experimental Psychology: Learning, Memory and Cognition, 10,* 483–95.

Anderson, J.R. (1983). *The architecture of cognition.* Cambridge, Mass.: Harvard University Press.

Anderson, J.R. & Bower, G.H. (1973). *Human associative memory.* Washington, D.C.: V.H. Winston and Sons.

Anderson, R.C. & Pichert, J.W. (1978). Recall of previously unrecallable information following a shift in perspective. *Journal of Verbal Learning and Verbal Behavior, 17,* 1–12.

Anderson, R.E. (1984). Did I do it or did I only imagine doing it?. *Journal of Experimental Psychology: General, 113,* 594–613.

Anschutz, L., Camp, C.J., Markley, R.P., & Kramer, J.J. (1985). Maintenance and generalisation of mnemonics for grocery shopping by older adults. *Experimental Aging Research, 11,* 157–60.

Baddeley, A.D. (1982). Domains of recollection. *Psychological Review, 89,* 708–29.

Baddeley, A.D. & Wilkins, A.J. (1984). Taking memory out of the laboratory. In J.E. Harris & P.E. Morris (Eds.), *Everyday memory, actions and absentmindedness.* London: Academic Press.

Baddeley, A.D., & Woodhead, M. (1983). Improving face recognition ability. In S.M.A. Lloyd-Bostock & B.R. Clifford (Eds.), *Evaluating witness evidence.* Chichester: John Wiley & Sons.

Bahrick, H.P. (1984a). Memory for people. In J.E. Harris & P.E. Morris (Eds.), *Everyday memory, actions and absentmindedness.* London: Academic Press.

Bahrick, H.P. (1984b). Semantic memory content in permastore: Fifty years of memory for Spanish learned in school. *Journal of Experimental Psychology: General, 113,* 1–35.

Bahrick, H.P. & Phelps, E. (1987) Retention of Spanish vocabulary over 8 years. *Journal of Experimental Psychology: Learning, Memory and Cognition, 13*, 344–9.

Bartlett, F.C. (1932). *Remembering.* Cambridge: Cambridge University Press.

Bartram, D. & Smith, P. (1984). Everyday memory for everyday places. In J.E. Harris & P.E. Morris (Eds.), *Everyday memory, actions and absentmindedness.* London: Academic Press.

Bates, E., Masling, M., & Kintsch, W. (1978). Recognition memory for aspects of dialogue. *Journal of Experimental Psychology: Human Learning and Memory, 4*, 187–97.

Battman, W. (1987). Planning as a method of stress prevention: Will it pay off?. In I.G. Sarason & C.D. Spielberger (Eds.), *Stress and anxiety, Vol.10.* New York: Hemisphere.

Beach, K.D. (1988). The role of external mnemonic symbols in acquiring an occupation. In M.M. Gruneberg, P.E. Morris, & R.N. Sykes (Eds.), *Practical aspects of memory: Current research and issues, Vol. I.* Chichester: John Wiley & Sons.

Bekerian, D.A. & Bowers, J.M. (1983). Eyewitness testimony: Were we misled? *Journal of Experimental Psychology: Learning, Memory and Cognition, 9*, 139–45.

Bekerian, D.A. & Dennett, J.L. (1988). Memory on trial. In M.M. Gruneberg, P.E. Morris, & R.N. Sykes (Eds.), *Practical aspects of memory: Current research and issues, Vol. 1.* Chichester: John Wiley & Sons.

Bjork, R.A. (1978). The updating of human memory. In G.H. Bower (Ed.), *The psychology of learning and motivation: Advances in research and theory, Vol.12.* New York: Academic Press.

Bower, G.H., Black, J.B., & Turner, T.J. (1979). Scripts in text comprehension and memory. *Cognitive Psychology, 11*, 177–220.

Bower, G.H. & Karlin, M.B. (1974). Depth of processing pictures of faces and recognition memory. *Journal of Experimental Psychology, 103*, 751–7.

Braine, M.D.S. (1978). On the relation between the natural logic of reasoning and standard logic. *Psychological Review, 85*, 1–21.

Bransford, J.D. & Franks, J.J. (1972). The abstraction of linguistic ideas: A review. *Cognition, 1*, 211–49.

Bransford, J.D. & Johnson, M.K. (1973). Consideration of some problems of comprehension. In W.G. Chase (Ed.), *Visual information processing.* New York: Academic Press.

Brewer, W.F. (1986). What is autobiographical memory?. In D.C. Rubin (Ed.), *Autobiographical memory.* Cambridge: Cambridge University Press.

Brewer, W.F. & Dupree, D.A. (1983). Use of plan schemata in the recall and recognition of goal-directed actions. *Journal of Experimental Psychology: Learning, Memory and Cognition, 9*, 117–29.

Brewer, W.F. & Treyens, J.C. (1981). Role of schemata in memory for places. *Cognitive Psychology, 13*, 207–30.

Bricker, P. & Pruzansky, S. (1966). Effects of stimulus content and duration on talker identification. *Journal of the Acoustical Society of America, 40*, 1441–9.

Broadbent, D.E. (1958). *Perception and communication.* London: Pergamon.

Broadbent, D.E., Cooper, P.F., Fitzgerald, P., & Parkes, K.R. (1982). The cognitive failures questionnaire (CFQ) and its correlates. *British Journal of Clinical Psychology, 21*, 1–18.

Brown, N.R., Rips, L.J., & Shevell, S.K. (1985). The subjective dates of natural events in very long-term memory. *Cognitive Psychology, 17*, 139–77.

Brown, N.R., Shevell, S.K., & Rips, L.J. (1986). Public memories and their personal context. In D.C. Rubin (Ed.), *Autobiographical memory.* Cambridge: Cambridge University Press.

Brown, R. & Kulik, J. (1982) Flashbulb memory. In U. Neisser (Ed.), *Memory observed: Remembering in natural contexts.* San Francisco: W.H. Freeman & Co.

Brown, R. & McNeill, D. (1966). The "tip of the tongue" phenomenon. *Journal of Verbal Learning and Verbal Behavior, 5*, 325–37.

Bruce, D. (1985). The how and why of ecological memory. *Journal of Experimental Psychology: General, 114*, 78–90.

Bruce, V., & Young, A. (1986). Understanding face recognition. *British Journal of Psychology, 77*, 305–27.

Buckhout, R. (1982). Eyewitness testimony. In U. Neisser (Ed.), *Memory observed: Remembering in natural contexts.* San Francisco: W.H. Freeman & Co.

Byrne, R.W. (1977). Planning meals: Problem-solving on a real data-base. *Cognition, 5,* 287–332.

Byrne, R.W. (1979). Memory for urban geography. *Quarterly Journal of Experimental Psychology, 31*, 147–54.

Camp, C.J. (1988). Utilisation of world knowledge systems. In L.W.Poon, D.C. Rubin, & B.A. Wilson (Eds.), *Everyday cognition in adulthood and later life.* Cambridge: Cambridge University Press.

Camp, C.J., Lachman, J.L., & Lachman, R. (1980). Evidence for direct access and inferential retrieval in question answering. *Journal of Verbal Learning and Verbal Behavior, 19,* 583–96.

Cavanaugh, J.C. (1988). The place of awareness in memory development across adulthood. In L.W. Poon, D.C. Rubin, & B.A. Wilson (Eds.), *Everyday cognition in adulthood and later life.* Cambridge: Cambridge University Press.

Chaffin, R. & Herrman, D.J. (1983). Self reports of memory abilities by old and young adults. *Human Learning, 2,* 17–28.

Chase, W.G. & Ericsson, K.A. (1982). Skill and working memory. In G.H. Bower (Ed.), *The psychology of learning and motivation: Advances in research and theory, Vol. 16.* New York: Academic Press.

Chase, W.G. & Simon, H.A. (1973). Perception in chess. *Cognitive Psychology, 4,* 55–81.

Chi, M.T.H., & Koeske, R.D. (1983). Network representation of a child's dinosaur knowledge. *Developmental Psychology, 19,* 29–39.

Christie, D.F.M. & Ellis, H.D. (1981). Photofit constructions versus verbal descriptions of faces. *Journal of Applied Psychology, 66,* 358–63.

Clark, H.H. & Clark, E.V. (1977). *Psychology and language: An introduction to psycholinguistics.* New York: Harcourt Brace Jovanovich.

Clark, H.H. & Haviland, S.E. (1977). Comprehension and the given-new contract. In R.O. Freedle (Ed.), *Discourse production and comprehension.* Norwood, N. J.: Ablex Publishing.

Clifford, B.R. (1983). Memory for voices: The feasibility and quality of earwitness evidence. In S.M.A. Lloyd-Bostock & B.R. Clifford (Eds.), *Evaluating witness evidence.* Chichester: John Wiley & Sons.

Cohen, G. & Faulkner, D. (1984). Memory in old age: "Good in parts". *New Scientist,* October 11, 49–51.

Cohen, G. & Faulkner, D. (1986). Memory for proper names: Age differences in retrieval. *British Journal of Developmental Psychology, 4,* 187–97.

Cohen, G. & Faulkner, D. (1988a). Life span changes in autobiographical memory. In M.M. Gruneberg, P.E. Morris, & R.N. Sykes (Eds.), *Practical aspects of memory: Current research and issues.* Chichester: John Wiley & Sons.

Cohen, G. & Faulkner, D. (1988b). The effects of ageing on perceived and generated memories. In L.W. Poon, D.C. Rubin, & B. Wilson (Eds.), *Cognition in adulthood and later life.* Cambridge: Cambridge University Press.

Collins, A.M. (1979). Fragments of a theory of human plausible reasoning. In D.L. Waltz

(Ed.), *Theoretical issues in natural language processing*. Hillsdale, N.J.: Lawrence Erlbaum Associates Inc.

Collins, A., Warnock, E.H., Aiello, N., & Miller, M.L. (1975). Reasoning from incomplete knowledge. In D.G. Bobrow & A. Collins (Eds.), *Representation and understanding*. New York: Academic Press.

Conway, M.A. & Bekerian, D.A. (1987). Organisation in autobiographical memory. *Memory and Cognition, 15*, 119–32

Craik, F.I.M. & Lockhart, R.S. (1972). Levels of processing: A framework for memory research. *Journal of Verbal Learning and Verbal Behavior, 11*, 671–84.

Crovitz, H.F. & Schiffman, H. (1974). Frequency of episodic memories as a function of age. *Bulletin of the Psychonomic Society, 4*, 517–8.

Dudycha, G.J. & Dudycha, M.M. (1941). Childhood memories: A review of the literature. *Psychological Bulletin, 38*, 668–82.

Duncker, K. (1945). On problem solving. *Psychological Monographs, 58* (whole no. 270).

Dywan, J. & Bowers, K. (1983). The use of hypnosis to enhance recall. *Science, 222*, 184–85.

Ebbinghaus, H.E. (1885). Memory: A contribution to experimental psychology. Republished 1964. New York: Dover.

Egan, D.E. & Schwartz, B.J. (1979). Chunking in recall of symbolic drawings. *Memory and Cognition, 7*, 149–58.

Ellis, H.D. (1975). Recognising faces. *British Journal of Psychology, 66*, 409–26.

Ellis, H.D., Shepherd, J.W., & Davies, G.M. (1975). An investigation of the use of the Photofit technique for recalling faces. *British Journal of Psychology, 66*, 29–37.

Ericsson, K.A. & Simon, H.A. (1980). Verbal reports as data. *Psychological Review, 87*, 215–51.

Field, D. (1981). Retrospective reports by healthy intelligent elderly people of personal events of their adult lives. *International Journal of Behavioral Development, 4*, 77–97.

Fischhoff, B. (1977). Perceived informativeness of facts. *Journal of Experimental Psychology: Human Perception and Performance, 3*, 349–58.

Fitzgerald, J.M. & Lawrence, R. (1984). Autobiographical memory across the life span. *Journal of Gerontology, 39*, 692–8.

Flavell, J.H., Flavell, E.R., & Green, F.L. (1983). Development of the appearance-reality distinction. *Cognitive Psychology, 15*, 95–120.

Flavell, J.H. & Wellman, H.M. (1977). Metamemory. In J.W. Hagen (Ed.), *Perspective on the development of memory and cognition*. Hillsdale, N. J.: Lawrence Erlbaum Associates Inc.

Fodor, J.A. (1983). *The modularity of mind*. Cambridge, Mass.: M.I.T. Press.

Foley, M.A. & Johnson, M.K. (1985). Confusions between memories for performed and imagined actions: A developmental comparison. *Child Development, 56*, 1145–55.

Foley, M.A., Johnson, M.K., & Raye, C.L. (1983). Age-related changes in confusion between memories for thoughts and memories for speech. *Child Development, 54*, 51–60.

Freud, S. (1901). *The psychopathology everyday life*. Republished 1953. In J. Strachey (Ed.), *The standard edition of the complete psychological works of Sigmund Freud, Vol. 6*. London: Hogarth Press.

Galton, F. (1883). *Inquiries into human faculty and its development*. London: Macmillan.

Garnham, A. (1985). *Psycholinguistics: Central topics*. London: Methuen.

Gentner, D. & Gentner, D.R. (1983). Flowing waters or teeming crowds: Mental models of electricity. In D. Gentner & A. Stevens (Eds.), *Mental models*. Hillsdale, N.J.: Lawrence Erlbaum Associates Inc.

Giambra, L.M. (1979). Sex differences in daydreaming and related mental activity from the late teens to the early nineties. *International Journal of Aging and Human Development, 10*, 1–34.

Gick, M.L. & Holyoak, K.J. (1980). Analogical problem solving. *Cognitive Psychology, 12,* 306–55.

Gilhooly, K.J., Wood, M., Kinnear, P.R., & Green, C. (1988). Skill in map reading and memory for maps. *Quarterly Journal of Experimental Psychology, 40,* 87–107.

Glucksberg, S. & McCloskey, M. (1981). Decisions about ignorance: Knowing that you don't know. *Journal of Experimental Psychology: Human Learning and Memory, 7,* 311–25.

Goldstein, A.G. & Chance, J. (1971). Visual recognition memory for complex configurations. *Perception and Psychophysics, 9,* 237–41.

Graesser, A.C. & Clark, L.F. (1985). *Structures and procedures of implicit knowledge.* Norwood, N.J.: Ablex.

Graesser, A.C. & Nakamura, G.V. (1982). The impact of a schema on comprehension and memory. In G. Bower (Ed.), *The psychology of learning and motivation: Advances in research and theory, Vol. 16.* New York: Academic Press.

Greene, E., Flynn, M.S., & Loftus, E.F. (1982). Inducing resistance to misleading information. *Journal of Verbal Learning and Verbal Behavior, 21,* 207–19.

Grice, H.P. (1967). Logic and conversation: William James lectures. Partly reproduced in P. Cole & J.L. Morgan (Eds.), *Syntax and semantics, Vol. 3: Speech acts.* New York: Seminar Press, 1975.

Gruneberg, M.M., & Sykes, R.N. (1978). Knowledge and retention: The feeling of knowing and reminiscence. In M.M. Gruneberg, P.E. Morris, & R.N. Sykes (Eds.), *Practical aspects of memory.* London: Academic Press.

Harmon, L. (1973). The recognition of faces. *Scientific American, 229,* 71–82.

Harris, J.E. (1980). Memory aids people use: Two interview studies. *Memory and Cognition, 8,* 31–8.

Harris, J.E. & Wilkins, A.J. (1982). Remembering to do things: A theoretical framework and an illustrative experiment. *Human Learning, 1,* 123–36.

Harris, R.J. (1978). The effects of jury size and judges' instructions on memory for pragmatic implications from courtroom testimony. *Bulletin of the Psychonomic Society, 11,* 129–32.

Harris, R.J. & Monaco, G.E. (1976). Psychology of pragmatic implication: Information processing between the lines. *Journal of Experimental Psychology: General, 107,* 1–22.

Hasher, L., Attig, M.S., & Alba, J.W. (1981). I knew it all along: Or did I? *Journal of Verbal Learning and Verbal Behavior, 20,* 86–96.

Hayes-Roth, B. & Hayes-Roth, F. (1979). A cognitive model of planning. *Cognitive Science, 3,* 275–310.

Hayes-Roth, B. & Thorndyke, P.W. (1979). Integration of knowledge from texts. *Journal of Verbal Learning and Verbal Behavior, 18,* 91–108.

Herrman, D.J. (1984). Questionnaires about memory. In J.E. Harris & P.E. Morris (Eds.), *Everyday memory, actions and absentmindedness.* London: Academic Press.

Holding, D.H., Noonan, T.K., Pfau, H.D., & Holding, C. (1986). Date attribution, age and the distribution of lifetime memories. *Journal of Gerontology, 41,* 481–5.

Hudson, J.A. (1986). Memories are made of this: General event knowledge and development of autobiographical memory. In K. Nelson (Ed.), *Event knowledge: structure and function in development.* Hillsdale, N.J.: Lawrence Erlbaum Associates Inc.

Hunter, I.M.L. (1979). Memory in everyday life. In M.M. Gruneberg & P.E. Morris (Eds.), *Applied problems in memory.* London: Academic Press.

Intraub, H. & Nicklos, S. (1985). Levels of processing and picture memory: The physical superiority effect. *Journal of Experimental Psychology: Learning, Memory and Cognition, 11,* 284–98.

James, W. (1890). *The principles of psychology,* New York: Holt.

Johnson, M.K. (1985). The origin of memories. In P.C. Kendall (Ed.), *Advances in cognitive behavioural research and therapy, Vol.4.* London and New York: Academic Press.

Johnson, M.K. & Raye, C.L. (1981). Reality monitoring. *Psychological Review*, *88*, 67–85.

Johnson, M.K., Raye, C.L., Foley, H.J., & Foley, M.A. (1981). Cognitive operations and decision bias in reality monitoring. *American Journal of Psychology*, *94*, 37–64.

Johnson, M.K., Raye, C.L., Wang, A., & Taylor, T. (1979). Facts and fantasy: The role of accuracy and variability in confusing imaginations with perceptual experiences. *Journal of Experimental Psychology: Human Learning and Memory*, *5*, 229–46.

Johnson-Laird, P.N. (1981). Comprehension as the construction of mental models. *Philosophical Transactions of the Royal Society of London: The Psychological Mechanisms of Language*.

Johnson-Laird, P.N. (1983). *Mental models*. Cambridge: Cambridge University Press.

Jones, G.V. (in press). Back to Woodworth: Role of interlopers in the tip of the tongue phenomenon. *Memory and Cognition*.

Kausler, D.H. & Hakami, M.K. (1983). Memory for topics of conversation: Adult age differences and intentionality. *Experimental Aging Research*, *9*, 153–7.

Keenan, J.M., MacWhinney, B., & Mayhew, D. (1977). Pragmatics in memory: A study of natural conversation. *Journal of Verbal Learning and Verbal Behavior*, *16*, 549–60.

Keller, F.S. (1953). Stimulus discrimination and Morse code learning. *New York Academy of Science*, Series 2, *15*, 195–203.

Kemper, S. & Thissen, D. (1981). Memory for the dimensions of requests. *Journal of Verbal Learning and Verbal Behavior*, *20*, 552–63.

Kintsch, W. & Bates, E. (1977). Recognition memory for statements from a classroom lecture. *Journal of Experimental Psychology: Human Learning and Memory*, *3*, 150–9.

Kintsch, W. & van Dijk, T.A. (1978). Toward a model of text comprehension and reproduction. *Psychological Review*, *85*, 363–94.

Kirasic, K.C. & Allen, G.L. (1985). Spatial performance and spatial competence. In N. Charness (Ed.), *Ageing and human performance*. New York: John Wiley & Sons.

Koriat, A., & Lieblich, I. (1974). What does a person in a "TOT" state know that a person in a "don't know" state doesn't know. *Memory and Cognition*, *2*, 647–55.

Kosslyn, S.M. (1981). The medium and the message in mental imagery: A theory. *Psychological Review*, *88*, 46–65.

Kosslyn, S.M., Ball, T.M., & Reiser, B.J. (1978). Visual images preserve metric spatial information: Evidence from studies of image scanning. *Journal of Experimental Psychology: Human Perception and Performance*, *4*, 47–60.

Kozlowski, L.T. & Bryant, K.J. (1977). Sense of direction, spatial orientation and cognitive maps. *Journal of Experimental Psychology: Human Perception and Performance*, *3*, 590–8.

Kreutzer, M.A., Leonard, C., & Flavell, J.H. (1975). An interview study of children's knowledge about memory. *Monographs of the Society for Research in Child Development*, *40* (No.159).

Krinsky, R., & Krinsky, S.J. (1988). City size bias and the feeling of knowing. In M.M. Gruneberg, P.E. Morris, & R.M. Sykes (Eds.), *Practical aspects of memory: Current research and issues, Vol. I*. Chichester: John Wiley & Sons.

Lachman, J.L., Lachman, R., & Thronesberry, C. (1979). Metamemory through the adult life span. *Developmental Psychology*, *15*, 543–51.

Levy, R.L. & Loftus, G.R. (1984). Compliance and memory. In J.E. Harris & P.E. Morris (Eds.), *Everyday memory, actions and absentmindedness*. London: Academic Press.

Ley, P. (1978). Memory for medical information. In M.M. Gruneberg, P.E. Morris, & R.N. Sykes (Eds.), *Practical aspects of memory*. London: Academic Press.

Lichtenstein, E.H. & Brewer, W.F. (1980). Memory for goal directed events. *Cognitive Psychology*, *12*, 412–45.

Linton, M. (1982). Transformations of memory in everyday life. In U. Neisser (Ed.), *Memory observed: Remembering in natural contexts*. San Francisco: W.H. Freeman & Co.

List, J.A. (1986). Age and schematic differences in the reliability of eyewitness testimony. *Developmental Psychology*, *22*, 50–7.

Loftus, E.F. (1974). Reconstituting memory: The incredible eyewitness. *Psychology Today*, *8*, 116–9.

Loftus, E.F. (1975). Leading questions and the eyewitness report. *Cognitive Psychology*, *7*, 560–72.

Loftus, E.F. (1979a). *Eyewitness testimony*. Cambridge, Mass: Harvard University Press.

Loftus, E.F. (1979b). Reactions to blatantly contradictory information. *Memory and Cognition*, *7*, 368–74.

Loftus, E.F. & Greene, E. (1980). Warning: Even memory for faces may be contagious. *Law & Human Behavior*, *4*, 323–334

Loftus, E.F. & Loftus, G.R. (1980). On the permanence of stored information in the human brain. *American Psychologist*, *35*, 421–34.

Loftus, E.F. & Marburger, W. (1983). Since the eruption of Mount St. Helens has anyone beaten you up? Improving the accuracy of retrospective reports with landmark events. *Memory and Cognition*, *11*, 114–20.

Loftus, E.F., Miller, D.G., & Burns, H. (1978). Semantic integration of verbal information into a visual memory. *Journal of Experimental Psychology, Human Learning and Memory*, *4*, 19–31.

Loftus, E.F. & Palmer, J.C. (1974). Reconstruction of autombile destruction: An example of the interaction between language and memory. *Journal of Verbal Learning and Verbal Behavior*, *13*, 585–9.

McCloskey, M. & Bigler, K. (1980). Focused memory search in fact retrieval. *Memory and Cognition*, *8*, 253–64.

McCloskey, M. & Zaragoza, M. (1985). Misleading postevent information and memory for events: Arguments and evidence against memory impairment hypotheses. *Journal of Experimental Psychology: General*, *114*, 1–16.

McGehee, F. (1937). The reliability of the identification of the human voice. *Journal of General Psychology*, *17*, 249–71.

McKeithen, K.B., Reitman, J.S., Rueter, H.H., & Hirtle, S.C. (1981). Knowledge organisation and skill differences in computer programmers. *Cognitive Psychology*, *13*, 307–25.

McKenna, P. & Warrington, E.K. (1980). Testing for nominal dysphasia. *Journal of Neurology, Neurosurgery and Psychiatry*, *43*, 781–8.

McKoon, G. & Ratcliff, R. (1981). Comprehension processes and memory structures involved in instrumental inference. *Journal of Verbal Learning and Verbal Behavior*, *20*, 671–82.

McWeeny, K.H., Young, A.W., Hay, D.C., & Ellis, A.W. (1987). Putting names to faces. *British Journal of Psychology*, *78*, 143–9.

Mandler, G. (1967). Organisation and memory. In K.W. Spence & J.T. Spence (Eds.), *The psychology of learning and motivation: Advances in research and theory, Vol.1*. London: Academic Press.

Mandler, J.M. (1978). A code in the node: The use of a story schema in retrieval. *Discourse Processes*, *1*, 14–35.

Mandler, J.M. (1984). *Stories, scripts and scenes: Aspects of schema theory*. Hillsdale, N.J.: Lawrence Erlbaum Associates Inc.

Mandler, J.M. & Parker, R.E. (1976). Memory for descriptive and spatial information in complex pictures. *Journal of Experimental Psychology: Human Learning and Memory*, *2*, 38–48.

Martin, M. (1986). Ageing and patterns of change in everyday memory and cognition. *Human Learning*, *5*, 63–74.

Martin, M. & Jones, G.V. (1984). Cognitive failures in everyday life. In J.E. Harris & P.E. Morris (Eds.), *Everyday memory, actions and absentmindedness*. London: Academic Press.

Meacham, J.A. & Singer, J. (1977). Incentive in prospective remembering. *Journal of Psychology*, *97*, 191–7.

Means, B., Mingay, D.J., Nigam, A., & Zarrow, M. (1988). A cognitive approach to enhancing health survey reports of medical visits. In M.M. Gruneberg, P.E. Morris, & R.N. Sykes (Eds.), *Practical aspects of memory: Current research and issues, Vol. 1*. Chichester: John Wiley & Sons.

Metzler, J. & Shepard, R.N. (1974) Mental rotation of three-dimensional objects. *Science*, *171*, 701–3.

Meyer, B. (1975). *The organisation of prose and its effect on memory*, Amsterdam: North Holland.

Miller, G.A. (1956). The magical number seven plus or minus two. *Psychological Review*, *87*, 252–71.

Morris, P.E. (1984). The validity of subjective reports on memory, In J.E. Harris & P.E. Morris (Eds.), *Everyday memory, actions and absentmindedness*. London: Academic Press Inc.

Morris, P.E., Gruneberg, M.M., Sykes, R.N., & Merrick, A. (1981). Football knowledge and the acquisition of new results. *British Journal of Psychology*, *72*, 479–83.

Morris, P.E., Tweedy, M., & Gruneberg, M.M. (1985). Interest, knowledge and the memorising of soccer scores. *British Journal of Psychology*, *76*, 415–25.

Morton, J., Hammersley, R.H., & Bekerian, D.A. (1985). Headed records: A model for memory and its failure. *Cognition*, *20*, 1–23.

Moscovitch, M. (1982). A neuropsychological approach to memory and perception in normal and pathological ageing. In F.I.M. Craik & S. Trehub (Eds.), *Aging and cognitive processes*, New York: Plenum Press.

Murphy, G.L. & Wright, J.C. (1984). Changes in conceptual structure with expertise: Difference between real-world experts and novices. *Journal of Experimental Psychology: Learning, Memory and Cognition*, *10*, 144–55.

Nakamura, G.V., Graesser, A.C., Zimmerman, J.A., & Riha, J. (1985). Script processing in a natural situation. *Memory and Cognition*, *13*, 140–4.

Neisser, U. (1978). Memory: What are the important questions?. In M.M. Gruneberg, P.E. Morris., & R.N. Sykes (Eds.), *Practical aspects of memory*. London: Academic Press Inc.

Neisser, U. (1982a). John Dean's memory: A case study. In U. Neisser (Ed.), *Memory observed: Remembering in natural contexts*. San Francisco: W.H. Freeman.

Neisser, U. (1982b). *Memory observed: Remembering in natural contexts*. San Franciso: W.H. Freeman.

Neisser, U. (1982c). Snapshots or benchmarks?. In U. Neisser (Ed.), *Memory observed: Remembering in natural contexts*. San Francisco: W.H. Freeman.

Neisser, U. (1984). Interpreting Harry Bahrick's discovery: What confers immunity against forgetting? *Journal of Experimental Psychology*, *113*, 32–5.

Neisser, U. (1986). Nested structure in autobiographical memory. In D.C. Rubin (Ed.), *Autobiographical memory*. Cambridge: Cambridge University Press.

Neisser, U. (1988). The present and the past. In M.M. Gruneberg, P.E. Morris, & R.N. Sykes (Eds.), *Practical aspects of memory: Current research and issues, Vol. 2*. Chichester: John Wiley & Sons.

Nelson, K. & Gruendel, J. (1986). Children's scripts. In K. Nelson (Ed.), *Event knowledge: Structure and function in development*. Hillsdale, N.J.: Lawrence Erlbaum Associates Inc.

Nickerson, R.S. (1977). Some comments on human archival memory as a very large data base. *Proceedings of the Third International Conference on Very Large Data Bases*, Tokyo (October).

Nickerson, R.S. & Adams, M.J. (1982). Long-term memory for a common object. In U. Neisser (Ed.), *Memory observed: Remembering in natural contexts*. San Francisco: W.H. Freeman.

Nigro, G. & Neisser, U. (1983). Point of view in personal memories. *Cognitive Psychology*, 15, 465–82.

Nisbett, R.E. & Wilson, T.D. (1977). Telling more than we can know: Verbal reports on mental processes. *Psychological Review*, 84, 231–59.

Norman, D.A. (1980). Twelve issues for cognitive science. *Cognitive Science*, 4, 1–32.

Norman, D.A. (1981). Categorisation of action slips. *Psychological Review*, 88, 1–15.

Norman, D.A. & Bobrow, D.G. (1976). On the role of active memory processes in perception and cognition. In C.F. Cofer (Ed.), *The structure of human memory*. San Francisco: W.H. Freeman.

Norman, D.A. & Bobrow, D.G. (1979). Descriptions: An intermediate stage in memory retrieval. *Cognitive Psychology*, 11, 107–23.

Paivio, A. (1969). Mental imagery in associative learning and memory. *Psychological Review*, 76, 241–63.

Parkes, K.R. (1980). Occupational stress among student nurses. *Nursing Times*, 76, 113–6.

Parkin, A.J. (1987). *Memory and amnesia: An introduction*. Oxford: Blackwell.

Patterson, K.E. & Baddeley, A.D. (1977). When face recognition fails. *Journal of Experimental Psychology: Human Learning and Memory*, 3, 406–17.

Peper, R.J. & Mayer, R.E. (1978). Note taking as a generative activity. *Journal of Educational Psychology*, 70, 514–22.

Perlmutter, M. (1978). What is memory ageing the ageing of? *Development Psychology*, 14, 330–45.

Phillips, R.J. (1978). Recognition, recall and imagery of faces. In M.M. Gruneberg, P.E. Morris, & R.N. Sykes (Eds.). *Practical aspects of memory*. London: Academic Press.

Pylyshyn, Z.W. (1981). The imagery debate: Analogue versus tacit knowledge. *Psychological Review*, 86, 383–94.

Read, J.D. & Bruce, D. (1982). Longitudinal tracking of difficult memory retrievals. *Cognitive Psychology*, 14, 280–300.

Reason, J.T. (1979). Actions not as planned: The price of automatisation. In G. Underwood & R. Stevens (Eds.), *Aspects of consciousness, Vol. 1*. London: Academic Press.

Reason, J.T. (1984). Absentmindedness and cognitive control. In J.E. Harris, & P.E. Morris (Eds.), *Everyday memory, actions and absentmindedness*. London: Academic Press.

Reason, J.T. & Lucas, D. (1984). Using cognitive diaries to investigate naturally occurring memory blocks. In J.E. Harris & P.E. Morris (Eds.), *Everyday memory, actions and absentmindedness*. London: Academic Press.

Reason, J.T. & Mycielska, K. (1982). *Absentminded? The psychology of mental lapses and everyday errors*. Englewood Cliffs, N.J.: Prentice-Hall.

Reiser, B.J., Black, J.B., & Abelson, R.P. (1985). Knowledge structures in the organisation and retrieval of autobiographical memories. *Cognitive Psychology*, 17, 89–137.

Reitman, J.S. (1976). Skilled perception in Go: Deducing memory structures from inter-response times. *Cognitive Psychology*, 8, 336–56.

Rips, L.J. (1987). Mental muddles. In M. Brand & R.M. Harnish (Eds.). *The representation of knowledge and belief*. Tucson, Ariz.: University of Arizona Press.

Robinson, F.P. (1946). *Effective study*. New York: Harper.

Robinson, J.A. (1976). Sampling autobiographical memory. *Cognitive Psychology*, 8, 578–9.

Rosch, E., Mervis, C.B., Gray, W.D., Johnson, D.M., & Boyes-Braem, P. (1976). Basic objects in natural categories. *Cognitive Psychology*, 8, 382–439.

Rowntree, D. (1970). *Learn how to study*. London: MacDonald.

Rubin, D.C. (1977). Very long-term memory for prose and verse. *Journal of Verbal Learning and Verbal Behavior*, 16, 611–21.

Rubin, D.C. (1982). On the retention function for autobiographical memory. *Journal of Verbal Learning and Verbal Behavior*, 21, 21–38.

Rubin, D.C. & Kozin, M. (1984). Vivid memories. *Cognition*, 16, 81–95.

Rubin, D.C., Wetzler, S.E., & Nebes, R.D. (1986). Autobiographical memory across the life span. In D.C. Rubin (Ed.), *Autobiographical memory*. Cambridge: Cambridge University Press.

Rumelhart, D.E. & Norman, D.A. (1978). Accretion, tuning and restructuring: Three models of learning. In J.W. Cotton & R. Klatzky (Eds.), *Semantic factors in cognition*. Hillsdale, N.J.: Lawrence Erlbaum Associates Inc.

Rumelhart, D.E. & Norman, D.A. (1985). Representation of knowledge. In A.M. Aitkenhead & J.M. Slack (Eds.), *Issues in cognitive modelling*. London: Lawrence Erlbaum Associates Ltd.

Sachs, J.S. (1967). Recognition memory for syntactic and semantic aspects of connected discourse. *Perception and Psychophysics*, *2*, 437–42.

Salaman, E. (1982). A collection of moments. In U. Neisser (Ed.), *Memory observed: Remembering in natural contexts*. San Francisco: W.H. Freeman.

Schachtel, E.G. (1947). On memory and childhood amnesia. *Psychiatry*, *10*, 1–26.

Schank, R.C. (1982a). *Dynamic memory*. Cambridge: Cambridge University Press.

Schank, R.C. (1982b). Reminding and memory organisation. In W.G. Lehnert & M.H. Ringle (Eds.), *Strategies for natural language processing*. Hillsdale, N.J.: Lawrence Erlbaum Associates.

Schank, R.C. & Abelson, R.P. (1977). *Scripts, plans, goals, and understanding*. Hillsdale, N.J.: Lawrence Erlbaum Associates Inc.

Searle, J.R. (1969). *Speech acts*. Cambridge: Cambridge University Press.

Sheingold, K. & Tenney, Y.J. (1982). Memory for a salient childhood event. In U. Neisser (Ed.), *Memory observed: Remembering in natural contexts*. San Francisco: W.H. Freeman.

Shepard, R.N. (1984). Ecological constraints in internal representation: Resonant kinematics of perceiving, imagining, thinking and dreaming. *Psychological Review*, *91*, 417–46.

Shepherd, J.W., Davies, G.M., & Ellis, H.D. (1978). How best shall a face be described? In M.M. Gruneberg, P.E. Morris, & R.N. Sykes (Eds.), *Practical aspects of memory*. London: Academic Press.

Shiffrin, R.M. & Schneider, W. (1977). Controlled and automatic information processing. II: Perceptual learning, automatic attending, and a general theory. *Psychological Review*, *84*, 127–90.

Smith, E.E. & Medin, D.L. (1981). Categories and concepts. Boston: Harvard University Press.

Spilich, G.J., Vesonder, G.T., Chiesi, H.L., & Voss, J.F. (1979). Text processing of domain related information for individuals with high and low domain knowledge. *Journal of Verbal Learning and Verbal Behavior*, *18*, 275–90.

Stevens, A. & Coupe, P. (1978). Distortions in judged spatial relations. *Cognitive Psychology*, *10*, 422–37.

Sunderland, A., Harris, J.E., & Baddeley, A.D. (1983). Do laboratory tests predict everyday memory? A neuropsychological study. *Journal of Verbal Learning and Verbal Behavior*, *22*, 341–57.

Tenney, Y.J. (1984). Ageing and the misplacing of objects. *British Journal of Developmental Psychology*, *2*, 43–50.

Thompson, C.P. & Cowan, T. (1986). Flashbulb memories: A nicer interpretation of Neisser. *Cognition*, *22*, 199–200.

Thorndyke, P.W. & Hayes–Roth, B. (1982). Differences in spatial knowledge acquired from maps and navigation. *Cognitive Psychology*, *14*, 560–89

Thorndyke, P.W., & Stasz, C. (1980). Individual differences in procedures for knowledge acquisition from maps. *Cognitive Psychology*, *12*, 137–75.

Tulving, E. (1972). Episodic and semantic memory. In E. Tulving & W. Donaldson (Eds.),

Organisation of memory. New York: Academic Press.

Tyler, S.W. & Voss, J.F. (1982). Attitude and knowledge effects in prose processing. *Journal of Verbal Learning and Verbal Behavior, 21*, 524–38.

Van Dijk, T.A. & Kintsch, W. (1983). *Strategies of discourse comprehension* New York: Academic Press.

Wagenaar, W.A. (1978). Recalling messages broadcast to the general public. In M.M. Gruneberg, P.E. Morris, & R.N. Sykes (Eds.), *Practical aspects of memory*. London: Academic Press.

Wagenaar, W. (1986). My memory: A study of autobiographical memory over six years. *Cognitive Psychology, 18*, 225–52.

Wagenaar, W.A. & Visser, J. (1979). The weather forecast under the weather. *Ergonomics, 22*, 909–17.

Wason, P.C. (1960). On the failure to eliminate hypotheses in a conceptual task. *Quarterly Journal of Experimental Psychology, 12*, 129–40.

Welford, A.T. (1958). *Ageing and human skill*. Oxford: Oxford University Press.

Wetzler, S.E. & Sweeney, J.A. (1986). Childhood amnesia: An empirical demonstration. In D.C. Rubin (Ed.), *Autobiographical Memory*. Cambridge: Cambridge University Press.

White, S.H. & Pillemer, D.B. (1979). Childhood amnesia and the development of a socially accessible memory system. In J.F. Kihlstrom & F.J. Evans (Eds.), *Functional disorders of memory*. Hillsdale, N.J.: Lawrence Erlbaum Associates Inc.

Whitten, W.B. & Leonard, J.M. (1981). Directed search through autobiographical memory. *Memory and Cognition, 9*, 566–79.

Wilding, J. & Mohindra, N. (1980). Effects of subvocal suppression, articulating aloud and noise on sequence recall. *British Journal of Psychology, 71*, 247–61.

Wilkins, A.J. (1976). A failure to demonstrate effects of the retention interval. Cited in J.E. Harris, Remembering to do things: A forgotten topic, in J.E. Harris & P.E. Morris, (Eds.), *Everyday memory, actions and absentmindedness*. London: Academic Press.

Wilkins, A.J. & Baddeley, A.D. (1978). Remembering to recall in everyday life: An approach to absentmindedness. In M.M. Gruneberg, P.E. Morris, & R.N. Sykes (Eds.), *Practical aspects of memory*. London: Academic Press.

Williams, M.D. & Hollan, J.D. (1981). The process of retrieval from very long-term memory. *Cognitive Science, 5*, 87–119.

Wilson, B. Baddeley, A.D., & Hutchins, H. (1984). The Rivermead Behavioural Memory Test. *Rivermead Technical Report* 84/1.

Wilson, B. & Moffat, N. (1984). Rehabilitation of memory for everyday life. In J.E. Harris & P.E. Morris (Eds.), *Everyday memory, actions and absentmindedness*. London: Academic Press.

Wilton, R.N. (1979). Knowledge of spatial relations: The specification of the information used in making inferences. *Quarterly Journal of Experimental Psychology, 31*, 133–46.

Winograd, E. (1976). Recognition memory for faces following nine different judgements. *Bulletin of the Psychonomic Society, 8*, 419–21.

Winograd, E. (1978). Encoding operations which facilitate memory for faces across the life span. In M.M. Gruneberg, P.E. Morris, & R.N. Sykes (Eds.), *Practical aspects of memory*. London: Academic Press.

Winograd, E. & Killinger, W.A. (1983). Relating age at encoding in early childhood to adult recall: Development of flashbulb memories. *Journal of Experimental Psychology: General, 112*, 413–22.

Wood, G. (1978). The knew-it-all-along effect. *Journal of Experimental Psychology: Human Perception and Performance, 4*, 345–53.

Woodhead, M., Baddeley, A.D., & Simmonds, D.C.V. (1979). On training people to recognise faces. *Ergonomics, 22*, 333–43.

Yekovich, F.R. & Thorndyke, P.W. (1981). An evaluation of alternative models of narrative schemata. *Journal of Verbal Learning and Verbal Behavior, 20*, 454–69.

Yin, R.K. (1969). Looking at upside-down faces. *Journal of Experimental Psychology, 81*, 141–5.

Young, A.W., Hay, D.C., & Ellis, A.W. (1985). The faces that launched a thousand slips: Everyday difficulties and errors in recognising people. *British Journal of Psychology, 76*, 495–523.

Young, A.W., McWeeny, K.H., Ellis, A.W., & Hay, D.C. (1986). Naming and categorising faces and written names. *The Quarterly Journal of Experimental Psychology, 38A*, 297–318.

Zaragoza, M.S., McCloskey, M., & Jamis, M. (1987). Misleading postevent information and recall of the original event: Further evidence against the memory impairment hypothesis. *Journal of Experimental Psychology: Learning, Memory and Cognition, 13*, 36–44.

Zelinski, E.M., Gilewski, M.J., & Thompson, L.W. (1980). Do laboratory tests relate to self-assessment of memory ability in the young and old? In L.W. Poon, J.L. Fozard, L.S. Cermak, D. Arenberg, & L.W. Thompson (Eds.), *New directions in memory and ageing*. Hillsdale, N.J.: Lawrence Erlbaum Associates Inc.

Zimbardo, P.E. (1984). Social psychology: What it is, where it came from, and where it is headed. In V. Sarris & A. Parducci (Eds.), *Perspectives in psychological experimentation: Toward the year 2000*. Hillsdale, N.J.: Lawrence Erlbaum Associates Inc.

Author Index

Subject Index